# A Beautiful Woman in Venice

by

Kathleen Ann González

Ca' Specchio
San Jose
2015

Cover portraits from left to right:

First row - Veronica Franco, Cassandra Fedele, Maria Boscola, Sarra Copia Sulam

Second row - Modesta Pozzo, Giustina Renier Michiel, Angela del Moro, Lucrezia Marinella Vacca

Third row - Giustiniana Wynne, Margherita Vitturi, Elisabetta Caminer Turra, Antonia Padoani Bembo

Fourth row - Isabella Teotochi Albrizzi, Gaspara Stampa, Elena Cornaro Piscopia, Luisa Bergalli Gozzi, Barbara Strozzi

Fifth row - Cencia Scarpariola, Morosina Morosini Grimani, Marina Querini Benzon, Rosalba Carriera

Kathleen Ann González, 1965 –
*A Beautiful Woman in Venice*
www.kathleenanngonzalez.com

Cover by RJ Wofford II
Photographs by Kathleen Ann González
ISBN 978-0-9850972-8-8
First Edition
Printed in the United States of America

# Table of Contents

*Dogaressa Morosina Morosini Grimani Disembarking at Saint Mark's*
by Andrea Vicentino

# *Introduction*

$\mathcal{A}$ stately woman in a deep gold brocade gown shot through with golden threads steps off a fabled golden boat. A mirror merchant in simple white blouse and shawl takes action to preserve her republic. An elegant singer poses in a private salon wallpapered in patterned red velvet. Standing at a university podium, a woman with hair coiled atop her head holds forth in Latin on women's education. A cloistered nun in a walled up convent uses the only power she has—her pen. Artists hold in their hands pastels or pens or glass or thread to document or protect or adorn or embellish those around them. A hostess orchestrates the conversation, entertainment, and refreshments to keep culture alive.

All these beautiful women represent Venice, Italy's city of water and light. Venice, associated with Venus, the goddess of love, was a city ruled by men, their elaborate republican model meant to offer equality and justice rather than dispense favors to monarchs. Ruled by the elected doge, with a dogaressa sometimes at his side for stately functions, Venice had no kings or queens, princes or duchesses, though it did revere its original twenty-four noble families in the *Libro d'Oro*, the Book of Gold. Though men wielded the power and made the decisions, Venice was still a city of women: women who maintained its culture, who attracted tourists and lovers, who entertained in both sacred and secular venues, who founded refuges for others or prayed for their wellbeing, who sold or delivered the goods and foods that maintained life. Women who were mothers, wanting the best, fair education for their children. Women who were daughters, dutiful or seeking or devout. Women who were wives, working alongside their husbands or forging their own talented paths. Women who prayed faithfully. Beautiful women, each in her own way.

Libraries of books have been written about Venetian history and Venetian men's roles in shaping it. But little is written about the lives of its women. *La Serenissima*, the Most Serene Republic as Venice was known, ruled the seas and a good chunk of Europe and the East for a thousand years. While men made the navy's boats or passed the laws or declared wars, women did what women do to support those men: manage households; bear and raise children; run shops or tend gardens; entertain and create; provide comfort and advice and pleasure; and teach, often in subtle ways. Some of these women also traveled new paths, seeking education, learning languages, speaking publicly, or writing letters, madrigals, poems, and novels. Women often prodded men to be better, to remember their values and families. Venetian women may have been limited in their life choices, especially those women in the upper classes, yet they still found ways to effect change or influence their surroundings or leave things better than they were.

In this book you'll find some of their stories.

It was not easy to track down Venetian women as they lurk in history's corners. Sometimes I'd find only a few sentences in a few books and have to piece together a story with details about a neighborhood or an era. But for the last two decades, monumental work, most notably through consortiums at the Universities of Chicago, Toronto, and Padua, has commenced to uncover the lives of remarkable Italian women. One by one, these women's lives are being chronicled and assessed, their works gathered and translated. Researchers are combing through archives in search of details, and their work made mine immeasurably easier. For the academic analysis or more details on any of these women, please peruse the bibliography where you will find leads to more information. *A Beautiful Woman in Venice* is not intended to be a scholarly work for other academics but instead one to introduce these often-overlooked Venetian women to a world of readers and travelers who can delight in their contributions and characters. I hope to make these women's stories accessible to all, whether my readers are fueled by an interest in women's rights or Italian history, a love of Venice, hope for inspiration, or a desire for a good story.

With this background in mind, I set up criteria to determine which women to include: women who did something remarkable; women who made their neighborhoods or their city a better place; women who protected others, provided succor, or inspired people; women who forged new paths. Although these women's physical beauty was often mentioned, they were beautiful in so many other ways as well.

While the Venetian government ruled much of the Veneto mainland for many years, I chose to focus on women who lived the bulk of their lives in Venice itself. This decision resulted in omitting some highly successful or fascinating women. For example, Isabella Andreini, a playwright and actress especially noted for her improvisation skills and groundbreaking theatrical innovations, lived on the mainland rather than on the island of Venice. Zanetta Casanova, mother of the famous lover and writer Giacomo Casanova, was a theatrical superstar who catapulted playwright Carlo Goldoni to fame and who toured Europe, living most of her life away from her birthplace, as did Faustina Bordoni, a beguiling soprano who sang throughout Europe but lived only the beginning and end of her life in Venice. Teresa Imer, who left Venice when she was a teen, was later known as Mrs. Cornelys during her years in London where she created the fabulous Carlisle House, which became the talk of London society and was frequented by British nobility. Anna Renzi, noted as the first opera diva, sang for years to great fame in Venice, though she was born and raised in Rome. Caterina Cornaro, who became Queen of Cyprus, was much beloved by Venetians but actually lived her days in Cyprus or later on the mainland city of Asolo.

I chose to develop whole chapters around some women's lives; however, if there was little information available and the women were similar to others discussed at length, I mention them briefly in the related chapters. This includes people like painters Marietta Robusti or Francesca Sartori, poet Francesca Baffo, composer Marieta Morosina Priuli, and Dogaressa Giovanna Dandolo. I would like to do justice to each of these women's lives, but without some boundaries, this book would never have been completed.

Many of these women were proto-feminists, meaning they were espousing feminist ideals up to two centuries before the idea of feminism even existed. As I read their life stories, I also read much commentary and analysis on feminist theory and history and impact. While this book highlights the contributions of women who forged new paths for women or argued for women's rights, I don't consider this a purely feminist work. I have not attempted to outline major trends or these women's roles in them, beyond the places where their writings and thoughts intersected with later feminist thought. Yes, these are heroic women, sometimes outspoken women, women who were not always content with the roles that society offered them, yet this book is not expected to live in the feminist pantheon.

One of the very first Venetian women to garner my attention was actually a living person: Giorgia Boscola, the first woman gondolier. Gondolas are a uniquely Venetian vessel, a symbol of the city, an icon from its history. Yet you will not find a chapter here on Giorgia. Instead, I chose to focus on historical women, those who set in motion, sometimes centuries earlier, the accomplishments being realized by Venetian women today. Perhaps Maria Boscola, regatta champion, inspired Olympic swimmer Federica Pellegrini. Or journalist Elisabetta Caminer Turra forged a path followed by Teresa Sensi, twentieth century journalist. Perhaps I'll write these modern women's stories later, or another can come along to record their accomplishments.

Of course, each of the women featured in *A Beautiful Woman in Venice* represents more than just herself. These are the women whose stories have survived, if even in only a few sentences here and there, a painting or a signature or a name on a will or court record. How many of their sisters' stories are lost to us? How many remarkable creators and writers, mothers and daughters and wives, left no trace? How many women—talented, ambitious, thoughtful, intelligent, beautiful women—were silenced or their stories erased? For example, when I saw the index of 250 women poets published by Luisa Bergalli Gozzi in 1726, I realized that each of them had her own story to tell, but I found biographies on fewer than a dozen of them. The women whose stories are rescued in these pages bear some burden of representing others whose stories cannot be told.

With telling their stories comes a great responsibility. From the outset, I wished to find these women's voices whenever possible, to quote their writings and their words, whether in letters, poems, books, wills, or court records. I wanted their words to help build the stories of their lives, and in places I have chosen to limit quotes by men who defamed them; though these malicious men are part of the stories, I don't want to give their demeaning words more power or space on the page. If a chapter contains no quotes by that woman, this means that I was unable to locate any. Some quotes appear to be of doubtful authenticity, and I note those places but chose to include the quotes as at least a semblance of that woman's voice. I only hope that I have done right by these women, each of whom I fell in love with as I learned about her unique experiences. Where my ability to research might be lacking, I hope my devotion and caring can make up for the deficiencies.

Related to the feelings I developed for these women was my decision about how to use their names. Academic writing calls for referring to subjects by their last names. But which last name? When Venetian women married, they generally appended their husband's last name to their own. Some women changed the spelling of their name; for example, poet Veronica Franco, as she's most often known, published under the name "Franca," using the feminine final "a" in the Italian language. Some names appear spelled in a variety of ways, so I chose the spelling most frequently used by other scholars or the spelling on legal documents, and I noted other spellings (though this was not always clear either, as in the case of Hermonia Vivarini). And some women had no last names, such as Giovanna of Corte Nova or Anna Maria, an orphan. As I read and wrote more about these remarkable women, I found that referring to them by their first names felt the most natural, as though they are women you would have a cup of hot chocolate with, or borrow a book, or discuss a sonnet. Most of these women were from the patrician class and would have been addressed with loftier titles, and I intend no disrespect, but I hope that readers can feel their human warmth by getting to know them on a first name basis.

And why Venetian women? Why not Florentine, or Roman, or women from other great European centers of culture, or the overlooked women of the working class? To state it simply, I love Venice. It is a city that draws me back again and again, as it does for many women and men who fall for its allures. I keep meeting women who feel an almost inexplicable draw to the city of canals, and it's time that they had the stories of the women who came before them. Perhaps others will find a connection to our predecessors, as I have.

Venetian women faced unique cultural challenges in a society that granted them few choices beyond arranged marriage, a convent, or the sex trade. And yet Venice also offered unprecedented opportunities as a city with a great deal of autonomy from Roman and papal rule, a city at the heart of the publishing explosion, a city that drew thousands of pilgrims, both religious and hedonistic, to sample what Venice had to offer. Its founders created a system of checks and balances of power, otherwise unknown in Europe at that time. Venice had more convents than any other city, but also more theaters. It was the birthplace of credit banking and also public opera. Marriage contracts elicited the highest dowries, so necessary for proper noble families, but the Carnevale season engendered the most debauchery among citizens of all classes. Dozens of laws were passed to control women's fashions and household extravagances. Venice's artists contributed greatly to the birth of Rococo as well as the craze for lace, glass, and periodicals. Women had a hand in all these enterprises. The women in these pages span the fourteenth through nineteenth centuries, their stories bringing to life the cultural milieu in which they lived.

Beauty comes in countless guises and packages. I won't attempt to define it, though I hope that the stories of these beautiful Venetian women will illuminate the term and help us all redefine beauty.

# Morosina Morosini Grimani

## A Woman Beckoning

The new dogaressa stands at the apex of a triangle formed by women. Morosina gazes directly at the viewer, her eyes prominent under curving brows, her wide face passive, calm, despite the tumult around her. She leans back slightly while stretching out her left hand, palm up. Is she thinking about the thousands of people gathered to pay her tribute? Besides pride and delight, she must feel a bit humbled by the great pageant created in her honor. Below her at the left point of the triangle stoically stands an image of Lady Justice, blindfolded, holding her scales, here seen on the prow of the Venetian state boat. To the right lounges the allegorical woman of Venice (sometimes depicted as Venus, the goddess of love), swathed in flowing fabrics, her feet in the sea. Morosina Morosini Grimani, newly sworn in at her coronation ceremony, holds the position of honor, placing her as the prime symbolic woman representing this feminine city, as depicted in Andrea Vicentino's 1597 etching *Dogaressa Morosina Morosini Grimani Disembarking at Saint Mark's*. Scholar Bronwen Wilson points out that "The procession . . . dramatizes the transformation of an individual woman into a symbol of the state" (76). The dogaressa was the wife of the doge, Venice's head of state, as close to the monarchy as this republic would allow, and the woman with the most power in a state where women had almost none. Morosina held a position very few women ever held, and she did so with grace and honor.

This image may seem unremarkable. How many times are nobles lionized, magnified, or exalted as symbols of a great country? Morosina made of herself an important symbol in a city that generally silenced her sex. Venetian patrician women were kept indoors, allowed to be viewed on their balconies, or paraded out as decoration on a father's or husband's arm for visiting dignitaries or state festivals. More than in other European cities, Venice had gendered spaces—that is, places women occupied, such as the drawing room, the kitchen, and the church, while men inhabited other spaces, such as the public streets and squares, governmental offices, and the front rooms of the house. Rules strictly demarcated women's movements, bodies, dress, and images. Sumptuary Laws delineated what they could and couldn't wear. Restrictive social mores limited their independence and even their personal identities. Writer Giovanni Battista de Luca wrote in the seventeenth century that women should add "to the quality of the husband, as if she were a kind of moon that received all light and splendor from the sun, that is the husband" (qtd. in B. Wilson 102). True, Morosina's husband the doge held far more power than she, but she was not a dim candle. A handful of her sisters who preceded her had clawed their way out of this restrictive box, but for the most part Morosina stood alone in her assertion of herself into a public space. She may have simply been enjoying the costly extravaganza, the clothing, food, and processions, or she may have had designs to elevate women's status by becoming a role model for others.

With these strictures in mind, Morosina Morosini Grimani's image—and of course her actual actions that led to that image—become more remarkable.

Born in 1545 into a wealthy and prestigious family, Morosina lived the life of the very upper classes of the *nobili*. This meant a home in the splendid Palazzo Morosini near San Canzian (or Cancian), with its celebrated gardens full of statuary, and a name positioned in Venice's Golden Book of the most exalted class of families. Morosina married Marino Grimani on November 27, 1560, joining together her family with the Grimani, another family whose lineage stretched back to the original twelve families that elected Venice's first doge in 697. After their wedding at the Church of San Cristoforo, she moved from her family's palace to the imposing, white marble Palazzo Grimani on the Grand Canal near San Luca, replete with frescoed ceilings and a domed roof. No Grand Canal palace feels more solid or stately.

Marino and Morosina were an immensely popular couple, and in 1595 Marino was unanimously appointed to replace Pasquale Cicogna to become the eighty-ninth doge. For his coronation the State held a three-day feast for every working woman and man in the city, with jugglers and singers in the streets and plays performed in the squares. Free bread and wine were distributed generously so that all citizens, not just the nobles, could enjoy the beneficence of their new ruler. Morosina and her daughters threw silver and copper coins to the populace from the balcony of the Palazzo Ducale, displaying their brocade dresses shot through with silver and gold thread.

Of Marino and Morosina's four daughters, Beatrice became a nun, while the other three, Donata, Laura, and Maria, married well, a sign of great affluence as each of those daughters would have required an extravagant dowry. (Many noble families could only afford to marry off one daughter.) Morosina would have had the pleasure of spending evenings with her daughters to prepare their trousseaus, embroidering their linens, counting their cutlery, and placing all into elaborate wooden chests to transport to their husbands' homes.

The family had delayed Morosina's coronation as dogaressa for two years, till May of 1597, so they could plan an event like no other and so she need not share the limelight with her husband the doge. Only three other dogaressas had been crowned; other wives hadn't lived long enough to have a coronation, one doge had died too soon in office, and somewhere in there came a war with the Turks. Perhaps Morosina was ambitious, pompous, even vain to so publicly display such wealth and power. Or can her coronation be read as an opportunity for a woman to place herself in a public realm at a time when women were never allowed this position? History didn't retain her thoughts on the subject, yet it's hard to imagine that her presence didn't inspire other women to both admire her and aspire to have a public life, too.

In fact, Morosina's coronation surpassed her husband's. Over 2,000 people turned out to view the ceremony, clogging the Grand Canal with boats and the Piazza with bodies. "Most singular and Most Serene Lady, words fail to assure your Highness of the devotion of your enthusiastically admiring servants," cried out her fans who lined her path (qtd. in Staley 285). As Morosina rode on the Bucintoro, the gilded state barge, from the Palazzo Grimani up the Grand Canal to Piazza San Marco, she passed palaces festooned with bouquets of damask roses, the Morosini emblem. In her wake followed trade-guild boats decorated with sea creatures and deities. Young women tossed roses upon the waters, and liveried gondoliers bowed as she passed. Wooden platforms rocked upon the waters as people danced each of the three nights of festivities. In the Bacino at the mouth of the Piazzetta San Marco floated the "*Teatro deto il Mondo*" or Theater of the World barge, a floating playhouse constructed for their enjoyment.

Morosina's procession and disembarkation is recorded in a number of paintings and etchings, including the aforementioned painting by Andrea Vicentino (aka Andrea Michieli) now at Venice's Museo Correr. It shows the decorated boats lined along the *fondamenta,* the sidewalk that runs alongside the water, and the gowned and bejeweled people crowding the Piazzetta to view the festivities. The painting's size is imposing, taking up an entire upper wall. Similarly, the sheer magnitude of the spectacle is overwhelming, with everyone turning their faces towards Morosina in her gown of brilliant gold, servants holding up the edges of her dress, and everyone seeming to remark, "Have you seen her?"

Attired in cloth embroidered with gold thread and silver floral designs, Morosina flouted the Sumptuary Laws. These edicts, first proclaimed in 1299 and added to over the centuries, attempted to restrict people, particularly women, from spending so lavishly and outshining their neighbors in clothing and other accouterments. But this didn't stop

Morosina, who was out to create of herself a new icon. At her coronation, a floor-length veil studded with jewels cascaded from her small ducal cap, which was likewise covered with precious gems. Though a flared and stiff Burano lace collar rose behind her head, her chest above her bodice was still visible through a thin fichu of fabric. Morosina attired herself magnificently in fabrics she had designed herself—novel floral designs done in silver thread, and a frothy, airy fabric of gold so fine it resembled tissue. She also bedecked herself liberally with Burano lace, in the form of a fine white silk veil studded with jewels and a fichu on her bosom embedded with pearls. Historian Edgecumbe Staley wrote that Morosina's coronation "raised the tone of society, and materially improved the condition of employment" (384). Though fashion may not appear as weighty a contribution as other accomplishments, these preparations certainly created countless jobs.

Four hundred ladies accompanied Morosina at her coronation, a truly remarkable number of women to be seen in public. They were fabulously attired in brocade gowns, lace collars, golden chains, white feather fans in hand, and their hair in the popular coif of the day that appears as two horns of tall curls. For nearly all of her procession, Morosina did not travel alongside her husband Marino, the doge. Only once did they stand side by side, rendering the crowd speechless, since Venetian law generally forbade the Republic's rulers from appearing together like king and queen, which they were not. Despite the fact that women had no political power or presence, Morosina created this weighty persona and came as close as anyone could to holding an influential position. Her coronation was an event separate from her husband's, giving it equal weight. Morosina became the female face of Venice, a potent symbol for the state. A potent symbol for women.

Morosina didn't forget to reward those who had helped to create this spectacle, nor those who had elected her husband in the first place. For those who served her on the second festival day as she opened gifts, she gave each an *osello*, a medallion that featured Morosina's likeness on one side and her new title on the back. The forty voting senators received bags of gold ducats. Day three found feats of valor in her honor by the city's Castellani and Nicolotti factions, as hearty men built human pyramids called the Feats of Hercules or held daring fist fights on city bridges. Navies from England, Holland, and Flanders paraded across the Lagoon, showing off their battleships and exploding cannons. Gondoliers and sailors wearing red and white performed "aquatic sports" and proved their speed in a regatta (Staley 288). Elaborate banquets provided exotic feasts; one such featured forty-seven courses, starting with spiced sturgeon and ending with "apples of paradise" (Staley 287). No expense was spared.

Besides all this pomp and presentation, though, Morosina also spent her time and money on good works. She used her own money to restore the Church of San Sebastiano in Venice's Dorsoduro neighborhood. This was one of Venice's votive churches dedicated to a saint whose intervention helped to end the bubonic plague. Though the church's exterior is plain, inside it holds works by Titian, Tintoretto, and Veronese, who is buried there. Morosina may have lived in physical isolation from other classes of Venetian citizens, but she didn't forget to include them in her generosity and charitable works.

During her husband's eleven-year reign as doge, a time of peace and prosperity, Morosina Morosini Grimani took it upon herself to promote the lace industry, just like Dogaressa Giovanna Dandolo Malipiero had 140 years earlier. With her own money, Morosina founded a school at Santa Fosca directed by Caterina Gardin, educating women in this original Burano artistry. There, 130 women sat at their work cushions stitching or twisting bobbin thread to form lace "intended for personal use or as rich presents for foreign courts" (qtd. in Davanzo Poli, *Lace* 19). Morosina initiated a committee to promote this craft among the upper classes, encouraging wealthy women to place orders for cuffs, ruffles, veils, wraps, scarves, and linens. This not only provided her fellow nobles with beautiful fashions to adorn themselves, but also, more importantly, it provided livelihoods for countless women who could supplement their family incomes and perhaps set aside dowries for their daughters. Venetian lace is one of Venice's homegrown arts, like glass making and book printing, that put it on the map as a shopping destination for all Europe.

For her patronage of the lace industry, in 1597 Pope Clement VIII presented Morosina with a Golden Rose, a solid gold, life-size flower "as a special mark of honour," write historians Thomas Jonglez and Paola Zoffoli (315). Seven such roses were presented by popes to Venetians, but only one of the recipients was a woman—Morosina. "Its presentation as a gift expresses the pontiff's wish that the heart and spirit of the recipient will be bathed in an equally divine perfume," (315) demonstrating the high esteem in which Morosina was held, not only by Venetians but as far away as Rome.

All of these lavish fabrics, jewels, and accouterments served to make women into symbols of their husband's wealth, not to mention the State's prosperity. Bedecked women were the embodiment of success, money, and power, objects to be shown off to visiting dignitaries as well as an admiring populace. Scholar Stanley Chojnacki contends that Venetian women wore elaborate clothing and gemstones to compensate for having no political clout. Clothes and jewels increased women's visibility. They demanded notice. "In a culture that narrowly limited women's activities in the public sphere, heavy spending on lavish dress could be viewed as doubly assertive, calling visual attention to individual identity and demonstrating the autonomous possession of wealth," concludes Chojnacki (159). At her coronation Morosina stood, a woman alone and admired, unapologetic, strong in her image of Venice personified. She seemed to be making the rules work for her. As Bronwen Wilson writes, "Through the power of the representations of her public appearance, Morosina threatens to establish an autonomous female identity, which seems very dangerous indeed to such a system" (107). Women had few ways to be seen, so when they did get the opportunity, they garnered all the attention they could, sometimes in ways that transgressed the status quo (Price 97). Perhaps men kept women concealed and suppressed because they feared the power that women might commandeer. For those three days of festivities, and perhaps for her tenure as dogaressa, Morosina didn't just adorn a man or create a scenic backdrop. She may not have had a public political voice, yet she didn't merely disappear behind closed doors, either. Sumptuary Laws and patriarchal constraints wouldn't hinder her.

Curiously, Morosina's coronation as dogaressa was the last. On January 10, 1645, the Senate decreed that no future dogaressa could hold such a festival. She would not be allowed to ride in state in the Bucintoro, she would not be allowed a lavish procession, and sadly, she would not be allowed to wear that symbol of power, the red *corno* cap. Were the patriarchs threatened by Morosina's ostentation, her potential power amongst the populace? Morosina's husband Marino died in 1605, and then Morosina followed nine years later on January 21, 1614, when she was given an elaborate funeral, her body laying in state in the Palazzo Ducale, with all the senators attending. Inside the Church of Sant'Iseppo in the Castello district, Vincenzo Scamozzi designed an elaborate monument for the couple, with sculptures by Girolamo Campagna. The smooth stone panels reach the ceiling and take up much of one church wall with their enormous cool white marble columns and cornices, a final memorial to the Grimani family's glory. Two sarcophagi hold the once-beloved doge and dogaressa, with robed classical figures atop every column and pediment.

Vicentino's painting shows Morosina at the zenith of the triumvirate including justice and love. In it, Morosina looks directly at the viewer, beckoning.

# Giustina Rossi

## Thanks to the Old Woman

$G$iustina peers out her window, arm outstretched after dropping her spice-grinding mortar, which now lies alongside the gruesomely bleeding head of a hapless standard bearer. Blood pools below his head while his legs are gently crossed at the ankles, his arm slung out like one asleep. His rebel flag lies on the stones. Around him men run in all directions, gesticulating wildly, as soldiers in round black helmets brandish lances. Gabriel Bella captured this moment in his painting *Bajamonte Tiepolo's Conspiracy.*

Giustina had just turned the tide of history. The date was June 15, 1310.

Right outside the Piazza San Marco, on the Merceria dell'Orologio street that leads under and then behind the Clock Tower, a low relief carving above the Sotoportego e Calle del Capello Nero captures Giustina at that fateful moment. The carving shows a window framing an older woman with a shawl wrapped round her shoulders, her hair pulled back in a bun. A curtain hangs down one side. One of her hands rests on the sill, while the other is poised above a mortar that is tipping out of the window. It is as if Giustina were grinding her cornmeal with her pestle and stopped in her work. She looks intent, serious, her head tilted to one side and mouth in a line. Giustina was a patriotic Venetian citizen, fed up with the hooligans running through the streets below her, and she was going to do something about it. Perhaps Giustina also feared the turmoil that these rebels brought, and as a shopkeeper wanting to maintain a business and protect her family, she did her part to safeguard her own and her city's interests.

For a while, Venice had been at war in Ferrara, and not with any ordinary foe, but with the Pope. From its earliest inception, Venice had prided itself on its independence, both political and religious. When Italy was just a conglomeration of kingdoms and states, the Pope in Rome ruled as the spiritual leader, and all bowed before his edicts concerning not only matters of religious but also governmental affairs. Except Venice. While Venetians undeniably embraced Catholicism, they simultaneously embraced an independence from Rome's mandates; "Venetian first, Christians second" was the saying at the time. In this case, the Pope threatened Venice with an interdict—an official prohibition barring the city from church functions—plus excommunication from the Church. Venice's Doge Pietro Gradenigo would have none of it. He wanted to rule Ferrara, and he wanted to maintain Venice's standing with the Church. Giustina Rossi, described as "*una vecchia*" or older woman, would have cherished the legacy of Venetian independence, a point of pride for Venetian citizens of every rank.

But not for every Venetian. A few patrician families—perhaps disgruntled with their doge's stance, perhaps more loyal to the Pope, or perhaps making a power grab—instigated a rebellion. Querinis and Tiepolos hoped to overthrow Doge Gradenigo. Marco Querini enlisted his son-in-law Bajamonte Tiepolo to lead a group of men. This branch of the Tiepolo family made its home at Campo Sant'Agostin in the San Polo district. The Querini and Tiepolo groups would each commence in different parts of the city—Tiepolo from San Polo and Querini from the Rialto fish market—and converge at the Piazza San Marco, stampeding through the narrow alleys and small *campi* or squares that make up the city. They were to be joined by Badoero Badoer, arriving with a fleet of ships at the water entrance to the Piazza.

Unfortunately for them, the three groups were not synchronized in their attack. A sudden storm had broken out and delayed Badoero's fleet, which didn't arrive in time to help the conspirators. Moreover, a loyal citizen named Marco Donato had tipped off the doge about the rebellion, so the Palazzo Ducale guards waited at the ready for their arrival. Bajamonte Tiepolo's band was nearly rioting; they had paused on their journey to plunder the treasury building near the Ponte di Rialto, and their pockets must have clinked with the weight of their stolen wealth while their hearts soared with their triumph. Yelling slogans and brandishing swords, they careened through Venice's narrow streets past shops selling fabrics, shoes, glass, paper, dresses, doublets, and hats. Tiepolo's group raced through the Merceria towards the Piazza San Marco while Marco Querini's faction advanced along the Calle dei Fabbri. These two groups could see each other along the narrow and gloomy Calle del Capello Nero, probably wondering where Badoero was. Giustina must have heard them coming as their stomping boots echoed off the stone walls and cobblestones. As the rebels emerged from under the covered walkway of the Sotoportego del Cappello Nero, their flag bearer reached the Merceria dell'Orologio, right below Giustina's window, carrying the flag bearing the word "*Libertá*."

Here is where the facts become murky. Some reports claim that Giustina knocked a stone mortar, or perhaps a flower pot, off her window sill. Others say that she intentionally dropped the heavy stone mortar onto the standard-bearer's head. Traveler Margaret Oliphant writes, "One woman, looking out, in the mad passion of terror seized the first thing that came to hand, a stone vase or mortar on her window-sill, and flung it down at hazard into the midst of the tumult" (86). Whatever the case, something heavy struck the man's head hard enough to kill him instantly. A white stone set into the street marks the spot where he expired. Apparently, Giustina was not the only loyal Venetian to act. Soon neighbors in nearby houses leaned out their windows to pelt the rebels with crockery, stones, roof tiles, or whatever was at hand, calling out for the ruffians to flee. The citizen uprising worked, jangling the traitors' nerves, and the death of their flag bearer wrecked their confidence.

The rebels panicked. Already a motley lot of untrained citizens, they had little discipline and less direction. Giustina's timely stone from above so startled Tiepolo's band that they immediately turned and fled back towards the Rialto, pursued by the Palazzo Ducale's guards, who had amassed due to Marco Donato's tip. Unbeknownst to Tiepolo's men, Marco Querini's group was thwarted and Querini himself killed. Bajamonte Tiepolo's band wreaked havoc as they retreated, burning the wooden Ponte di Rialto en route to Campo Sant'Agostin, hoping to prevent the doge's men from following them. Who knows what Giustina did after derailing the rebellion: perhaps she returned to preparing her meal—though she wouldn't be able to finish grinding the corn for her polenta with her mortar lying in the street next to a dead man.

Doge Gradenigo was quite pleased with the day's outcome. The loyal informant Marco Donato was elevated to the patrician class and later became a member of the Great Council that decided Venetian State policy. The surname Donato was contracted to Doná, or Doná delle Rose, another branch of the Doná family, and grew to become one of Venice's illustrious noble families.

The doge also wanted to reward Giustina Rossi. Being a humble merchant of a mirror shop, she didn't ask for much. But she did have two requests. One, Giustina wished to fly the Venetian flag from her balcony window on all feast days and State holidays. Venice's flag in the early fourteenth century featured the winged lion of San Marco, a halo behind his head, a fierce look on his face, and his paw upon the open Bible (Schmoger). The doge gladly granted Giustina's patriotic request, and her flag must have stood out boldly against the pale stone of her building. Two, Giustina asked that her rent never be raised for her or her daughters. The Procuratie or governmental offices owned her building and were her landlords. The doge was so happy to comply that he granted her request in perpetuity. Giustina's rent of fifteen ducats a month would never increase, he declared.

June 15 became a State holiday, commemorating the rebellion's crushing defeat. It had already been a special day, the feast day of San Vio and San Modesto, when the doge and a retinue of clerics and elected officials processed from Piazza San Marco to the Church of San Vio and Modesto in Dorsoduro. Each year, to thank the saints for their intercession to foil the uprising, the doge lit twelve candles in a church ceremony, which was followed by a banquet and a musical performance. After the rebellion, the church was actually rebuilt using stones from Bajamonte Tiepolo's house, which was demolished as punishment for his role; in fact, the Tiepolo palace door became the new church door. (Sadly, the church fell into disrepair and was demolished in 1813, and then a house was built on that site, again using some of the Tiepolo house fragments.)

Bajamonte Tiepolo, being of the patrician class, was not executed, but exiled. His family's *palazzo* or palace in Campo Sant'Agostin was demolished and marked by a Column of Infamy, which stood there for many years before being moved to the Museo Correr. A similar marker in Campo San Luca also commemorates Bajamonte's defeat. According to the diary of writer Francesco Sansovino, this site marks the geometrical center of Venice and the location where loyalists to the doge gathered on that fateful day of the rebellion (Freely 99). Members of the Scuola della Caritá and the Scuola dei Pittori came to the State's aid and were honored for this by the flagpole bearing their coats of arms. The *scuole* in Venice were charitable or religious fraternities that provided social services like burying the destitute, overseeing hospitals, or organizing festivals, and in this case they rallied to aid the State against the rebels.

Giustina Rossi apparently returned to quietly selling her mirrors and raising her daughters. The history books tell little else about her. Chronicler Pompeo Molmenti recorded that the legal documents list her name as Lucia, while he added that State Archive records by Cecchetti gave her name as Maria de Oltise (Part 1, Vol. 1, 144). Venetians to this day refer to her affectionately as "*La vecia del morter.*" With pride she would have draped her flag from her window for every Sensa (Ascension Day), Festa di San Marco, Festa delle Marie, and of course every June 15.

Giustina's heirs enjoyed the generosity of the State for over a century. But in 1436, the rent on the apartment was increased. Giustina's great-grandson Nicolo Rossi was the official inhabitant, but he had been away from Venice, serving in the navy. After his return, in 1468 he appealed to the State and won his suit; the rent was returned to its initial fee of fifteen ducats. The agreement lasted through Venice's prosperous and powerful fifteenth and sixteenth centuries, and through its decline in the seventeenth, a total of 487 years. When the Venetian Republic fell to Napoleon in 1797, this rental agreement became null and void. However, the historical significance of Giustina Rossi's home did not diminish. Around 1888, writer Margaret Oliphant wrote that a shop in this location bore the sign *"Della grazia del morter,"* expressing thanks for Giustina's hunk of stone (92). In 1861, the home's inhabitant, Elia Vivante Mussati, had a plaque made that bears the date "15 June 1310."

One other significant institution developed after that fateful day. The Venetian Great Council created the Consiglio dei Dieci or Council of Ten, a body designed to oversee sentences of exile, such as the one against Bajamonte Tiepolo. The Ten's Capi or heads also became watchdogs to thwart potential rebellions and oversee a group of security police. This body proved quite useful in securing more government power, and its authority was broadened to oversee secret cases that the leaders didn't want the full Senate to know about. In the sixteenth century, the Council of Ten expanded even further, adding three State Inquisitors who employed spies, guarded State secrets, and prosecuted crimes committed by nobles. This Council struck fear into the hearts of generations of citizens.

Great things can come from mishaps. If a scientific discovery was made by accident, does that diminish its importance? Whether Giustina Rossi intended to thwart the rebels that day or not, the outcome was the same. Her mortar stopped the forward momentum of a rebel band, securing the doge's continued reign and Venice's independence from the Pope. Despite the power, prestige, and wealth of the patricians, it was an elderly shopkeeper, and a woman, who played a pivotal role in the doge's reign, preserving the Republic when it was still clay being formed.

*Bajamonte Tiepolo's Conspiracy* by Gabriel Bella

# Cassandra Fedele

## The Clearest Testimony

 $\mathcal{M}$ en wearing robes and ruffled collars, scores of them ranged in a great hall, leaned in to hear every word of this woman's speech. Standing at the podium, Cassandra Fedele must have known that some of them would doubt her, would question the very legitimacy of her position as the principal speaker at the University of Padua, where, as a woman, she would not have been permitted entry as a student. Yet she did not shrink from them. She raised her voice and began, speaking of her young cousin Bertuccio Lamberti, "Because our Bertuccio, even when he was a boy, always applied all his energy and enthusiasm, his superb memory and intellectual acuity to eloquence, he has now become an orator of the first order and a uniquely gifted speaker" (Fedele 157). Though it was his graduation, Cassandra could have been describing herself as a speaker— and she richly deserved similar accolades and also a university degree. In 1487 for Cassandra, at age twenty-two, to present a Latin oration at her cousin's university commencement was quite an anomaly and an accomplishment. An anonymous engraving shows Cassandra's smooth, narrow face, with eyes downcast, an unsmiling mouth, and hair coiled atop her head, a few curls allowed to frame her face. She wears a thickly gathered scholar's gown edged by a band of darker, embroidered ribbon. She radiates a mood more contemplative than contented.

Irony lay in the fact that Fedele had been invited to speak by university professors at a school that she was not allowed to attend. The University of Padua is the second oldest in Italy, after Bologna's. Its Palazzo Bo, near the center of the original walled city, has porticoed halls facing a central courtyard. Upon the walls and ceilings of hallways and lecture halls are painted coats of arms or sculpted medallions, listing each professor's name and subject, including the likes of Copernicus and Galileo. Their coats of arms in Vesuvian red, honey orange, and midnight blue cover nearly every surface, hammering home the presence of these men's places in academia. Men had been attending the school since 1222, when it was founded by a group of students from Bologna who hired their own teachers to begin a new school. Women were not allowed to attend classes nor lectures, so for Cassandra to be both present and a featured speaker was an oddity indeed. Her speech topic was the value of an education and particularly the skill of oration. "For it is speech," she contended, "that makes men superior to all other animals" (157). Did the men in the audience realize this statement applied to all women, too, and not just the woman standing before them?

Perhaps they did. This was the age of Renaissance Humanism after all, when classical Greek and Latin texts were revived and the liberal arts became the center of any worthy education. The liberal arts were the soul of learning, and a number of enlightened fathers were educating their daughters. Cassandra was one of these. History tells few details about Angelo Fedele, Cassandra's father, except that the family was from Milan and he had studied Latin and Greek literature and philosophy. Cassandra's mother Barbara Leoni bore five children: a son named Alessandro, and three other daughters named Cristina, Maddalena, and Polissena (Pignatti). Cassandra, probably born in 1465, was the only one who appeared to relish learning, so her father tutored her in Latin and Greek. She later wrote in a letter to the son of her fellow scholar Francesco Camosi, "For there is nothing sweeter, more excellent, or more pleasurable to human beings than [the pursuit of knowledge]" (Fedele 132).

Though the family was not of the noble class, they were above the common *popolani* or workers class; at some point in her life, Cassandra lived in the more working-class neighborhood of Venice's Castello district, in an apartment on the long street Calle de la Testa near Campo Santi Giovanni e Paolo. Homes here shared the three and four story buildings with others, with a common entrance and staircase and a breeze from the northern lagoon if one was lucky enough to live on an upper floor. As her abilities progressed, by age twelve she began studying with a Servite monk named Gasparino Borro. At about age sixteen, Cassandra settled into studies with tutors at home, perhaps a room set aside as a study or the dinner table piled with books that had to be swept aside for each meal. How she must have hungered for knowledge, willingly putting in countless hours and probably anxious about how she would be perceived by others.

Fortunately, everyone initially hailed Cassandra as a prodigy. By age twelve she had mastered classical languages and moved on to philosophy and dialectics. She would compose Latin verses and then sing them, accompanying herself on the guitar. These things simply were not done by young women. She was so rare that Florentine scholar and poet Angelo Poliziano likened her to "violets [that] were to grow in ice, roses in snow, or lilies in the midst of frost" (qtd. in Fedele 90). Her fame spread throughout Europe as scholarly men and monarchs learned of this young woman who had spoken to such an assembly of educated men. Cassandra corresponded with Angelo Poliziano and with a number of other scholars, which helped to develop her reasoning and writing skills. These admirers often praised her. "Even if I say I have thought of you as unique," wrote Jacopo Ponzano, a Servite professor, "I do not think I err" (qtd. in Fedele 119). As Lodovico da Schio of Vicenza wrote to Cassandra, "But when I think of your not simply human but divine eloquence, when I consider your physical gestures suitable to oratory, when I ponder your constantly ornate style, I don't know what else to say about you unless I may adapt the following passage from Virgil to describe you: 'I believe—nor are these empty words—that you are descended from the race of the gods'" (qtd. in Fedele 65). This praise may seem hyperbolic to modern ears, but it was the style of the age. It must have brought Cassandra a sense of vindication for her toils.

Cassandra wrote similar praise about others, including the contention that one's gifts were divine. So perhaps the most important thing to note in all this praise is the shock that her skillful university oration emanated from a woman. Only one previous woman, Isotta Nogarola, had given a public oration before Cassandra. As historian Margaret L. King points out, Cassandra's oration is "unoriginal;" (69) in other words, the ideas she presents do not break new ground. Yet, "It is remarkable not in itself," King continues, "but because a woman had acquired the skills necessary to compose it without error and to deliver it with poise to an audience of some of Europe's most learned men" (69.). Her speech represented years of intense study, first learning Latin and Greek and then reading the original classic texts. Perhaps she read her books stooped over a wooden table, books stacked high around her, wan light falling from the window or a guttering candle. Cassandra overcame not only fatigue and the rigors of a liberal arts education not taught in one's native tongue, but walking a gender expectation tightrope as well. Her every utterance was scrutinized.

In 1587 in Italy, a hundred years after Cassandra Fedele reached her apex of fame for her erudition, only about thirty-three percent of men were educated, and only about twelve percent of women could read and write (Datta 177). Women weren't allowed to attend school, except for the very rare exception of Bonifacio Bembo's Humanist school in Castelfranco and a handful of girls who gleaned small learning at home alongside their brothers. Texts were written in Latin, so studies in philosophy, literature, history, mathematics, and the sciences couldn't even be attempted until one mastered Latin, and usually Greek as well. Noblemen's sons walked this path in scholar's robes, while women remained at home. Against these obstacles, Cassandra's success is that much more impressive.

After her speech, Cassandra launched into an epistolary career, what translator and biographer Diana Robin calls "the obligatory humanist oeuvre" (3). This being before the explosion of Venetian publishing, writers had little chance to publicly share their works. Instead, the learned wrote to the powerful, connected, and intelligent scholars of Europe. Later they might publish these correspondences (and often the companion replies) in small runs for their literary circle. Besides her reading and studies of the classics, Cassandra would have spent countless hours drafting and revising letters every day, scratching out missives on parchment, repeatedly dipping her quill in the ink pot, taking great care with each word as the process of editing errors was so laborious. Each letter probably entailed multiple drafts, a penknife for sharpening her quill, a dictionary in Latin, Aristotle or Dante or the Bible at hand for handy reference, with Cassandra's fingers ink-stained by its completion.

Cassandra cultivated relationships across the continent, from Italian philosophers and writers like Pico di Mirandola and Francesco Gonzaga of Mantua, to King Louis XII in the French court and members of the Spanish throne; in fact, Queen Isabella and King Ferdinand of Spain repeatedly entreated Cassandra to come serve them in Madrid. "Come, then, at our urging," (qtd. in Fedele 20) wrote Isabella, but as France threatened war with the Italian city-states, Cassandra felt it was unwise to travel so far. She would travel "when I do regain my former health," she replied to the Queen, "and when I see that there is peace, tranquility and serenity in Italy (for in these turbulent times and particularly with Italy preparing to go to war it is not advisable for me, a young maiden, to take so much as a stroll, nor could even you, most prudent one, persuade me to do so)" (Fedele 23). Climbing into a carriage, then a boat to travel hundreds of miles was a major undertaking for anyone, but particularly daunting for a young woman. Dirt roads were rough and fraught with bandits, inns were shabby and often of questionable safety, and passports were needed at each frontier. For a modest and often ill young woman, this journey would seem formidable indeed. Furthermore, the Venetian State didn't want Cassandra to leave because she was seen as a valuable asset (King & Rabil, *Immaculate* 22). Her orations and famed abilities brought honor and prestige to the Venetian Republic, and similarly, Cassandra could help raise the Fedele family's status by gaining connections to lofty and powerful people.

In letters, Cassandra often mentioned a chronic, mysterious illness that left her weak and unable to study or correspond. "Ill health, with which I have been afflicted for a long time now," she wrote to Queen Beatrice of Hungary in 1497, "has deterred me from the duty of writing" (Fedele 28). King and Rabil posit that Cassandra might have suffered from psychosomatic illness due to her precarious role in society "stemming from the conflict between personal desire and social necessity" (King & Rabil, *Immaculate* 26). She must have felt the immense pressure of expectation from her family, her government, and her fellow scholars.

She was in a unique position to benefit from the fame and pleasure her learning brought, while simultaneously it raised expectations for her literary output, increased by the fact that these feats were accomplished by a woman. Despite her recurring illness, however, Cassandra corresponded with monarchs, nobles, popes, clergy, and scholars, including some of the most important men and women of her era. Such correspondence was the prime literary activity of her time, and Cassandra was prolific, though few of her numerous letters have survived.

Though she corresponded with many powerful women and sought their patronage, Cassandra didn't seem to develop close friendships with many women near her (or if she did, any such evidence has disappeared). By entering the scholarly world, Cassandra found herself in a world of men, mostly much older than she. According to Angelo Poliziano, she "dare[d], though a maid, to run with men" (qtd. in Fedele 91). Cassandra cultivated a sort of "father as patron" relationship with many of them, a non-sexual definition that allowed her to write to them and learn from them. "You should know that I love you as I would a father," (Fedele 142) she wrote to Andrea Campagnola. To Doctor Ambrosius Miches, after receiving a letter of praise, she penned, "I recognize here the performing of a father's duty" (130). Defining the relationship in these terms made it possible for Cassandra to continue her education and correspondence. Sadly, a woman in the man's scholarly world made herself vulnerable to attack. Cassandra needed patronage and protection from men like these. "Be the guardian of my reputation if I am deserving of this," (67) she beseeched Lodovico da Schio, rector at the University of Padua. Women of the patrician class were rarely seen outside their homes, and when they were, they were usually escorted on the arm of a male family member; a woman's place was to produce children, accompany her husband to social functions, or attend church services.

Cassandra's gender was her bane and her boon. Any young man with her accomplishments might win praise but not continental acclaim; her gender, which made her a rarity in academia, elevated her abilities to a higher status. Though they loved to hear her "perform" at her home as she discussed Aristotle or dialectics in Latin, these same men never invited her to attend classes at the university. By many, Cassandra was never treated as an equal but more as an impressive and entertaining anomaly. She was referred to as "unique glory and jewel of the female sex" by Lodovico da Schio of Vicenza (qtd. in Fedele 65).

Cassandra was in a precarious position. She must appear both non-threatening and still alluring at the same time. Many male Humanists welcomed her to their world and made much of her skills and learning— while simultaneously noting her beauty and maidenhood. Her male correspondent Angelo Tancredi noted her "sweetest lips" (111) and "shining blue eyes . . . like divine stars" (83) and "pure maiden's face" (91). As much as they praised Cassandra's mind, these learned men were not blind to her body. This attention to her looks outlines her dilemma: as Cassandra grew older, she couldn't continue to remain single. She must either sequester herself—to the convent or to what Margaret King calls a "book-lined cell," ("Book" 71) or she could marry, which generally ended any scholarly career.

Over and over Cassandra's male correspondents refer to her chastity. For women, public speaking was seen as akin to promiscuity; a woman who opened up her mouth was as likely to open up her body for others, they believed (Robin 26). Cassandra's correspondents commanded her to "be counted among the virtuous maidens so that [she] may be received by the Lord," (qtd. in Fedele 129) or refer to her "maidenly purity" (113) or her "purity of body and soul" (111). She couldn't exist in this scholarly world without purity as her protection. Girolamo Broianico (as well as others) compared her to Lucretia, who was known in ancient times for valuing her chastity so much that she committed suicide after being raped. Cassandra was expected to be modest while debating great ideas. Many marveled at her ability to do this—and it deserved praise because she carried this added burden, one which men need not consider for themselves. Not only did she need to display her intelligence, but also Cassandra must remain a paragon of chastity. Cassandra's intelligence could be a threat to many men, even those liberal Humanists. They may have respected learned women, but as Margaret King and Albert Rabil point out, many men feared women like Cassandra, and "in response to that fear [they showed] the desire to restrain them by exceptionally rigid demands of chastity" (*Immaculate* 13). A woman's powers must still be controlled.

To attain this balance between purity and erudition, one of Cassandra's tactics was to minimize herself. Professor Diana Robin points out how Cassandra often used Latin word endings as diminutives, creating phrases like "your little servant," (Fedele 24) "a little newcomer," (28) and "so very young a maiden" (51) though she was in her twenties by then. Granted, male writers were sometimes wont to use self-deprecating terms themselves, but Robin notes that this is a trope particular to Cassandra (Robin, "Editor's Introduction" 9). "Such diminutives are designed not only to circumscribe her attributes and thus allay male fears," writes Robin, but also "they are meant to stress her youthful sexual innocence and to arouse male desire" (9). Cassandra must appeal to her male audience, but not too much! She must appear chaste, intelligent, and yet non-threatening. She also referred to her "audacity" to write to monarchs, for she was only a "young girl" (Fedele 49). Cassandra created a charming picture of herself as she stood before the Venetian Senate in 1556 to present her second oration, the topic being women's education. "I blush to do so," she said, "and am ever mindful that I am a member of the female sex and that my intellect is small" (159). In the grand hall of the Palazzo Ducale, darkly stained wooden walls and enormous oil paintings glowering from the ceiling, Cassandra must have appeared particularly fragile in this world of men's politics and power.

Cassandra may have told her audience that she had little talent or learning, yet the beauty of the moment came when she proved otherwise. How many naysayers clapped shut their skeptical mouths or widened their eyes in shock as this erudite woman began to speak? Cassandra was a nimble speaker, with "subtle, elegant, articulate Latin missives" and her oration was "erudite, eloquent, sonorous, brilliant, and full of felicitous talent," (qtd. in Fedele 90) as her correspondent Angelo Poliziano put it. He could write these things about her, but self-deprecation was a survival skill for a woman navigating the Humanist man's world. Fortunately, a number of Cassandra's works were saved and published in 1636 by Giacomo Filippo Tomasini, under the title *Cassandrae Fidelis Ventae epistolae & orationes posthumae: nunquam antehac editae* (*Letters & Orations of the Most Illustrious Venetian Woman, Cassandra Fedele, Posthumous, Having Never Previously Been Edited*). Unfortunately, none of Cassandra's original manuscripts have survived, her rounded or spiky, forceful or gentle handwriting unknown to later readers.

Though so many of Cassandra's remarks are self-deprecating—her armor against envious attack—she showed bolts of confidence and pride. In a letter to Accorsio Maynerio, orator to King Louis XII of France, she referred to herself as "a female warrior" (Fedele 48). To Lodovico Sforza, Duke of Milan, she acknowledged that some men were envious of her talents and responded, "Even so, I am accustomed to laugh at these men, following the habit of the philosophers" (51). Dwelling on these "malevolent" men only slowed her down, she remarked (51). It's tempting to believe, (and perhaps it's wishful thinking), that these tidbits represent her true voice.

Society didn't have a standard role for women like Cassandra. She was neither the silent wife relegated to the drawing room nor the cloistered nun sealed in a cell, and neither was she the educated yet socially shunned "honest courtesan." Many struggled to place her. "It is amazing to think," wrote Angelo Poliziano, "that such a letter came from a woman (but why do I use that word?): I should say instead: a girl and one not yet married" (qtd. in Fedele 90). He said this in awe and wonder and wrote to her with great reverence, and yet this letter helps to outline a woman's definition. General Pier Dabuson, after visiting Venice but not being allowed to meet Cassandra, added in his subsequent letter to her, "[Cassandra] has demonstrated that a manly mind can be born in a person of the female sex and that women, though their sex be unchanged, can acquire traits that clearly belong to the male" (qtd. in Fedele 110). This was certainly meant as a compliment (after all, he was trying to win an audience with her), but again such comments show that a learned woman was a rare flower—and maybe not a "woman" at all.

Once she grew older and her fame as a child prodigy had waned, Cassandra saw the invitations dwindle and the stipends taper off. She seems to have married happily, though, in 1499 to a doctor named Gian-Maria Mapelli. Diana Robin believes that Cassandra's two warm letters to an unnamed doctor were probably to him (35). Cassandra wrote, "You ought to know that you are loved by me as a father and nothing would please me more, nor could anything more pleasant happen, than that I be allowed to contribute to your honor and utility" (Fedele 41). After posting for a number of years in Cyprus or Crete for Gian-Maria's work, however, the couple lost all their belongings in a shipwreck as they returned to Venice, wooden boxes floating wrecked upon the waves, cloth bundles quickly sinking below. How many of Cassandra's precious letters and books were lost to a watery fate? Within a year of the shipwreck Gian-Maria was dead, and Cassandra had nothing. Looking down upon her husband's coffin at his funeral service, scents of incense filled the air and chanting punctuated the service, but Cassandra's thoughts must have drifted towards her uncertain future.

In her twenty years of married life, (which apparently produced no children), Cassandra seems to have written nothing. Learned women of the fifteenth and sixteenth centuries had virtually no freedom within marriage to pursue their studies or their writing, which is why, as historian Patricia Labalme contends, they might instead choose to sequester themselves to seek "psychic freedom" (78). Unfortunately, psychic freedom didn't pay the rent. Apparently, Cassandra did not feel a religious calling, either, that might lead to withdrawing into a convent. Instead, Cassandra needed support from her web of correspondents in the form of recommendations to the State, which might result in patronage, an allowance, housing, or other financial support. When she was younger and single, she had received a small monetary stipend from the government, which she used to help support her family. But after her husband's death, while she lived with her sister Polissena and her family, Cassandra returned to her desk and penned letters to her network, asking for recommendations and financial help. In 1521 she wrote to Pope Leo X, "In this tragedy, then, I am in need of your protection," and requested, "I ask you to provide assistance to my family and me" (Fedele 106). Unfortunately, she received no reply (King & Rabil, *Immaculate* 22).

Later, in 1547 Cassandra beseeched Pope Paul III for help. He granted her the position of Prioress at the orphanage at the Church of San Domenico di Castello in Venice, which came with spare yet adequate housing. She would have lived in a simple cell with a straw bed, hopefully a desk and a few books as companions, and no details are offered to explain if Cassandra had to take religious vows for this position. The footfalls and calls of the children in her charge would have permeated her days, and church services, prayers, chants, and readings would have provided her daily routine. A double, carved wooden door to this institution, which is all that now remains of it, is surmounted by white stone carvings of saints offering succor to all who enter; certainly, this residence offered a refuge for Cassandra's final years.

Despite having dropped out of the literary world, Cassandra was not completely forgotten. In 1556 at age ninety, Cassandra was invited to publicly welcome Bona Sforza, the Queen of Poland, to Venice. During days of entertaining boat races, solemn church services, and sumptuous banquets, crowds gathered once again to hear Cassandra speak. "In glorifying you," said Cassandra to the Queen, "I might hope that my life too might be consigned to immortality" (Fedele 163). The Venetian State still valued its learned orator and gave her pride of place. Though having connections to the rich and powerful gave Cassandra a boost, it was her own studies and speeches that earned her immortality.

Cassandra Fedele was not a sixteenth century feminist. There were none. But she did prepare the ground for her sisters who followed. Diana Robin writes, "It was Cassandra Fedele who first paved the way for women in the republic of letters" ("Introduction" 12) in Venice, and her inspiration spread outwards. She may have belittled her own talent at times, and she faced censure from some and pity from many who claimed to adore her but saw no place for her in their society. "But in our own time when few men have achieved much in literature," wrote her admirer Angelo Poliziano, "only you, a girl, exist, who would rather comb a book than wool, paint with a quill rather than rouge, stitch with a pen rather than a needle, and who would rather cover papyrus with ink than her skin with white powder" (qtd. in Fedele 90). Cassandra held her own in that man's world, though it turned aside from her talents when she was no longer young and fresh. Yet that is no reason for history to also diminish her accomplishments. What she achieved cannot be erased. Cassandra corresponded with high-ranking and educated women, displaying that not only men excelled in the epistolary genre (Ross 159). Perhaps most importantly, Cassandra proved that women could speak publicly, in fact be invited by men to do so, for male audiences, with eloquence, erudition, and grace. The balancing act she employed to stay atop that tightrope is a testament to her ability to overcome the obstacles before her. Of the precious few women who were allowed any education at all, Cassandra made her way to the pinnacle.

In a final act of dignity, Cassandra wrote parts of her own will, in

Latin in her own hand, at age ninety-one. She passed away two years later on March 24, 1558. She left her estate, including her literary works, to Antonia, the wife of a lawyer listed as her "*nepote*," (sic) a vague term in those days that denotes a relation or friend who is like family (Robin 48). Besides setting aside money for masses for the salvation for her soul and her husband's, Cassandra also willed furniture to a trusted female servant. She seemed to be balancing justice by providing for women in her life. Cassandra's lengthy and solemn funeral procession ended at the Church of San Domenico in Castello, which faced San Francesco di Paolo and was nearby to the orphanage where Cassandra had finished her days. In her coffin, Cassandra's head was crowned with a laurel wreath symbolizing her great learning, and some of her beloved books were placed in her hands. A monument by Giovanni Bellini originally adorned her tomb, though it is now lost (Pignatti). Although nothing remains of her tomb or the Church of San Domenico, Cassandra is memorialized in the pantheon of notable Italians at the Istituto Veneto di Scienze, Lettere ed Arti in Campo Santo Stefano, where a carved medallion of her rests among fifty-four busts to men and only two others of women.

Perhaps rather than focusing on Cassandra as a rare bird or a rose growing in the snow, historians and modern readers alike can take her accomplishments on their own merits, with no comparisons to either men or women contemporaries. Through sheer will, Cassandra triumphed over the pressures and expectations placed on her, as well as braving the long hours of studious toil. In his biography on Cassandra Fedele, Giuseppe Betussi said it well: "I think that it would be better to have recorded just her name, so that by saying little I would not seem to defraud her worth of its right, since she herself has given the clearest testimony to the world of how great her virtues were" (qtd. in Ross 98). The hours she dedicated to study, and the resulting words that flowed through her voice and pen, can stand alone, just as she stood alone at her cousin's graduation at the Palazzo Bo.

# Marietta Barovier and Hermonia Vivarini

## A Recipe for Success

Marietta was entrusted with the recipe book. Her father Angelo did not give it to his five sons: Marino, Francesco, Giovanni, Nicolo, or Alvise, but to his one daughter, Marietta. Not because she was a better cook. No, this recipe book held the secrets to the family's formulas for making glass, very valuable secrets indeed, especially considering that Angelo Barovier was the inventor of clear *cristallo* glass. A glassmaker's secrets were his livelihood and were also greatly valued by the Venetian State, which wanted to protect its assets and craftspeople. Marietta's heart must have swelled with pride at her father's trust in her, while she simultaneously felt the heavy burden she now carried to protect this treasure.

Legend has it that Marietta accidentally left the book out one day, where Giorgio Ballarin discovered it. Not being a Venetian by birth, he couldn't own his own glassmaking furnace. But with the secrets stolen from the Barovier workshop, Giorgio was able to marry the daughter of a rival furnace, where he soon began making glass on par with the Baroviers' (Long). How angry Marietta must have been, to be betrayed by a conniving colleague. But nothing ever got her down. Her determination to succeed only increased.

This thief Giorgio hadn't counted on the creativity, skill, and business acumen of Marietta Barovier and her clan. After their father's death, in 1460 Marietta and her brother Giovanni inherited the family workshop, called all'Anzolo or all'Angelo (Borella). The furnace had operated under the leadership of their brother Marino, who had focused his skills on stained glass windows. Taking a different focus, Giovanni and Marietta spearheaded production of glass painted with enamels, known as *smalto*. Women often did the painting and other detail work; in fact, between 1443 and 1445, a woman named Elena de Laudo specialized in *smalto* at Salvatore Barovier's workshop, one of the many furnaces run by this large and prolific family of glassmakers (Syson & Thornton 191).

Marietta was probably a principal painter as well, as her workshop was hailed for this kind of work.

Back around 1440, the masterpiece goblet, now known as the Barovier wedding cup, was fashioned from deep blue glass and painted with scenes of riders on horseback tramping across the grass. The opposite side of this large goblet shows a party of nude bathers in a fountain, enjoying the sunshine, the trees, the lively company. The finely detailed painting displays the artist's patience, attention to detail, and eye for composition. Though no document proves it, many scholars believe that this cup was painted by Marietta Barovier herself (Moretti 25). It is one of the most prized glass pieces from the fifteenth century, now on display at the Museo del Vetro on Murano, near where it was created five centuries ago. Marietta could feel great pride in her artistic creations—in addition to showing Giorgio Ballarin that she would not be crushed by a competitor.

Besides Marietta's ability to paint such lovely scenes, manage the family business, direct her workers, order supplies, and sell their productions, she was an innovator as well. In 1480 she developed the rosetta bead, using the Venetian technique first called *murrine* and later *millefiore*, or "a thousand flowers." Invented by Giacomo Franchini, for *murrine* the glassmaker takes canes of colored glass and lays them together, heating them so they fuse into a single cane. This cane can be heated and stretched and then laid alongside other canes to repeat a pattern (Lane 160). Marietta's rosetta design took this basic principle, employing six layers with white at its center in a star shape, adding layers of blue, white, and brick red. The finished canes were cut to make individual beads. Rosetta beads quickly became highly prized commodities. As far away as Africa, they were worn only by kings and high-ranking authorities (Moretti 25). But the beads were not utilized only as jewelry. Marietta's rosetta beads were used as currency, to trade for goods, services, or privileges. Some say that even Christopher Columbus paid with rosetta beads to procure safe passage on treacherous seas (Glass of Venice).

Luckily, Marietta obtained a patent for her precious design, protecting its secret from people like Giorgio Ballarin. Of course, the bead was still copied, as other glassmakers saw it and worked out for themselves how to create the design. Next Marietta applied to Doge Agostino Barbarigo for permission to build a special small furnace or *muffola* exclusively for her own work, particularly for firing enamel painting. A document from July 26, 1497, confirms Marietta's permission for this right (Mariacher). Theoretically, women were not allowed to work glass or to own businesses except temporarily when their husbands had died. Furthermore, in the fifteenth and sixteenth centuries, virtually no women worked in the arts. Marietta wasn't about to accept these social norms, however, and employed her talents in multiple ways. Perhaps the prestige, wealth, and value of the Barovier name and workshop procured her greater privileges and freedom from censure.

Marietta showed a strong independent streak, preceding by centuries the idea that a woman could forsake marriage in favor of a life dedicated to her work and art (Moretti 28). Marietta's mother Donna Apollonia recorded her will in 1431, bequeathing sixty ducats for her only daughter's wedding dowry, which Marietta never needed. This is the first document naming Marietta (whose given name was Maria); birth or baptism records no longer exist. Maybe after seeing the lengths that Giorgio Ballarin went to, stealing her family's secrets in order to get himself a glassmaker bride, Marietta might have mistrusted the men around her. Besides, she had a prestigious and lucrative workshop to run.

Marietta Barovier inherited not only her family's workshop, but also the long, rich tradition of glass work in Venice. Since Venice was a trading hub between East and West, arts and goods all passed through the city; glassmaking techniques were adopted from Rome as well as from eastern countries. Remains of a furnace dating from around 800 were found on Murano, showing how far back reached the connection between Murano and this craft. According to the Museo del Vetro on Murano, a notarized document signed by a man named Domenico mentions a *fiolario* or maker of glass bottles and is dated 982, confirming that glass was being produced in Murano at this early date. Glassmaking furnaces were originally spread across the Venetian archipelago, but in 1291 the Senate passed a law moving all furnaces to the island of Murano. They claimed that the furnaces posed a fire danger in a city where most dwellings were still made of wood; however, the State also wanted to contain one of its most valuable assets—glassmakers—on the island where their trade secrets could be protected. By 1295 a new law forbade glassmakers from leaving. Severe punishments were meted out to those who betrayed the State by divulging their knowledge.

What made Venetian glass so special? Historian Frederic Lane contends that materials made all the difference (160). The best sand was that which washed down from the nearby Alps to the Adige River, and clay for making furnaces came from Vicenza. Rather than the typical soda ash made from burnt hardwoods, Venetians used burnt seaweed that produced what they termed "maritime glass." Huge quantities of this seaweed were hauled into the port as ballast inside ships coming from the East. Glassmakers guarded the secrets of their materials to protect their trade. They also formed the Glassmakers Guild to help guard these secrets and to increase their profits, even pressuring the State to pass a law banning foreign workers or materials. Guild bylaws gave masters and furnace owners authority over contracts but also freedom when dealing with their workers. A female artist such as Marietta, regardless of her skill or renown, was forbidden from guild membership.

Glassmakers' great pride led them to develop never-before-seen techniques. As early as 1285, factories were producing large sheets of window glass. Bright and clear Venetian mirrors were highly prized everywhere. Spectacles may have been invented in Venice, Lane maintains (160); certainly, in 1302 the crystal workers, originally a separate guild, were then allowed to make clear glass disks for eyeglasses. In the fourteenth century, artists emerged with techniques for making glass that looked like pearls and precious stones. In the 1400s, records show a recipe for *smalti d'oro* or gold glass employed in the San Marco mosaics. Other innovators created *aventurine*, glass containing threads of gold, and *lattimo*, a milky white glass. The sixteenth century brought innovations such as diamond-point engraving and *ghiaccio* or ice glass, with its surface that appears cracked. Marietta's artistic contributions fit into this history of Venetian innovation. Despite the prohibitions against women working in the glass industry, another ingenious woman, Hermonia Vivarini, followed in her footsteps.

Hermonia probably learned the glassmakers' art from her great-grandfather Michele. The family had originally moved from Padua to Murano in the fourteenth century. Perhaps Hermonia first did preparation work or chores in the factory, from sweeping the floors to cleaning the tools. She would have picked up on the craft by being surrounded by it, or she may have been inspired by Marietta Barovier, whom everyone on Murano would have known. Like Marietta, Hermonia came from a prestigious family, though it was her father, uncle, and grandfather who were known for their painting, not their glasswork.

With great patience, Hermonia spent countless hours in front of the furnace, heating globs of raw glass at the end of a long pole called a pontil or punty. She would then whip or twist the pole to manipulate the gob, letting gravity assist her as the glass sank or twisted into curlicues, threads, shells, and arcs. The heat would have blasted her face, more welcome in winter, but withering in the scorching summer months. Her hair bundled back and a heavy apron protecting her, she would use pincers to twist the glass into the hull of a boat, the turn of a sail, producing her unique design for a *navicella*, a glass pitcher shaped like a sailing ship. Perched on a wooden stool, Hermonia would have sat at her workbench stained with burn marks, using smaller pincers, tweezers, and clips to manipulate the hot glass. Glassmakers must work rapidly while their element is hot, their errors tossed aside. Once it was done, the finished piece was briskly snapped off the pontil, leaving its telltale scar. Did Hermonia's children, Simon and Isabeta, stand and watch their mother work, marveling at her dexterous hands that also formed the gnocchi for dinner or felt their feverish foreheads? Hermonia may have felt pulled in two directions—one to raise her family and run a household, while another part of her wished to create her visions in glass.

In the 1500s, glass artists developed a work style called *a mano volante* or "flying hand," a glass blowing technique that requires great dexterity and sensitivity, but it also allows the artist more freedom in creating the piece (Mentasti 85). The boat-shaped pitcher or *navicella* that Hermonia is known for would have required this masterful skill. Her hands would have gestured and twisted confidently, turning the pole so the hot glass would fall into shape. Furthermore, from the late 1400s on, glassmakers added a stem between the cup and the base, another innovation that Hermonia employed. Glass objects continued to become more ornate, with animals, the ubiquitous San Marco lion's head, rings or chains, or even flourishes representing wind or waves. The fifteenth and sixteenth centuries, when Hermonia was working, were known for their flights of fancy—elaborate additions, curlicues, ribbons, and peaks, to the main glass figure. Her mind must have teemed with designs that she couldn't wait to make a reality.

Hermonia's galley ship had full sail rigging and side ornaments, fashioned from thread-thin glass plus a thicker stem that it stood upon. Very few of these galleys survive now. One in the Musee de Cluny dates to the sixteenth century, while the one in the Museo del Vetro in Murano is probably older. The Museo Correr in Venice obtained this *navicella* in 1902 from the Neapolitan family Maglione, though it was passed on to the Museo del Vetro on Murano in 1932. Made of clear glass with blue edges and adornments, it sports crosses on its sides, which some believe indicates that it was used in church as an "*aquamanile*" or water pitcher for washing the hands during mass. Its tilted shape makes it appear to keel over upon the waves, and a beak at its prow serves as its spout. Delicate details are attached fore and aft, including a fluted blue cornucopia high atop its rigging. The Museo del Vetro owns a second one, another copy of Hermonia's design, made of bright, clear glass edged with gold. The gold leaf outlines the sails and the deck together with rosettes along the sides and a ball between the hull and stem. A golden serpent atop the mast bares its fangs and swishes its scaly tail.

Apparently Hermonia's design was so wildly popular that it was later replicated and could be found at all the glass stalls, even from the big factories like Barovier, Serena, and Ballarin. Early ones were often made of yellow glass called *giallino*, and though the design was popular, very few survived, indicating that production was not very high—and the piece was obviously very fragile. Highly ornate and extremely delicate pieces like this highlighted the owner's high status and wealth; families could afford to own an expensive though impractical object that would merely ornament their table. Such objects might be given as gifts to important guests, used for special church services, or displayed at weddings (Mentasti 28). Hermonia could have walked down the streets of Murano, her head held high, as one of the island's favored artists.

Another chronicler who noted Hermonia's glass ships was Marin Sanudo, indefatigable diarist of the 1500s. He recorded that on May 22, 1521, Venice's Great Council awarded Hermonia Vivarini exclusive rights to produce her glass ship for ten years. "Thus, a woman—daughter of painter Alvise Vivarini," Sanudo wrote, "had created new forms, worthy of being protected by a particular privilege" (qtd. from Brown, email). Evidently Hermonia's creation was of such beauty and value that government officials were impressed enough to grant her protective rights. Besides Marietta and Hermonia, other glassmakers were accorded special privileges, such as Andrea and Domenico d'Angelo dal Gallo, who won the right to make crystal mirrors, or Giuseppe Briati who revived the waning industry in 1737 with his patented version of Bohemian glassware. The glass producers (*verieri*) and crystal producers (*cristalleri*) fought over the exclusive right to create glass pearls, an extremely lucrative export item. Much was at stake—contracts, money, fame, reputation, privilege— valuable enough for men who worked in this trade but virtually unheard of for a woman to win such recognition and privilege.

Few records remain to provide details about Hermonia Vivarini. She was probably born in the early 1500s on Murano, and though these documents are missing, Hermonia's will still exists. Venetian women, despite the many obstacles and prohibitions in their lives, were allowed to have access to their marriage dowries upon their deaths, where they could bequeath their money and belongings to relatives or others. Researcher Pietro Paoletti unearthed documents showing that Hermonia (spelled here as Hermenia and elsewhere as Armonia) wrote her will on October 5, 1569. She left ten ducats to her daughter Isabeta, and five ducats to her granddaughter Bernardina, sweetly referred to as "the daughter of my daughter" (20 author's translation). The rest of her estate fell to her son Simon or, in case of his death, to her husband Domenico or her brother-in-law Giovanni Giacomo. Her home life and family details from this time can only be guessed at.

Hermonia's father Alvise (sometimes listed as Aloysius) Vivarini lived from 1441 to 1507 and painted religious works in the late fifteenth century in the family *bottega* or studio. (No records exist to confirm the location of the family's home and attached studio, though historian Marco Toso Borella believes it was located in the Campo Santa Maria Formosa.) Alvise Vivarini's father Antonio and uncle Bartolomeo were well-known painters of religious panels that hung in Venetian churches or were sent throughout the Venetian Empire and beyond; most of their works now reside outside Venice, though some of the churches as well as the Galleria dell'Accademia in Venice contain a fine sampling of their work. Decorating crowns and thrones at first with gold leaf, the family later developed a technique using yellow paint that replicated this gilding but at a fraction of the cost. The family of painters crossed the temporal line from the Gothic into the Renaissance, and some say they were more influential to Venetian painting than the Bellini clan who succeeded them (Steer 37). Hermonia would have grown up surrounded by pigments and paints, brushes and boards, the tools of fine artists, though given that glass was her medium, she probably lived on Murano near her furnace and among other glassmakers.

The Glass Guild was one of the most powerful in Venice. Their art brought great wealth to the city, be it from the clearest mirrors available in Europe or the glass beads used as currency or masquerading as emeralds, turquoise, and rubies. Glass treasures were worn as jewelry, graced tables as vases, bowls, and pitchers, or as goblets sipped from by priests at the altar. Though commoners, glassmakers were highly prized members of the Venetian State. Marietta and Hermonia proved that women could be successful artisans, innovators, and business people. Protecting and preserving such enterprising women proved to be a recipe for success.

The Barovier Cup

# Founders and Funders

## A Testament to their Contributions

$A$ petite woman in a long brown tunic points to the bricks and calls to the stonemason, "Move them here. This is the spot where you will erect the altar of the new church." With a wimple covering her hair and cross upon her breast, she stands alone, as her sisters seclude themselves within the walls of their small, spare cells nearby. This nun has petitioned patrons, collected funds, and received permits from Venice's governing bodies in order to erect this new church. She hopes to provide a place of refuge, serenity, and piety for herself and her sisters, away from the often dangerous, secular world. Rather than waiting for someone else to protect or care for her and her sisters, she has taken that initiative herself.

Venice's history books are filled with stories of women's oppression, harassment, and ridicule. But not all of the city's history was so, and throughout the centuries examples of independent and empowered women do crop up. One sentence here or a couple there, a footnote perhaps, and these women peek out to the present from behind church doors, convent grills, hospice windows, and palace balconies. These are the women who founded or funded numerous Venetian institutions that would provide succor for untold numbers of their sisters.

One of the oldest of these institutions, and one about which the most is known, is the church and convent of Corpus Domini, which used to stand at the far western tip of Venice, an area then called Capo de Zirada. The church was entirely demolished when the train station was built in the 1860s. Thanks to Sister Bartolomea Riccoboni, who kept a chronicle, readers know not only about the convent's founding in 1375 but also about the daily lives of the remarkably devout women who made it their home.

One such woman, Sister Lucia Tiepolo from a noble family line, had taken the veil three decades earlier and had resided at the Benedictine convent of Santa Maria degli Angeli on Murano. Having begun her tenure there at age eleven, she rose to become the Abbess. But her managerial talents were needed elsewhere, and Lucia was posted to Sant'Apostolo on a remote Venetian island, where she served as Abbess. The area was half-abandoned, especially after the plague of 1348 had decimated the population. Lucia felt that she had little opportunity to help others in such a desolate convent, so she yearned for a change. The request came from Jesus himself, who sent her a vision. He appeared covered in blood, wearing the thorny crown and tied to a column. "Go to Venice and build me a convent in my name," (26) he told her in the tale recounted roughly thirty years later by Sister Bartolomea Riccoboni in her history of the convent, later published as *Life and Death in a Venetian Convent*. "I'm a poor little woman," Lucia replied. "I have no relatives or friends who I might hope would give a penny to help me" (27). But Lucia was determined, and, after consulting Venice's patriarch Francesco Querini, she resolved to make her vision a reality. She even used some small funds she had "earned by practicing medicine," Bartolomea noted, revealing another of Lucia's talents. Lucia took six years to obtain permission and land, but she succeeded in founding a church in 1375 to honor the body of Christ, the Corpus Domini. Its attached dormitory housed only Lucia, another nun, and two lay sisters and was quite isolated from other habitations. Still, Lucia fervently believed that one day this convent would become home to over sixty nuns.

However, others doubted Lucia's visions. Her food and upkeep were paid for only by offerings from those who visited the church, and the simple wooden chapel and dormitories must have been spare, cold, and isolated places to pass her days. A young priest named Francesco Rabia visited often, pitying Lucia and remarking, "Good mother, you'll see sixty hens" before seeing sixty sisters enter this convent (29). "When it pleases my Lord God," Lucia believed, "he will see to what he has promised me" (28). Nearly three more decades passed, but eventually more visions assured Lucia of this future coming true. One winter, an unusually persistent snow fell, a kind of premonition, and on that site of the snow that would not melt, Lucia had a stone altar laid. Lucia never faltered, and being a resourceful person, she procured means to rebuild the wooden church in stone, over the new altar.

Around this time, two sisters also received visions that they must honor Christ with a church. Orphaned girls from another noble family, Isabetta and Andreola Tommasini offered up their marriage dowries to pay for Corpus Domini's construction. Their guardian, Margarita Paruta, spoke to Father Giovanni Domenici, their confessor, at the Church of San Zanipolo (also known as Santi Giovanni e Paolo), who himself received a heavenly command to begin a convent next to the church. Though he at first hesitated, the women's devotion and the visions convinced him; Bartolomea wrote, "But the Lord Jesus made his heart race so while he was praying and saying mass that he could resist no longer" (31). Father Giovanni went on to treat the enterprise and the women with devotion and tireless energy. He invited a happy Lucia Tiepolo to become the first Prioress to head the house, though it meant that she would change from following the rule of Benedict to that of the Dominicans. The sisters' dowries were employed to purchase materials, and within a year the buildings were finished, "and the amazing thing was that for the entire year it never rained on workdays, but only at night or on holidays," added Bartolomea (31).

By the time the convent of Corpus Domini was officially consecrated on June 29, 1394, on the feast day of San Pietro and Paolo, Lucia was nearly eighty years old. She was officially named the convent's Abbess, its highest ranking leader, receiving help from Isabetta Tommasini as subprioress and Lucia Dandolo as vicaress. Father Giovanni Domenici visited the rooms and "designating the cells with their altarpieces, he blessed them all with holy water," Bartolomea recorded (33). "Just imagine what joy lingered in those minds that had for so long yearned to be enclosed for love of the Lord Jesus Christ!" They numbered twenty-seven that first day, and a week later seven more joined them, and nine days later seven more had arrived, women of all ages and stations, from inexperienced teenaged girls to those who had lived a cloistered life for many years, to widows of all ages who wished to devote their remaining years to God. "By the end of the year there were seventy-two of us," wrote Bartolomea (34). Lucia lived to see her vision become reality. Born of the women's fervent perseverance, this community grew into a safe haven where they could devote themselves to a life centered around their beliefs.

Sister Bartolomea's distinctive history of convent life is similar to the life lived by thousands of Venetian women over the centuries. "Some of the sisters were so given to devotion and meditation that as they walked they seemed to speak with God," Bartolomea declared (35). "Perfect silence was observed, such that from the time compline was said until mass the following day was finished (that is, the one that is said after the hours), no one would utter a single word" (34-5). Theirs was a life of routine, divided between prayer, chores, and sleep. They held property in common, being issued a tunic and scapular, a blanket and quilt, which they changed four times a year. "It was lovely to see so many—indeed all of them—so clean," reported Bartolomea (37). The convent was a well-run machine. Women managed this world, at a time when it was believed that they had little agency or independence.

Rather than choosing to be wives and mothers and to take care of others in those roles, the women of Corpus Domini took care of each other or devoted their lives to prayer and religious exaltation. Sister Bartolomea compiled a necrology from year to year to record each sister's death, plus of course her good deeds and devout life. She wrote of Sister Chiara Buonio who "out of humility . . . performed the most demeaning chores in the convent with the greatest joy," (66) or Sister Domenica who "at table . . . never ate anything good but took the worst bread and the worst things and gave the good to her companions" (73). Many of the sisters saw illness as a "gift from God" to test their faith (67), and they took great care of those who were suffering. Sister Paola, mother of the priest Giovanni Domenici, was widowed at age seventeen and entered the convent at age fifty-eight, where she became known as "the mother of the poor" for her charitable works for the needy and for the nearby monks (78). One after another, these women are described as dying peacefully, with great joy or even laughter, knowing they were joining their God. According to Bartolomea's account, theirs were lives of great contentment and meaning.

The women of Corpus Domini lived there by choice, not compulsion, and were very ardent in their beliefs. Some chose to sleep on bare planks and go without food. Bartolomea continued, "The vicaress had to command them to go easy and temper their great fervor, and she gave them a direct order to take food, since they were so fervent they did not want to eat" (35). But often they went too far in other ways besides starvation. Bartolomea recounts that many did penance using "hair shirts, chains, and whips . . . and they scourged themselves with great shedding of blood" (36). They were convinced that these actions pleased God, who sent them visions, miracles, and sensations of ecstasy. However, this lifestyle also led to many illnesses, and the priest finally ordered the nuns to refrain from those practices. They obeyed, as obedience, along with chastity and poverty, constituted the principal elements of a monastic life. Though it may be difficult for modern readers to fathom why these women would choose to live lives of pain and privation, it's worth remembering that it was replaced by spiritual and corporeal security in a medieval world that was largely unstable and unsafe, especially for unmarried women.

Regrettably, Sister Bartolomea's chronicle is a rare document, virtually the only one of its kind in Venice. But it provides a sense of the daily lives of Venetian nuns or a glimpse into why women would provide funding for other women to live a monastic life. Tribute should be paid to these women for their generosity and service to others. For other convents, churches, or *ospedale*—the institutions that provided safety for orphans, abandoned children, widows, reformed prostitutes, or those who converted faiths—the records provide scant details of their benefactresses. For example, in 1403 at Campo Santa Margherita, Meneghina Bocco left funds in her will for a hospice to provide shelter for twelve unmarried women (Giordani 547). Undowered daughters, women with physical disabilities, those past what was considered a marrying age—these women established a home and built a community in this busy and boisterous square. They might have laughed over the laundry basin or gossiped at the hearth, creating a world not steered by men. Meneghina wanted to make sure women who never married had an alternative home, a safe place within their community but not tied to its usual expectations.

Meneghina's institute stood near another hospice for the poor, founded by Maddalena Scrovegni, a wealthy and educated woman from Padua. This home was located on Fondamenta Scoazzera (546), a *fondamenta* that no longer exists; a canal used to run in front of the row of buildings at the end of the *campo* opposite from the church, and the *fondamenta* was the sidewalk between the houses and the canal. It was filled in and is now called the Rio Terá Canal, but a plaque remains where the word "*hospiti*" can still be made out. Those who may have been pitied for their poverty or derided for their tattered clothing instead found here solace in community, plus a warm bed in a dry room. In this bustling square, a crossroads between busy sections of Venice, Maddalena made sure that poor women were included in its center and not relegated to the edges. She was looking out for not only their physical well-being but also their emotional needs.

While these institutions usually had men at the helm making final decisions, in reality daily life was run by women. Women assigned the chores and directed others in their duties. Women managed the funds for food, clothing, and other necessities. Women saw problems that needed fixing, such as enlarging a building or organizing jobs for the residents, and they found ways to resolve matters. Women also worked in useful employment. They gathered in the sunniest rooms to embroider, stitch lace, or weave fabrics. As evidenced by paintings that show Venetians' daily lives, the women likely wore long skirts of simple cotton or linen, in earth tones of russet and sage, flax, mahogany, and mustard yellow. A white blouse was covered by a fitted bodice, an apron protected the clothing, and a scarf or straw hat covered the head, a shawl their shoulders.

Across town in Castello, in 1418 Lucia Foscola willed money to build an asylum for poor widows, initially housing sixteen of them. Called the Ospizio Foscolo, it was located on the Fondamenta Sant'Anna in Castello (Freely 33). Its original entryway remains, with a curved alcove over the wooden door that contains a bust of "Maternity," a mother suckling her child. This doorway leads into the ancient and now abandoned Corte de le Donne, the women's courtyard. Women could sit there in the sun while doing their mending or lace work. Two floors provided a refuge for these impoverished women who had little other protection in the world. How lovely to breathe through each day, without the fear of men's blows or harsh words. The Ospizio remained in operation until the early 1800s. The *ospedale* provided safe havens for women where they need not fear sexual assault, loveless or abusive marriages, or the desperation of turning to prostitution. Lucia ensured that at least a small community of women could count on this refuge.

Unfortunately, many Venetian women were pushed into the sex trade. Convent life or marriages were safer, but if a woman had no dowry, lived in poverty, or if she were raped, prostitution often provided her only means of support. One such woman was Margherita Vitturi, who as a young woman worked in the sex trade but in a later turn of fortune used her wealth and station to provide a place of healing for others. Nothing is known about her very early life except that she was a courtesan, of the higher class of Venice's sex workers who were also educated, talented women working to provide entertainment for men, both locals and visitors. Did Margherita turn to this work because her mother initiated her into it? Or because it was her only source of income? In 1608 the British traveler Thomas Coryat visited Margherita's home and in his journal *Coryat's Crudities* cataloged the delights he encountered there. "The walles round about being adorned with the most sumptuous tapistry and gilt leather [ . . . and also] the picture of the noble Courtezan most exquisitely drawen" (qtd. in Brown 160). Her bedroom, or "chamber of recreation," contained even more delightful objects, such as "many faire painted coffers wherewith it is garnished round about, a curious milke-white canopy of needle worke, a silke quilt embroidered with gold, and generally all her bedding sweetly perfumed."

Furthermore, Margherita, like other courtesans, was multi-talented. Thomas Coryat described Margherita's skills as a singer and musician when she played the lute and sang "with as laudable a stroake as many men that are excellent professors in the noble science of Musicke; and partly with that heart-tempting harmony of her voice" (160). She was also "a good Rhetorician, and a most excellent discourser, so that if she cannot move thee with all these foresaid delights, shee will assay thy constancy with her Rhetoricall tongue." *Coryat's Crudities* provided a drawing showing Margherita greeting Thomas in her entryway. She wore a sumptuous gown of swirling fabric trimmed with fringe, and she was "decked with many chaines of gold and orient pearle like a second Cleopatra." Thomas was astounded by Margherita's typical Venetian dress that bared her breasts, while an upstanding, formal lace collar rose behind her neck and mingled with her tightly curled hair. Despite Thomas Coryat's impression of Margherita as a dissolute and cunning woman, he also remarked that she kept "a picture of our Lady by her bedde side, with Christ in her armes, placed within a cristall glass." A woman might be compelled to work in the sex trade, but that didn't preclude her from a sense of religious devotion. Margherita must have felt torn or tormented within to be a courtesan but to also revere the Virgin Mary and keep her constantly by her side. How often did Margherita look at this picture and feel remorse? Or perhaps she felt more strongly compelled to devise a way out of her life style and prayed fervently for another option.

Actually, this appeared to be the situation with Margherita. She eventually married a nobleman named Giovanni Miani (sometimes spelled as Emiliani) and became a devoted wife. In her will from 1427, Margherita bequeathed a sum of money to Venice's Procuratori of San Marco for the State to erect a chapel to honor her husband and to express her piety. Thomas Coryat commented that "I have not heard of so religious a worke done by so irreligious a founder in any place of Christendome: belike she hoped to make expiation unto God by this holy deede for the lascivious dalliances of her youth" (Coryat 387). This may indeed be the case, though Margherita's thoughts on the subject haven't survived. A century passed before the Procuratori began work on this, the Capella Emiliana, which is attached to the Church of San Michele in Isola on the cemetery island of San Michele. The chapel was consecrated in 1543 to honor Our Lady of the Annunciation, and Margherita's endowment, which had turned a nice investment over the years, also paid for upkeep. Statues of Santa Margherita and San Giovanni Baptista honor Margherita and her husband. Margherita requested that the chapel be accessible both from the outside as well as from the church, where monks at the attached monastery lived. The philanthropic group Venice in Peril completed restoration work on the Capella Emiliana in 2006. In a world where women had few options, a resourceful woman such as Margherita, using the means she had, left a legacy for others to enjoy.

In fact, a long catalogue of charitable women, whether wealthy or not, spans Venice's history, beginning even centuries before either Margherita or Lucia. Yet little is known about their daily lives, their families, their vocations, their pastimes, their fears or hopes or dreams. Did they wish for a blessed afterlife? Did they wish to show gratitude for safety or health or other blessings? Did they wish to honor a patron or saint who lightened their burdens? Did they wish to put their *zecchini* coins or their hands to charitable work that would alleviate another's pain? Perhaps these reasons as well as others that modern people cannot imagine all motivated Venice's founders and funders to do what they did.

One very early example is the creation of the Church of Angelo Raffaele in Dorsoduro, supposedly founded in 416 or 640 according to various records (Cotton). As Attila the Hun attacked the area, Genusio, Lord of Padua on the mainland, sent his family to safety to the high ground of the Rivo Alto, which later became the Rialto area of Venice. Genusio remained behind. His wife Adriana lived in terror that her husband would die in battle and leave her alone to raise their children. She vowed to erect a church if Genusio returned safely to his family's arms. The church was subsequently built; a wide, white façade faces a small canal, and light streams in from behind the altar at its opposite end. Adriana probably prayed there daily to give thanks for the safe return of her husband and for her children's safety. She didn't slacken her devotion and later saw to it that an oratory was included, which she bequeathed to the Benedictine nuns who used the space. They might have enjoyed the organ's deep tones and reverberating notes resounding in the lofty interior. The Church of Angelo Raffaele provides an example of a wealthy woman putting her money towards good works.

The fourteenth century was a busy time for church building, and while men usually erected churches, the women founders should also not be forgotten. In 1316 Giacomina Scorpioni, a nun from the convent of San Lorenzo d'Ammiana, founded the Church of Santa Marta along with its convent and an *ospedale* for the care of others. This large, boxy church sits on Venice's deserted southwestern edge and once housed Santa Marta's hand amongst its relics. The women who lived there passed quiet, pious lives, isolated from the bustle and thrum of mercantile Venice. One record from the sixteenth century even tells of a priest who urged the nuns to abstain from close friendships with each other, fearing that these earthly connections would distract them from a pious life (Laven 103). Santa Marta was a place for women wanting peace. The sisters did take in boarders, though, young girls who needed a safe home and basic education. Added to the nuns' daily life of prayers early and late, of group singing in the echoing church, they would have sat with their young charges for daily lessons. Nuns would have enjoyed basic literacy, enough to read of Santa Teresa's martyrdom or San Antonio of Padua's work with his beloved children. But apparently these boarders upset their quiet life, "wandering about in a disorderly fashion. . . . And they play cards all night long, scandalously" (qtd. in Laven 121). Still, the nuns persisted in their determination to provide guidance for their young charges. Their work at Santa Marta continued for centuries, and Giacomina could be proud that the institution she established provided refuge and education for generations of women.

Not far away, Sant'Andrea della Zirada was founded in 1329 by four noblewomen: Elisabetta Soranzo, Elisabetta Gradenigo, Francesca Cornaro, and Marianna (or Maddalena) Malipiero (Cotton). These four surnames come from the grandest of Venetian noble houses; as a matter of fact, the percentage of Sant'Andrea nuns culled from the nobility never fell below ninety-four percent (Laven 50). The convent followed Augustinian rules, including women shearing off their hair and wearing a habit and wimple that covered them decorously (4). The doge himself patronized the church with the command that the women should help tend to the poor. Destitute men in tattered shirts knew they could come to this church for a bowl of minestrone and hunk of bread, handed to them by the caring and generous nuns of Sant'Andrea. However, the women still had access to monies provided to them by their families. In 1609, Patriarch Vendramin wrote that "Since the nuns are prevented by their vow of poverty from having property, they are exhorted to follow the convention of other convents, that is to place their money in the safekeeping of the Mother Prioress" (qtd. in Laven 5). Elisabetta, Marianna, Francesca, and Elisabetta, privileged daughters used to a life of luxury, traded that home life for a more impecunious one that they funded with their families' legacies, providing not only for their own futures, but also for women down the centuries. They created a life for themselves that they shared with others.

Similarly, the Church of San Girolamo in the Cannaregio district was founded by a group—this time Augustinian nuns from the convent of Santa Maria degli Angeli on the island of Murano; in fact, they founded their convent in 1375 (though the present church was built later) (Cotton). Rectangular without the arms of the cross that most churches have, San Girolamo's interior is simple and without many frescoes or paintings. Its façade faces a small, unassuming *campo*, and the original cells faced an interior courtyard providing a secluded life for the nuns who passed their days there. These founders must have had a vision to create a community of their own, separate from the one on Murano, to meet their specific needs as they devoted their lives to God.

Not only nuns founded nunneries. In 1388, Antonia Venier, the doge's daughter, funded the Church and convent of Sant'Alvise in Cannaregio. She dedicated the church to Sant'Alvise from Toulouse (Alvise being the Venetian name for Louis), after being visited by him in a dream, in which he told her where to build a church to honor him (Nadali & Vianello 79). Sant'Alvise, robed in a blue and gold cloak over his plain brown habit, was known for ignoring his own needs in favor of aiding the poor. Antonia was attracted to this boy saint who died at twenty-three and is often depicted with a crown at his feet. After funding the church, Antonia elected to live out her life in the adjacent convent. The nuns would attend mass confined to their choir *barco*, an enclosed balcony with a wrought-iron grill that blocked them from the view of curious eyes. The boxy brick Church of Sant'Alvise contains a glorious trompe l'oeil ceiling, vaulting up to heaven, and outside a small statue of Sant'Alvise perches over the entrance. Many young women found a life of quiet service there thanks to Antonia's dedication.

The fifteenth century continued to see examples of women founding, funding, and maintaining religious and charitable institutions. In the Church of Santa Chiara, Sisters Sofia Veneziana and Agnese Ungara obtained permission to improve this site that had fallen into disrepair (and whose priests had reportedly fallen into disrepute). Sofia and Agnese built two new cells in 1470, which initiated a new convent (Giordani 407). While they began their monastic life completely isolated in their rooms bare of any adornment, they were soon joined by others to create a sisterhood in a large complex. Cells faced a central courtyard, and the women could have looked out upon the canals that nearly surrounded them. But a hundred years later, the nuns complained of excessive cold and windy drafts blowing through the convent and church (Laven 21), indicating that these austere habitations provided only the barest essentials, and the work that Sofia and Agnese had accomplished still left a lot more to be done. Despite the privations, Sisters Sofia and Agnese, clothed in simple tunics and living spare and modest lives, modeled a life of piety and penance that attracted others to join them.

In 1483 Maria Caroldo founded the Church of Spirito Santo in the Dorsoduro district, on the Zattere facing the wide Giudecca Canal, so close that the waters nearly lap at the entrance (Cotton). Maria was a nun at the convent of Santa Catterina in Venice and had the help of her brother Girolamo and the priest Giacomo Zamboni in erecting the building. Besides the church, Maria also established the attached Augustinian convent (which was plagued by sexual scandals about a decade later) (Tassini 619). Spirito Santo's convent had a parlor where nuns could converse with visitors, so though Maria led an enclosed life, it was not as isolated as one might suspect, as family, neighbors, and friends could enjoy a chat through the foyer grillwork. Nuns were known to gather for sewing or reading together in their cells, (Laven 6) and Maria must have enjoyed these pastimes with her sisters.

Similar to Maria, Catterina, a nun at the convent at Sant'Agnese in Dorsoduro, received permission to open a new convent in 1497. Santa Maria Maggiore in the Santa Croce district opened its church first, with a convent added later (Giordani 414). The Venetian State granted the land, and Catterina collaborated with the other Franciscans to bring the project to completion, similar to what occurred at the Church of Corpus Domini. Picture women in habit and headscarf directing gangs of stonemasons, carpenters, and bricklayers to construct the building, a nun petitioning red-robed senators for land grants and building permits, in between the daily prayers of prime and matins. Church records from 1594 list the jobs that the nuns held, from lowlier positions such as gardener, baker, loom worker, and spicer, to more skilled work such as bookkeeper and nurse. The senior members of the community held positions of higher authority and prudence, including counsel mother (*madre di consiglio*), gatekeeper, and novice mistress who taught the new sisters (Laven 9). The habitation that Catterina initiated in the fifteenth century lasted until the eighteenth.

Many people have heard the story of the Church of the Redentore on Giudecca, which was built in thanks for the end of the bubonic plague of 1575 to 1576, but few know that two women were behind the church's history. Originally, the Church of San Jacopo stood on this location, where Fiorenza Corner and Teodosia Scripiana, two noblewomen, lived as nuns after having the church and convent built to honor Santa Maria dei Angeli (carnivalofvenice.com). They gathered their ducats together to buy bricks and boards and build edifices where they could live and worship. Other young women arrived to join them, kneeling in the pews to show their obedience to God. In 1541 the rather mad Father Bernadino Ochino had the women expelled, but when he was tried as a heretic, the nuns returned to their devotional life. These two women, not to be suppressed, also established a second convent on Giudecca, called "*Monte dei Corni*" because the location was near the dumping ground for the horns (*corni*) of slaughtered animals. Surrounded by the stench of animal carcasses and tanneries, these women nevertheless raised their voices in spiritual song or daily gave their thanks to God for His gifts. After the plague, the Venetian State wanted to show its gratitude to the greater powers and had Palladio design the Church of the Redentore to replace the earlier church. Nowadays people still celebrate the feast of the Redentore (or Redeemer) in July each year, and nearly everyone has forgotten the original vision established by Fiorenza and Teodosia.

By the eighteenth century, times had begun to change, and rather than opening new convents or founding churches, women turned to providing places of refuge. Marina da Lezze used her own funds to open the Cannaregio Church of Santa Maria delle Penitenti with Maria Elisabetta Rossi in 1705. They wished to furnish a home to "shelter corrupt women who wanted to do penance" (Nadali & Vianello 75). For women who may have been forced by circumstances to support themselves by any means, whether legal or not, this home provided an opportunity to rebuild their lives. Were Marina and Maria harsh judges of these women's actions, or did they invite them in with compassion and forgiveness? Had they faced difficult circumstances and decisions themselves and then empathized with their sisters? The spare building looks more like a housing institution with an unfinished church façade placed in the center. It is built on the Greek cross plan with rather plain white walls, and a plaque outside attests to its function as a home for the "*penitenti*." Here the women no longer had to lift their skirts on men's orders or find a client that night so their children would have bread for breakfast. However, the Catholic idea of penance was no cake walk; nuns at such convents were expected to gather for communal prayer for much of the day, to "examine their consciences" for any sins, and in some cases to self-flagellate in order to tame their flesh (Laven 12). Still, Marina and Maria provided a safe haven for women escaping more worldly cares or dangers at others' hands, where all could gladly kneel and give thanks for this home.

This philanthropic trend continued into the nineteenth and twentieth centuries. After the fall of the Venetian Republic in 1797,

Napoleon took control of the city, and eventually it was ceded to the Austrians. During this unstable and impoverished era, many of the city's monasteries, convents, and churches were suppressed, disbanded, or even demolished. A large population of women now had nowhere to go. The Church of Cristo Re alla Celestia in Castello, which was originally founded in the fifteenth century, was suppressed like so many others. But in 1878 a group of Franciscan Nuns of Christ reopened the church. A new building was erected in the 1950s by Princess Benedetta Savoia Carignano and Angela Canal, Venetian noblewomen (Cotton). It's a small church with a coffered ceiling, bright white marble floor, and light pouring in from the windows placed high along each side. The site now serves as the Institute of the Franciscan Nuns of Christ the King, much as it did in the past, with nuns in white habits still praying fervently in the pews. After Benedetta and Angela's initial work, many women contributed to this community, building it, reclaiming it, and making of it a devout home.

Another charitable home was San Bonaventura in Cannaregio, which was originally opened in 1620 by Franciscan monks but later suppressed. Countess Paolina Giustinian-Recanti bought the site and built a convent for an order of barefoot (or discalced) Carmelites, which opened in 1875 (Cotton). These nuns followed an ascetic life with a vow of poverty, often barefoot and clothed in a robe and brown scapular, the length of cloth draped over the shoulders to cover their front and back. Their waking hours were divided between work, mass, and silent prayer. Fasting, solitude, and strict enclosure usually defined their days, in the belief that their fervent prayers would bring serenity not only to themselves but also to the larger world. Paolina, who came from a life of wealth and privilege, instead embraced a life of simplicity and privation, and joined with her sisters in daily devotion.

A founder similar to Paolina was Ana Maria Marovic, born on February 7, 1815, and living in the Montenegran community of Venice. She was a painter early on, though only a few of her drawings survive, and she also showed a talent for writing. At age twenty, Ana Maria published her first works and left behind some poems and some religious writings (Bakic). But this path was not enough for her; she was drawn to a spiritual vocation and dedicated herself to this life from 1838 on, sometimes being given the title "Servant of God." Desiring to serve others, in 1864, she collaborated with Canon Daniele Canal, and they obtained the site of the former Church of Santa Maria dei Servi in Venice's Cannaregio district. The monastery and church had been founded in the fourteenth century and were eventually destroyed by fire in 1769. These two religious souls established an asylum for women recently released from prison, which they called the Istituto Canal Marovic ai Servi. Ana Maria went on to begin a religious order called the Sisters of Reparation to the "Most Sacred Heart of Jesus and Mary Immaculate." In 2005 a short film was made about Ana Maria's life, with her name as the title, and the Catholic Church has been in process to launch her beatification. Paolina and Ana Maria represent many others who did good work in the service of others, whether they inaugurated places of refuge or worked within them to help those who had hit hard times.

The vast majority of Venetian history revolves around things men accomplished or built or began. Whole history books abound in these men's stories, and if women are mentioned, it's most often as some man's wife or mother. But Meneghina, Maddalena, Giacomina, Paolina, and Ana Maria prove that Venetian women did have agency and power, that they did run institutions, handle their finances, manage resources and people. Lucia, Margherita, Antonia, Maria, Catterina and their sisters confirm that women could follow their faith in erecting edifices to God's glory. Their words are mostly lost, but their buildings remain as testament to their contributions.

The Church of Corpus Domini

# Gaspara Stampa

## To Live Ablaze

Cassandra Stampa, burdened with the grief of her only sister's death, sat over a sheaf of handwritten manuscripts, laboring to create the highest gift she could for her younger sister Gaspara: a compilation of 311 of Gaspara's poems that had never been collected during her lifetime. Devastated at the loss of a sister who was only about thirty-one years old, Cassandra must have felt a great hole open in her life. Their friends urged Cassandra to instead devote herself to compiling these poems, but later readers ultimately have Cassandra to thank for preserving the work of her sister Gaspara, who has since been called by biographer Fiora Bassanese "one of the best, if not the best, poets of her century" (99). Portraits reveal Gaspara crowned with a laurel wreath on her luxuriant and wavy brown hair, her eyes focused on something off to her right, and the corners of her small mouth turned up. Her heavy velvet dress hangs low to display her shoulders, throat, and upper chest, giving her a certain vulnerability. In similar drawings from her publications, Gaspara holds a lute or scroll or books, tools for her talents.

Few exact details exist to complete Gaspara Stampa's biography. She was born around 1523 to 1525 in Padua. Her father Bartolomeo, a jewelry merchant, died, and her mother Cecilia moved with her three children to Venice, her home town. Cassandra, Gaspara, and their younger brother Baldassare were given a Humanist education in Latin, Italian literature, Roman history, philosophy, Greek grammar, art, rhetoric, and poetry. While Baldassare wrote poetry, the sisters studied the lute and singing, learning from their teacher Perissone Cambio the art of improvising poetry to specified tunes so that they might entertain in salons, the pleasure rooms that served the noble class.

Literary salons and academies, a vibrant part of Venetian society, provided men a place to gather amongst their friends for conversation. Usually, the same person hosted a salon at his palace or sometimes at his *casino*, a smaller, less-public apartment set aside for more casual gatherings. The host served refreshments, and the evening started late, often ending as the sun rose. The usual topics included poetics and literature, classic philosophies, religion, grammar, music, and more. Most academies developed their own focus, with the group centering itself around music or Petrarchan poetry, for example, or around a characteristic, such as the Academy of the Doubters or the Unknowns. Virtually the same were the salons, though they were perhaps a bit less academic and more casual. At either venue, the host or one guest would propose a theme, such as the exaltation of love or the suffering of the sinful. During the sixteenth and seventeenth centuries, academies and salons were attended almost exclusively by men; noble women were not allowed, and the only women present were entertainers, as writers, singers, musicians, or courtesans. Attired in yards of rich silks or brocades or velvets, multiplied by glittering mirrors in the drawing rooms where they performed, the Stampa sisters would sing. Gaspara and Cassandra would create a story with their words and a mood with their voices, filling the small chamber and moving their listeners' hearts.

After hearing her, Girolamo Parabosco, San Marco organist, wrote to Gaspara, "What can I say of that angelic voice that fills the air with its divine sound that, unlike the Siren, floods the spirit and life of those who hear, bringing them to tears?" (qtd. in Jaffe & Colombardo 242). He claimed that Gaspara's singing made him feel as though he were "burning and freezing at one and the same moment" (242). The two girls were in high demand as *virtuose*—not common theater entertainers, not courtesans who sang—but as women with a particular role within the strata of Venetian patrician society, where women might sing in private homes for a literary society. Sixteenth century music was ephemeral, however, and no recordings, of course, were ever made, so no one can hear Gaspara's artistry but only read the poetry that she left behind. Though outwardly modest, Gaspara and Cassandra must have swelled with pride to know their singing and verses brought pleasure to so many. Yet as such salon singers, did they also fear for their virtue and reputation? Would they be labeled as unchaste women and defamed because they attended a salon gathering? Despite any misgivings, though, Gaspara desired something more from life.

Apparently, Gaspara realized the fleeting nature of music and sought fame and immortality with her words. "I might have been already famous," Gaspara wrote in poem #12, "Perhaps all of the Adriatic and its shores / would resound today with my name—so great / thanks to the style he's given me" (Stampa 69). Though she attributed her inspiration and style to her lover Count Collaltino di Collalto, she still voiced her desire for immortality and recognized her own talent. Whereas some of her fifteenth century predecessors practically apologized for being women who wrote, Gaspara glorified it. Writing was challenging, but it was worthwhile. It is better, she wrote, "To struggle for a noble reason / that makes savage life gentle and blessed / than to enjoy vulgar, common pleasures" (Jaffe & Colombardo 255). No wine bar revels or empty chatter around a banquet table were enough for Gaspara. She was inspired to put pen to page and polish her work to the highest Petrarchan ideals.

Cassandra Stampa titled her sister's work *Rime (Rhymes)*, and the edition contained poems not only about Collaltino but also poems labeled *Varie*, a loose collection of laudatory poems directed to her friends and literary colleagues in Venice's salon scene. Fiona Bassanese argues that these poems reveal Gaspara Stampa the writer, through her "exercises in the art of writing; their inspiration is purely stylistic and literary" (44). Gaspara wasn't merely writing love poems; she was crafting her work with care and precision. Gaspara played with the many and varied tools in a poet's toolbox, such as personification, allusion, antithesis, oxymoron, and repetition. Her love for Collaltino initially inspired her to write, a clue found in her lines when Love tells her, "'Die to the good, to the bad be alive,' / he gives me as his final verdict; / 'that's enough for you, and that's what makes you write'" (Stampa 177). She personifies Love and adds juxtaposition to point out its positive and negative aspects that inspire her. Her friends' lively discussion of philosophy, love, art, language, and grammar inspired Gaspara to work on her verses and turn experience into poetry.

The great rage of the sixteenth century was still Petrarca, the Italian poet who had risen so high above his colleagues' rhymes that his Tuscan tongue became the standard vernacular and his poetic style the one to emulate for roughly four centuries. Like her contemporaries—and there seemed to be a sonneteer hiding in every household—Gaspara Stampa imitated the Petrarchan ideal, the loftiest goal for any poet. Bassanese points out, "For the sixteenth century, imitation represented a highly prized manner of writing" (51). Writers had followed Petrarca's model where the smitten gentleman pines for his perfect lady from afar, idealizing her in his noble though unrequited love. In these poems the lady is always passive, the beloved, but also a sort of princess-in-a-tower model rather than a real woman with her own desires. The lover will never be able to justly praise the romanticized beloved, "Since [to] the task my tongue is scarcely equal," (Stampa 75) wrote Gaspara as she admitted that her poems could not describe Collaltino's perfections. Of course it is the poet's task to attempt this description in verse.

Here is where readers can praise Gaspara and acknowledge her for her unique contributions to poetics. Writing in first person, Gaspara gave voice to a woman in love. She was the lover rather than the beloved. She took pen in hand, dipped in ink to fashion line after line lionizing her beloved, describing his handsome visage, his charm, how he sat on a horse or filled a room with his aura. Gaspara proved herself to be the faithful one rather than merely an object of desire. Finally readers heard what a woman was feeling, her griefs and exaltations and anxieties. The mythical Lady became flesh and blood and heart. "If lowly, abject woman I," Gaspara began, "can carry within so sublime a flame, / why shouldn't I draw out at least / a little of its style and vein to show the world?" (65). Her humility seemed counterfeit as she realized her power and gave it voice through her poems.

Gaspara defined herself. As a member of the Accademia dei Dubbiosi (The Doubtful), she took the name Anassilla, a play on the name of the River Anasso (also known as the Piave) that ran through the lands owned by her beloved Collaltino. In an attempt to recreate an idealized pastoral Arcadia, the literati often renamed themselves as "characters" within this classical world located in the Greek peninsula that was the mythical home of the god Pan. Arcadia became for artists and thinkers a place of harmonious living. Raising their conversations about philosophy, love, and letters to a higher plane, they reached back in time to converse like their Greek models. These writers pictured themselves as humble shepherds at one with a perfect natural world, and they penned plays, poems, and treatises praising this simple though intellectual life. As Professor Virginia Cox points out, "Texts such as these all helped establish the nymph-bard as a figure of Arcadian imagery, in a manner that reflected the place women had come to assume within the contemporary Petrarchan tradition" (*Prodigious* 95). Anassilla was no longer merely Gaspara; she became Collaltino's "little shepherdess," an epic hero on a quest for love (Stampa 237). "Ah, if your most faithful Anassilla / has ever been kind and sweet to you . . . ," she wrote in the third person, "it would do no harm to let a spark / of pity escape as a prize for her faith" (115). Gaspara was like Petrarca pining for his Laura, except for once readers heard from a woman what a woman was feeling.

Sadly, Count Collaltino di Collalto never requited her love; "to his Anassilla / he hasn't deigned to write a single verse," in the span of three years that her poems covered (131). Finally, as the love affair appeared hopeless, Gaspara wrote Anassilla's own epitaph: "Under this rough stone lies hidden / the loyal, most unhappy Anassilla, / rare example of great and amorous faith" (135). In the Petrarchan model where the man was always the hero, the lover, the most faithful, the one who acts, readers finally found a woman who took on this persona, making it possible for other women to leave their passive spaces and publicly and vocally declare themselves as heroic, as faithful as men. And though ninety percent of the time Gaspara exalted her beloved Collaltino, at times she inserted a sarcastic pinch, taking him down a notch, beseeching, "turn a compassionate eye / from your handsome self to my suffering, / so that the pity that will touch your heart / may match the pride you take in being you" (77). Could she not resist the spurned lover's jab?

In addition to her Arcadian salon persona, Gaspara also defined herself within her poetry. She might have been a suffering lover, but she was still full of brilliant life. "Love has fashioned me so I live in flame," she wrote, "the animal who also lives and dies / in one and the same place, no less strange" (241). She was indeed a bit "strange," a woman professing ardent love unapologetically, proclaiming her love and "erotic impulses," as researcher Giovanna Rabitti asserts (43). "If any woman ever so / enjoyed the fires and ice of love, it's me," Gaspara proclaimed (Stampa 197). Male writers seldom wrote from a female point of view, and so few women wrote at all that Gaspara's perspective was fresh and provocative. No passive, retiring woman, she. Unlike the mold society had fashioned for her, trying to keep her silent, chaste, and hidden, Gaspara Stampa blazed her love and lived ablaze, relishing it.

And yet, by modern standards, some aspects of Gaspara Stampa's poetry might be difficult for liberated twenty-first century women to praise. She wrote 220 poems about her beloved Collaltino di Collalto, sublimating her needs to him with a line like this: "If anything of worth from me is born, / none of it is mine, but yours; you guide me, / and to you goes all of value, and the crown" (Stampa 199). Or at times Gaspara seemed to revel in the pain of unrequited love, like when she wrote, "Love is suffering, but not wishing to complain / to the offender, turning your anger / against yourself, abasing yourself" (qtd. in Jaffe & Colombardo 263). It's like listening to Billie Holiday sing of her love for the man who betrays and leaves her. Furthermore, Gaspara's poems imitate Petrarca; lauded poets were those who most closely imitated Petrarca's style and themes. For modern readers who reserve the most praise for creativity and innovation, Gaspara seems like the antithesis of this.

Of course, today's readers can't measure Gaspara Stampa, a sixteenth century poet, with a twenty-first century yardstick. Upon further exploration, they can begin to understand Gaspara's particular talents and creativity, whose work, luckily for subsequent generations, was saved from obscurity by a loving sister. It makes one wonder how many other remarkable sisters, daughters, and mothers lived extraordinary lives that are now completely lost.

Unfortunately, being a woman with a voice brought on suspicion, attack, and revenge. Sperone Speroni, a fellow member of her salon the Accademia dei Dubbiosi, wrote a vulgar poem calling her a whore and asking which of the Stampa sisters made a better sexual partner. Because she never married and dared to write about her love for two different men, and because she frequented the literary salons amongst some people who were considered to have less than stellar morals, many labeled Gaspara a courtesan, the highest class of sex workers who were quite literate and musically talented. At that time, the literary salons were still a male society, where men gathered to discuss literature, philosophy, and ethics. The only women in attendance were courtesans or women who entertained the men with singing and playing music. Later, in the early 1900s, writer Abdelkader Salza combed through Venice's archives to find proof of Gaspara's supposedly illicit and unchaste lifestyle in the salon, publishing his work in his article *Madonna Gasparina Stampa secondo nuove indagini*. His "proof" was inconclusive—he never showed that she was sexually promiscuous or that she took money for sex. But what is the point of such questioning or slander? Is it to discredit Gaspara's work? To discredit all women writers of her time in order to push women back to a place of subservience and silence? Thanks to the diligence of Cassandra, Gaspara would not be silenced.

Sadly, no manuscripts in Gaspara's own hand remain. Three of her sonnets appeared in a 1553 anthology titled *The Sixth Book of Verse by Various Excellent Authors*. Bassanese points to the *Varie* poems that display crafting and styling akin to other writers of her day (44); the care Gaspara took with these and the time she invested in improving her writing indicate that she hoped to publish. Though her intended audience was probably wide, Gaspara also addressed some poems specifically to other women. "You women who have recently embarked / upon these waters full of treachery / . . . beware!" she warned. "Let me offer some advice: / find for yourselves noble lovers," (Stampa 113) meaning men who were honest and true and generous. She wished for others not to suffer as she had.

But her message was not only about love's dangers and how to avoid them. She also addressed women's laments, the "quarreling and torments / of children and husbands" (353). Gaspara wrote one poem that promoted a cloistered life—one that she certainly never chose for herself. For others, though, Gaspara proclaimed, "Happy [is] she who makes herself Christ's / handmaiden" (353). Was she indeed advocating taking vows and becoming a nun? Or was she simply questioning the few roles—and their consequences—that were open to women? This poem was published much later, in 1573, and some say it may not be written by Stampa at all (Tower & Tylus 350). It is ultimately out of step with her earlier writings and with the way she led her life.

Besides these messages to women, Gaspara influenced many who came later. She had a "disciple" in Olimpia Malipiero, a Venetian patrician woman who wrote of female friendship and other themes, and who published her own poems in 1559 and 1565 anthologies. Nearly two centuries later, Luisa Bergalli Gozzi helped to make a name for herself by republishing Gaspara's writings in 1738. The eighteenth century Romantic era saw a resurgence of interest in Gaspara's work, though a large portion of the allure was a mythologized version of her life that relied more on her personal identity as unrequited lover than as a powerful female author. Twentieth century audiences have begun to read her poetry as a distinctive female voice, and the most recent scholarship is beginning to drop the appellation of "female" before "writer" to give Gaspara her true due.

Gaspara didn't live long enough to see all her poems published. When she became ill, she took refuge at the home of Geronimo Morosini, the same family friend who had taken in the Stampa family when they first moved to Venice. Gaspara developed a high fever and coughing fits and withdrew to bed. Cassandra must have stayed faithfully by her side, applying cool cloths to Gaspara's forehead and changing the clinging bed sheets. As her symptoms rapidly worsened, Gaspara also developed "matrix pains" (qtd. in Bassanese 19) that seemed to emanate from her womb. She always intended to publish her poems and must have felt desperate as her illness worsened and she saw this dream disappearing. After a brief fifteen days, Gaspara died on April 23, 1554, so much potential still unrealized. Though thanks to her sister Cassandra, the world would remember her in her poetry. Cassandra's grief was acute and debilitating, but friends in their literary circle pushed her to collect and arrange Gaspara's work for publication. The work itself, and the tribute it represented, probably helped Cassandra work through her grief.

Not a helpless princess in a tower but a phoenix rising from the flames, Gaspara Stampa blazed a new path for women's voices in literature. Whether or not she was a courtesan seems less relevant than that fact that she was a virtuoso performer, a singer who could set a room afire with her voice, and a poet who articulated women's emotions. "My delight, my desire," she wrote, "is to live ablaze yet not feel the pain" (qtd. in Jaffe 239).

# *Veronica Franco*

## Taking up her Inks

"*A*mong so many women I will act first, / setting an example for them all to follow," wrote Veronica Franco ("Cap. 16," 165). Publicly slandered in vulgar poems written by nobleman Maffio Venier, Veronica must have felt not only insulted but also frightened of the public humiliation and personal harassment by one so highly-ranked. She may have been a courtesan, the highest class of sex workers, but that didn't mean she should suffer attacks. Instead of hiding in fear, though, Veronica retaliated with verses of her own, not only defending herself, but also all women. "And I undertake to defend all women / against you," (165) she continued, taking up "her inks" as she referred to her writing, as her surest weapon against cruel men. In the drawing room of a luxurious palace, part of the entertainment for the men gathered there for a literary salon, Veronica would have flounced her skirts, positioned her curls, and tilted her chin at just the right angle to make her point as she read her poems. She would not be cowed.

Veronica Franco knew the rules of the game that women in the public eye must play. She needed the patronage and protection of men, as a writer in a male-dominated literary world, and as a courtesan who was, as she herself wrote, "prey to so many men, at the risk of being stripped, robbed, even killed" (Franco 39). Besides being beautiful, exalted for her heart-shaped face, eyes like two suns, and her golden tresses, she was one strong woman—independent, intelligent, educated, not afraid to love to her fullest capacities, and strong enough to survive the harsh life of a sex worker. Her published letters, showing her intelligence along with the minutiae of a well-ordered life, silenced the stereotypes that all prostitutes lived chaotic, disorderly lives. In actuality, life in Venice was more stable than in most cities at that time; the State regulated its sex trade and collected taxes from it, so despite the definite dangers for the women themselves, the city was enhanced by their work (Rosenthal, *Honest* 16).

The Franco family lived in the Dorsoduro district of Venice on Calle Franchi where Veronica was born in 1546, though the exact address is unknown. Such a narrow street must have been a challenge to pass through for women wearing the wide, hooped skirts of the day. Veronica and her family attended the nearby Church of Sant'Agnese, where Veronica was baptized and where a medallion over the side door once showed the family coat of arms (though time has erased the painted details). With its shady, quiet *campo* or square, this residential district contrasts to Veronica's later bustling lifestyle. Growing up in this neighborhood, Veronica displayed an early love for learning. When her three brothers would return from their lessons, she ordered them to repeat the day's exercises for her. Her early hunger for knowledge became a great boon to her later career.

When Veronica's father Francesco, a member of the *cittadini* merchant class, couldn't provide enough income for his family, his wife Paola Fracassa resorted to the sex industry, ostensibly to help feed the family. Though Veronica's parents were able to arrange a wedding for her at age sixteen to Paolo Panizza, this marriage failed within a couple years. Veronica Franco was compelled into her profession as a courtesan by her mother, which may shock modern readers but was not so out of the ordinary in the sixteenth century. In the 1565 publication *Catalogo di tutte le principali et piu honorate cortigiane di Venezia (Catalogue of All the Principal and Most Honored Courtesans of Venice)*, Paola is listed as her daughter's procuress, and they each charged a lowly two *scudi* for their services (as compared to the thirty *scudi* required by Paolina Filla, the highest paid courtesan listed in the book). Paola was near the end of her career, Veronica at the beginning of hers, but it didn't take long for her to raise her status.

By the time Veronica was eighteen and pregnant with her first child, she wrote her will, a common practice for women of the time since death during childbirth was a distinct danger. This document, "Considering . . . the danger of our fragile life" (qtd. in Rosenthal, *Honest* 111, author's translation) dated August 10, 1564, showed her emerging pragmatism as she bequeathed money for a dowry if the child was a girl. Veronica believed the child's father to be Jacomo di Baballi, a wealthy nobleman from Ragusa (also known as Dubrovnik, Croatia), and she asked that he care for the child in the event of her death. But her will also showed her concern for others. Veronica must have earned—and saved—some income in her burgeoning career, for she set aside funds for her servants and also either for two poor Venetian girls' dowries or for two prostitutes to leave the profession. Even at this early date, Veronica was helping to protect women. Veronica gave birth to Achille, the first of six children she delivered, though three died in infancy. So often this tragic fact is drily noted in biographies, yet to lose even one child is for any mother a devastating wound, one that requires great fortitude to overcome. History has preserved stories proving Veronica's resilience, though she must have suffered great griefs and losses as well.

Having a child, though, didn't hinder her career or her prospects. As Professor Margaret Rosenthal points out, Veronica Franco was a "*cortigiana onesta*," translated as an "honest" or also an "honored" courtesan ("Introduction" 1), (or translated by Jaffe and Colombardo as "virtuous"). Courtesans were the highest strata of sex worker in Venice, an industry at its height in the sixteenth century. In a population of about 100,000 in the year 1500, Venice employed about 12,000 sex workers, so famous that they drew visitors from all over Europe (King, *Women* 78). Interestingly, prostitution was never illegal, but it was regulated. The industry thrived primarily due to Venice's marriage practices; families were reluctant to split up inheritances, so generally only one son married. This left the other men to seek pleasure from sex workers instead. Set above the *meretrice* or more common prostitute, the courtesan took her definition from the term "*cortigiano*" or courtier, one who "paid court" to nobles, so she was the more likely companion for these disenfranchised noblemen. A courtesan was expected to be well-educated—highly literate, well-read, fluent in several languages, witty and skilled in conversation, a musician or singer, refined, and graceful—as well as beautiful. Many of these qualities were quite atypical; among Venetian women, including the nobility, only ten to twelve percent were literate, compared to about thirty percent of men (Jones & Rosenthal 5). Veronica was "*onesta*" because she honored herself, and by extension her patrons, with her literary talents, an "honest" profession and also an honorable one. Still, this profession had a sort of twilight quality, set beside the official patrician society that lived in the limelight.

Often, however, courtesans sometimes tried to blend in to the noble class. A series of Sumptuary Laws decreed that Venetian women of all classes must curtail their luxurious and extravagant fashions. Women ignored these or found ways to thwart the regulations. For example, prostitutes were supposedly forbidden from donning pearls, yet numerous courtesans sported such adornment anyway. Women's dresses could not have elaborate trains that extended beyond their shoe height, so courtesans (and many noblewomen, too) famously began wearing *zoccoli*, shoes on such tall wooden soles (up to twenty-four inches!) that their wearers needed assistance so they would not topple over.

Fashionable Venetian women also wore dresses that bared their breasts or lightly covered them with a sheer fichu; interestingly, two areas of Venice have bridges or streets named for the "*tette*" or breasts because prostitutes were allowed to bare themselves at their windows in order to allure customers. In a series of drawings from the 1589 book *Diversarum Nationum Habitus*, women of different strata of Venetian society modeled typical clothing. One drawing of a courtesan depicts two versions—one where the courtesan's dress is flipped up as if a hurricane arose under her feet, displaying for all to see the gender-bending and thus titillating men's breeches under her skirt. "So silk and embroidery, silver and gold, / gems, crimson cloth, and all that's most precious," wrote Veronica Franco of women's fashions, "men used to embellish their highly placed treasure" ("Cap. 24," 247). In other words, men employed this finery to decorate their women, a comment Veronica may have made with a wry smile at the fact that women might enjoy this attire while also knowing that they were being used to show their value. As a leading courtesan, Veronica would have followed all these fashion trends. Her portrait, painted by the illustrious Venetian artist Tintoretto, depicts her wearing layers of heavy fabric, a rose colored overdress thickly embroidered with red thread and beading. Draped over one shoulder lays a netted lace shawl, while around her shoulders rests a stole of black satin. A small pearl necklace encircles her neck, while a larger string of ostentatious gems crosses her breast. Her bodice dips down to reveal the edge of one nipple, as she gazes off to the side.

By her early twenties, Veronica was hosting a small literary salon in her home near Campo Santa Maria Formosa. Most courtesans had their own richly appointed houses, often overflowing with luxurious draperies, chandeliers, mirrors, tables, and other furnishings they had received as gifts from clients. Sadly, she did not leave a description of her rooms. But she did divulge her greatest desires. In letter 17 of her published *Lettere Familiari a Diversi* (*Familiar Letters to Various People*), Veronica wrote telling lines about her life's wish—to learn the art of intellectual discussion. "And it's with great delight that I talk with those who know so as to have further chances to learn," she wrote about gaining education among those in a salon, "for if my fate allowed, I would happily spend my entire life and pass all my time in the academies of talented men" (qtd. in Jones & Rosenthal 34). Veronica began her literary career with a poetry anthology to honor Count Estor Martinengo who had passed away in 1575. His relatives had requested Veronica's service, indicating their trust in her judgment and an acknowledgement of her connections to many talented writers.

Besides hosting her own academic salon, Veronica got to achieve her goal to surround herself with literary men in another way. She became a member of Domenico Venier's celebrated salon at his home in Campo Santa Maria Formosa. Scores of the city's powerful, learned, and apparently lusty men attended. Domenico, the eldest of his patrician clan, suffered from gout and was unable to fulfill his duties in the Venetian Senate, so instead he had the city's literati come to him. His salon was known not only for brilliant conversation, but also for its literary output: members translated from Latin to Italian works by Ovid, Catallus, Propertius, Tibellus, and others, which Veronica greedily read and began incorporating into her own writing. In her poem "Capitolo 15" from her book *Terza Rima*, she wrote of being in Domenico's salon, "In that assembly of yours, so famous, / of learned men of distinguished judgment, / who know how to argue and discourse so well" (153). Though Veronica expressed modesty about her poetic abilities, she was able to hold her own amid this erudite company, taking center stage to improvise poems or sing, surrounded by the other guests, men in embroidered waistcoats of sage or cream, tight fitting breeches and powdered wigs. They would have arranged themselves around Venier's luxurious drawing room, which was furnished with inlaid wooden tables and damask-covered chairs, gilded mirrors on the walls. Although the Venier salon members often debated the ideals of Petrarchan love, Veronica broke new ground by writing poems in first person, giving women a voice for virtually the first time; in fact, a host of critics have noted ways in which Veronica subverted the genre in her unique approach and voice (Rosenthal, *Honest* 5). By listening to the arguments and discussing the literature, she gained an education here, incorporating her new knowledge into her own personal style.

Made famous in the 1998 film *Dangerous Beauty,* (which is an only partially accurate biography), were the poetic duels where Veronica contested with, among others, Maffio Venier, Domenico's nephew. Though Veronica and Maffio never physically duked it out with swords as did characters in the film, they did duel with words. As a writer himself, Maffio seems to have been threatened by her poetic prowess. Veronica taunted Maffio to choose any weapon he wished, "the common language spoken in Venice, / . . . Tuscan . . . of high or comic strain, / . . . the style that mixes Italian and Latin / . . . / for I am equally happy with them all, / since I have learned them for exactly this purpose" ("Cap. 16," 167). Maffio had written three vulgar poems defaming Veronica as a common whore; she never cringed to admit to her profession, but she was anything but common. Her quick wit matched any poet stanza for stanza, as her collection *Terza Rima* proved. It contains twenty-five poems, nineteen of which were written by Veronica, the others by men who replied to her in verse. This was a style called *proposta / risposta*, or challenge and response, according to Margaret Rosenthal (*Honest* 178*).* The resulting pairs of poems are termed *capitoli,* and the response always follows the same rhyme schemes as the challenge—a formidable medium since the writer must respond in the instigator's preferred style. Veronica rose to this challenge, probably with a twinkle in her eye and a tilt to her hip.

Before Veronica realized that Maffio Venier was the author of these defaming pieces, she believed them to have been written by Marco Venier, Maffio's cousin and brother of Domenico. In fact, the first poem of her *Terza Rima* collection was written by Marco, followed by her reply, and though later poems contain no names, it is believed that some *capitoli* were by Marco as well (Rosenthal, *Honest* 94). In this series, Veronica accused Marco of betraying her by writing insulting poems; he replied that he was not guilty, and she responded by suggesting that he teach her how to duel better, so she could prepare to defend herself against her real attacker. In Letter 47, in delicious double entendre she requested, "I entreat your lordship, as the perfect instructor, to teach me some secret stroke, or, rather, to take the sword into your own hand, not one with a sharp edge but one for play, and to engage me in a duel as virtuoso as you like" (Franco 45). These lines imply that Veronica and Marco enjoyed physical as well as literary intimacy, unlike her antagonistic relationship with Maffio. Witty, playful, sharp, and unafraid to speak frankly of sex, Veronica must have been a delightful change for men living in a Venice where women were normally so oppressed and silenced.

But where are Veronica's true feelings in this? Researchers Margaret Rosenthal, Ann Rosalind Jones, Irma B. Jaffe, Gernando Colombardo, Giorgina Masson, and others have offered many conjectures. Some contend that Veronica's bold lines about her sexual prowess reveal that she enjoyed her work. "So sweet and delicious do I become, / when I am in bed with a man / who, I sense, loves and enjoys me, / that the pleasure I bring excels all delight," (Franco, "Cap. 2," 69) she wrote to Marco Venier, referencing her experience with men other than just him. But notice here the referral to love. A courtesan didn't always have the prerogative to lie only with men who loved her. While a number of her poems do express deep love for a man, she must have had sex with scores with whom she shared no love. However, Veronica seemed to take some pride in being good at her job, as she wrote "that I, well taught in such matters, / know how to perform so well in bed / that this art exceeds Apollo's by far" (69). Though some contend that she showed delight in the art of love, these lines also hint that this skill was something she was taught, something she didn't necessarily seek of her own accord. Veronica made the best of this job she was compelled to do, and she excelled at it.

In "Capitolo 16," Veronica defended the prostitute's profession, and she aligned herself with this sisterhood, with whatever name it is given. Her poem responded to Maffio Venier's, in which he called her a *meretrice* or common prostitute, and she punned on the sound of merit, or goodness, in it, writing, "Whatever goodness prostitutes may have, / whatever grace and nobility of soul, / the sound of your word [*meretrice*] assigns to me" (Franco 171). She was not apologizing for her profession and in fact pointed out that these women had "grace and nobility of soul" like anyone else. Though the stereotype of the prostitute with a heart of gold or the noble whore may have entered common modern-day culture, this was most definitely not common thought in the sixteenth century. Veronica sought to change perceptions.

Veronica's poems and letters show that she could enjoy the game of love, and certainly the intellectual foreplay, yet other writings display a different attitude towards being a sex worker. As writers Jaffe and Colombardo point out, many of her writings show anxiety, anguish, and anger. She was the object of public humiliation in Maffio Venier's vulgar poems, and she used her wit and learning to defend herself and other women. If she were so happy in her profession, would she feel the need to declare that she should defend all women against the cruelties of men? Veronica was dependent on men for her livelihood, and while she could strive to achieve a higher class of clientele, her job was still to pleasure many men.

When King Henry III of France came through Venice, he spent a "secret" night with Veronica at her home in the San Giovanni Grisostomo neighborhood; many citizens knew all about this affair because it helped to glorify their city. But it is essential to remember that Veronica still was compelled to sleep with a stranger and that her body was a commodity of the Venetian State. "Even so disguised," she wrote in her first of two sonnets to Henry, "into my heart / he shone such a ray of his divine virtue / that my innate strength completely failed me" (Franco 27). Later, Veronica published a sonnet that she wrote for the king and also published her letter to him, which acted as a sort of introduction to her book of letters. She highly praised him and recounted her pleasure in his company. Yet she also hoped that he would fulfill his promise to help her publish her writing, as she wrote in a dedication, "Nor can I compensate even partly with any form of the thanks for the infinite merit of the kindly and gracious offers you made to me on the subject of this book, which I am about to dedicate to you" (Franco 24). She knew that her own worth increased by having been the king's lover. Veronica's flattery, like her enjoyment, were not necessarily insincere, yet her desire for patronage was also a factor when she wrote praising the king.

Veronica also commented over and over about virtue—praising the virtue of men like Domenico Venier when she was "longing for [his] virtue" (Franco, "Cap. 5," 85) or Cardinal Luigi d'Este with his "famous virtue" (Franco 23) or King Henry III's "sum of virtue and perfection" (28). She once admonished a lover that she might love him back if he proved himself through honorable deeds. Though many questioned the virtue of one who worked in the sex trade, a courtesan must actually hold herself to a high standard of virtue—meaning a sense of integrity, honor, and dignity. Her clients were the highest-ranking men, and they expected to be with a woman who provided them the illusion of being of equal rank. As this quest for honor or virtue was true for all in the courtesan class, Veronica aspired to it for herself as well as for her lovers and friends.

Despite Veronica's desire to be honorable and talented, she also revealed misgivings about her trade. In an oft-cited letter that Veronica wrote to a woman who was considering setting up her daughter as a courtesan, Veronica shared another opinion. Besides the religious argument that a prostitute's soul would be damned, and the social argument that a woman's reputation for chastity would be irreparably damaged, Veronica also stated in Letter 22, "this is a life that always turns out to be a misery. It's a most wretched thing, contrary to human reason, to subject one's body and labor to a slavery terrifying even to think of" (Franco 39). Pen in hand, she went on to list specific dangers, including injury, disease, and even murder, to which a courtesan was prey. "What wealth, what luxuries, what delights can outweigh all this?" (39) she asked with dismay. Any delights experienced in bed or in fraternizing with intellectual men were tempered by these thoughts. As Professor Ann Rosalind Jones points out, "For Franco, prostitution is wrong because it entails subjection and danger for women; it is a social, not a moral disease" ("Prostitution" 52). Women were not to be blamed for their roles in a society that set such expectations and limitations.

Though technically Veronica never recanted her profession, evidence reveals that she felt deep sympathy for women who had to work in the sex trade. Provisions in her wills (she penned them more than once, usually before giving birth) were set aside for women who wished to leave the profession. Then in 1577 she petitioned the Venetian government to open a Casa del Soccorso as a home for former prostitutes who had left their job. "There are many women who, having led a dishonest life because of poverty, sensuality, or other reasons, are sometimes touched by the Spirit of his Divine Majesty," wrote Veronica, "and thinking of the miserable end to which the path most often leads them with regard to body and soul, would easily change their wicked ways if they had some reputable place to repair to, and support themselves and their children" (qtd. in Rosenthal, *Honest* 131). She didn't live long enough to see this institution launched, though it was eventually built on the Fondamenta del Soccorso in Dorsoduro and opened its doors in 1581; the building still stands, with a plaque on the second level over the door reading "S. Maria del Soccorso."

Veronica wrote in defense of women not from the viewpoint of an unhappy nun cloistered from society, not as a woman compelled into a sterile political marriage, or not even as a happily married woman who still had to fight for individual identity and voice. Veronica wrote as one who had to share her body with others, some probably pretty undesirable, to put food in her mouth and the mouths of the six children she raised (three of her own and three adopted), and to put a roof over their heads. This provided her with some economic independence compared to women whose wealth was completely governed by their fathers, husbands, or male relatives. She furthermore presented a model to prove that women could be economically self-sufficient. No one compelled her to take up her inks and learn her "warrior's skills" (Franco, "Cap. 16," 163); she chose that on her own, and to her great delight. "When we women, too, have weapons and training, / we will be able to prove to all men / that we have hands and feet and hearts like yours," (163) she wrote. Her best weapons—and those allowed to her—were her mind and her body, which some might say were more powerful than any weapon forged of steel.

When Veronica died at age forty-five on July 22, 1591, she was living in poverty, having lost most of her savings during the plague years of 1575 to 1577 (which also took the life of her brother Girolamo). About 25,000 people died during this bout, and the fear of contagion would have caused clients to stay away from the sex workers. People lived these years in fear rather than in seeking pleasure. Also around this time, due to a spiteful accusation by her sons' tutor, Ridolfo Vannitelli, who claimed Veronica practiced witchcraft in her home, she faced trial but was eventually acquitted. These difficulties impoverished Veronica, and near the end of her life she was living in the San Samuele *contrada* or quarter that was inhabited by the poorer prostitutes. As an unmarried courtesan, she had no one to come to her aid. Records are a bit unclear, but apparently Veronica was originally buried at her family Church of Sant'Agnese, though her body was reportedly moved to the grandiose Church of San Moise. Probably her greatest joy in life had been that her profession as courtesan allowed her to be surrounded by men of letters—though this doesn't mean that she enjoyed her profession.

Whatever others might say about her and her occupation, Veronica knew that there was much more value to her. About herself, Veronica stated, "A woman whose fame makes her right to be proud, / who stands out for beauty or for courage, / and far exceeds all others in virtue-- / such a woman is rightly called 'unique'" (Franco, "Cap. 16," 169). She may have been a courtesan, she may have had to endure humiliations both verbal and physical, but she would do it honestly and virtuously and so well as to win fame as the best. That was her strength and her beauty.

# *Angela del Moro*

## Triumphant Venus

*G*uns. Knives. Brass knuckles. Fists. Swords. Humiliation. Rape. Poetry. All weapons men have used against women.

Those last three were leveled against Angela del Moro, a young courtesan who dared to turn away a client named Lorenzo Venier, who then swore to take revenge. Men endeavored to control her—and control her image—with poems, with letters, and with paintings, but Angela would overcome all these attempts through her perseverance and talent. Some saw her as a whore, as a victim, as a formidable foe, even as a goddess, but Angela would have the final say in shaping her destiny. She must have lived in fear more than once, and she certainly suffered extreme humiliation and possible physical assault, but she was a survivor. In fact, she triumphed.

Very few facts outline Angela's childhood. She grew up with a mother and father, or possibly stepfather, named Borrino (Rossi 239 n18). Sometimes called Giulia, she is most often known as La Zaffetta after her father's profession, a policeman or *zaffo*, though other records indicate that she was the illegitimate child of a procurator of San Marco, someone who regulates expenditures for the Basilica di San Marco and charitable institutions (Quaintance, *Textual* 82). One document states that Angela was born in 1525 (Rossi 239 n18), but this would make her only six years old at the time she clashed with Lorenzo Venier, supposedly in 1531. More likely Angela was a teenager at the time of the perceived offense and just beginning her career as a courtesan.

Although they were not born into the patrician class, courtesans still commanded much power in the upper echelons of society. Courtesans often set fashions for clothing, musical styles, and entertainments. As Venice's noblemen gained wealth, they had disposable income to spend on lavish entertainments, placing power in the hands of those who dispensed those pleasures (Rossi 225). While wealthy families only married off one son, this left the other sons (and many married men as well) to seek out courtesans' company. As Renaissance scholar Courtney Quaintance points out, "Part of her ideal role as a courtesan was to judge and choose only the worthiest of men as her suitors" (*Textual* 86). Imagine the fear of public rejection many men must have harbored. Courtesans' value to the male-dominated society gave them social standing, plus more freedom than many women enjoyed. Despite her youth (or perhaps because of it), Angela was early sought after by many elite men and members of the literary salons, including that of Domenico Venier, who was also an important patron to Veronica Franco. To be admitted to such an exclusive company, Angela must have been well-read, quick-witted, musically adept, and exceptionally beautiful. Lorenzo, in fact, was Domenico's brother, and their father was an influential senator. The family wielded power and as nobles would have been virtually immune to censure for any actions less than treason. Still, Lorenzo might have feared social rejection by his friends if Angela spurned him, so he felt the need to remind her of her inferior status.

Due to her wit and verve, Angela dined often with the painter Tiziano Vecellio (known as Titian in English) and the writer and wag Pietro Aretino at Casa Aretino, the Grand Canal palace halfway between the Ponte di Rialto and Ca' d'Oro. Named the Palazzo Bollani Erizzo, its land entrance is at number 5662 in Campiello Riccardo Selvatico. Pietro Aretino (most often referred to by his last name only) filled his house with art but not books, saying that he didn't want his writing to copy others (Aretino 26). For one such dinner, Aretino sent out an invitation to Titian and the architect and sculptor Jacopo Sansovino, stating that the menu included "two pheasants and Signora Angela Zaffetta" (qtd. in Masson 147). By using the title "*Signora*," Aretino ranked her in the higher class of courtesans, known for their learning, conversation, musical abilities, and other talents besides just those of the bedroom. She was also, apparently, scrumptious.

Considering that she dined at Aretino's often, Angela must have enjoyed his company as well, perhaps as a friend and not merely a client. Aretino mentioned Angela in some of his stories plus in four different letters. In one from 1548 he wrote, "Let it be known that the respect I have for your honour is twice as great now that I feel so very honest in my old age" (qtd. in Quaintance, *Textual* 83). At different times Aretino wrote scathingly but later warmly about Angela, so it's difficult to know their true relationship. Known to write to increase his own fame, Aretino might be fictionalizing his depiction of Angela for his own literary benefit, but his writings are virtually all that is left to chronicle her life (Quaintance, *Textual* 83).

For example, in Aretino's first volume *Lettere* (1537), he wrote to Angela, appearing to flatter her. "You don't exercise cunning, the heart of the courtesan's art, through betrayal," he said, "but with such dexterity that he who loses would swear he had gained" (qtd. in Ray 131). Though he appeared to compliment Angela, Aretino at the same time reinforced the negative stereotype that all courtesans were false, avaricious, and untrustworthy. According to his letter, Angela was the most cunning of them all, perhaps praiseworthy for Aretino who admired this quality. He continued to applaud Angela "because more than anyone else, you know how to make lust masquerade as respectability" (131). Was his praise genuine or backhanded? Aretino added that Angela was superior to other courtesans because she never faked orgasm; he wrote to her, "You embrace virtue and honor men of virtue, which is alien to the habits of nature of those who sell themselves for the pleasure of others" (qtd. in Hale 339). In Aretino's estimation, Angela was sincere and genuine, rather than false like others in her trade, though it can be difficult to unpack his compliments towards her considering the gender stereotypes of the day.

Angela, of course, had to survive in the male-dominant world of sixteenth century Venice. To make a living, she had to put up with such comments and writing. It must have often been quite tiresome. But Angela seems to have been different from other frivolous or shallow courtesans. Aretino wrote to her, "You abstain from the usual feminine chatter and keep away from silly people and pompous asses. Only those who honor you properly are allowed to enjoy your loveliness and the rare splendor of your person . . . . Lies, envy, malice—stuff of courtesan life—are not what motivated your heart and tongue." He went on to pledge himself to her, stating, "For all these reasons, you are worthy of having me call myself yours" (qtd. in Lawner 82). According to Aretino's depiction, Angela, with her superior personality, was a cut above most greedy sex workers. Witty, vivacious, beautiful, multi-talented, and overall pragmatic, Angela took the role that life had handed to her and embraced it.

In spite of these sometimes complimentary depictions of Angela, though, Aretino supported his friend Lorenzo Venier, a nobleman and aspiring writer who aimed to defame Angela. Supposedly Angela had committed an *arlasse*, sending away Lorenzo Venier at his usual appointed time with her so that she might entertain a different lover. Many courtesans kept standard appointments with their various lovers; Lorenzo, for example, may have had Tuesday evenings while Marco got Wednesdays. Matteo Bandello described this practice in his *Novelle* (1554),

> There is a certain custom in Venice . . . namely that a courtesan take six or seven lovers, assigning to each a certain night of the week when she dines and sleeps with him. During the day she is free to entertain whomever she wishes so that her mill never lies idle and does not rust from lack of the opportunity to grind grain. Once in a while, a wealthy foreigner insists on having one of her nights . . . . In this case, it is her duty to request permission from the lover whose evening that

would ordinarily be and to arrange to see him during the day instead. Each lover pays a monthly salary, and their agreement includes the provision that the courtesan is allowed to have foreigners as overnight guests. (qtd. in Lawner 9)

But Lorenzo, being of the patrician class and a man unused to being denied anything, was incensed that he could be treated this way by a mere "whore" or *meretrice* as he called her. He would have his revenge upon young Angela. Little did she know what horror awaited her.

Who knows why Angela turned away Lorenzo Venier on that day. Maybe he often skipped his appointments with her. Or maybe she had received a better offer. He may not have received her message. Perhaps she was happy to ditch him because he could be insufferable; indeed, he had proudly authored *La Puttana Errante* or *The Wandering Whore* to ridicule the courtesan Elena Ballerina, who Lorenzo claimed had robbed him, as well as Angela for fleecing her clients. He doesn't sound like a particularly nice person.

Then Lorenzo penned *Il trentuno della Zaffetta*, the story of a gang rape perpetrated on Angela del Moro. Aretino helped him produce it, probably in 1531 (Quaintance, *Textual* 70). Only Lorenzo's version of the story of this crime survives, and it may be highly fictionalized. In this poem, Lorenzo whines to Angela that "You laughed at me during *Carnevale*, / when I suffered the pains of your love" (qtd. in Rossi 235). He may be an earnest, spurned lover, or he may be looking for pity. Pietro Aretino, who could play king of vitriol himself, said that Lorenzo was "four days ahead" of him in his ability to inflict malice (qtd. in Masson 146). On the other hand, Aretino also claimed that Lorenzo was "my creation," his literary protégé whom he tutored through the writing process (qtd. in Quaintance, *Textual* 69). It could be that the two men were producing popular and scandalous tracts against the leading courtesans in order to bring themselves fame at the women's expense. Certainly, Aretino profited from his friendship with Lorenzo, this affluent and influential nobleman, who helped fill his pockets and lionize his name (Quaintance, *Textual* 70).

When Angela left Lorenzo knocking at her door in vain, he devised a plan. He first appeared especially attentive to her, not mentioning his displeasure at the missed appointment, as he invited her to dinner on the island of Malamocco, a long, skinny strip of land south of Giudecca. She dined ravenously on a whole hot roast partridge, allegedly "seized it and downed it in one gulp / and faster than you can say Ave Maria / guzzled six goblets of malmsey [wine]," (qtd. in Lawner) agreeing to then spend the night with him on Chioggia. In the poem, Lorenzo depicted Angela as silly, speaking in a chirpy voice, eating gluttonously, and embodying all the worst stereotypes. He tried to make Angela appear ridiculous, "wearing half a perfume shop on her person" where "here in Chioggia she wants to seem an empress" (qtd. in Lawner 76). They dined a second time before retiring to bed and intercourse.

This was when the night took a darker, violent turn.

After Lorenzo Venier had finished with Angela, a friend of his arrived and announced that it was time for a *trentuno*, a euphemistic term meaning a gang rape. *Trentuno* means thirty-one, the usual number for this type of punishment, but according to Lorenzo, eighty Chioggietti—fishermen, gondoliers, porters, peasants, even clerics—had their turn with her that night, Lorenzo making a point that these were men of the lowest class. This number for an *arcitrentuno* or "super trentuno" seems hyperbolic and incredible, but the point is the intense violence and humiliation inflicted on this woman.

Pietro Aretino brings this type of event to life in disturbing detail. In his dialogue titled "*Il Trentuno*" or "The Thirty and One" between Nanna, a courtesan, and her daughter Pippa, he recreates a horrifying experience similar to Angela's. "The drunken, foolish and wicked fellows replied to [their victim] with cruel jests: 'Signora, tonight you are under obligations to us and to our brother grooms of the stable,'" he writes. "'You may as well make up your mind to stay here'" (Aretino 140). Through the storytelling of his character Nanna, Aretino captures a fragment of the emotions that Angela must have felt, stating, "She was so overcome with grief that she was not able to speak a word" (140). The story continues by describing the first man who had his way with the poor woman in Nanna's story, the "big pig [who] dragged her to the trunk of an almond tree and, bending her head down there, drew her clothes over her head and did what seemed best to him, thanking her for the service with two cruel and resounding slaps on the rump," and the "screams she gave were the signal for the third tilter" (140). Nanna describes the crowd of men waiting their turn as making "the same uproar which starved dogs make when they are released from the chain" (140). The woman survived the night and her many assailants, "with her inflamed eyes, her pulpous cheeks, her rumpled hair, her dry lips, and her torn clothes" (141). She begged to be left alone and, according to Nanna, "she never recovered from the shame she had and, feeling that she had lost fortune and reputation, she was no longer herself but died of grief and want" (141).

By using a female narrator, Aretino's version of the *trentuno* shows some sympathy for the victim of such a crime, though the raucous laughter of the rapists and the extreme violence depicted virtually nullify that feeling. But Lorenzo Venier apparently felt little remorse. His version of the incident, published in 1536, reached nine hundred verses in *ottava rima*, the verse form of eight-line stanzas usually employed for epic poetry. With himself as narrator, Lorenzo recounted how eighty Chioggietti raped Angela on April 6, 1531. This date may actually be fictional; Quaintance points out that April 6 correlates with the famous first meeting between the poet Petrarch and his love Laura, and "thirty-one," the number of the *trentuno*, matches the year 1531 (*Textual* 87). Speaking of himself using the third person, Lorenzo explained, "The man craves vengeance, not lovemaking" (qtd. in Lawner 76). Lorenzo wrote specifically to publically humiliate Angela, saying that "every brothel is full of talk of Angela, and the news of her *trentuno* has spread throughout Venice" (qtd. in Quaintance, "Defaming" 201). He also hoped to garner praise for himself, writing, "In the entire city, not one man can be found who does not praise the man who did it to her" (201). Lorenzo wanted to remind Angela, and deliver a clear message to other courtesans, that he held the power over their reputations, careers, and safety. In fact, historian Georgina Masson explains that after this incident, many courtesans refused to leave home, even for one hundred ducats (147).

Though in his poem *La Puttana Errante* Lorenzo Venier described women's sex as a weapon, he reinforced that men's arsenal was still more powerful: *Il Trentuno* contains numerous lines about Angela's humiliation or displays her as begging for mercy (Quaintance, "Defaming" 200). In *Il Trentuno* he explained that after the rape, Angela remained hidden in her home "as if she were dead" (qtd. in Quaintance, "Defaming" 201). Lines in the poem explain that when Angela's mother attended to her after the rape, she "saw her beaten, / so swollen and red on all sides / she was sure that her daughter would be in her grave within two hours" (qtd. in Rossi 234). Angela even laments, "Ah! Why don't I just stab myself through the heart" (qtd. in Quaintance, *Textual* 95), contemplating suicide rather than continuing pain and shame. But six days later Angela was again displaying herself on her balcony in typical courtesan fashion, "cheekier than ever" according to Lorenzo (qtd. in Quaintance, "Defaming" 201).

For Lorenzo, writing his poem was a necessity to remind Angela and to record for all time Angela's humiliation. He even went a step further, blaming Angela for the poem's existence: "So what am I supposed to do if everyone wants me to make a poem out of your *trentuno*?" he wrote (Quaintance, "Defaming" 201), as if others were clamoring for him to disgrace her. However, he also ended one stanza with the phrase about his "crazy love of revenge," (Veniero, author's translation) giving away his own motives. He also included Angela's desire for revenge, when he recorded her saying, "That traitor . . . should be burned and killed" (qtd. in Rossi 234). Lorenzo ended the poem by admitting that courtesans were powerful and were a necessity among men who have such driving sexual desires; courtesans such as Angela, therefore, must be courteous and know their station so that society would not crumble (Lawner 76-77). Historian Daniella Rossi contends that many Venetian noblemen felt threatened by the power that courtesans held over them, so humiliating these courtesans reminded them that women were meant to be silent and obedient (235). Rather than continue to feel humiliated, though, it appears that Angela became incensed and determined to not be a victim.

Despite the poem's great detail and length, many historians debate whether or not the rape actually occurred. Professor Ian Moulton points out that "Prostitutes were undoubtedly gang-raped, and the '*trentuna*' was a recognized cultural form of shaming, whether actually performed or merely rumored to have occurred" (Moulton, email). Rape, even today, is used as a weapon. Rossi states that "group rapes, which occurred in a broad range of social groups in urban Renaissance Italy were seen as a form of punishment or discipline for women who did not adhere to community standards of sexual conduct" (227). For a highly-ranked courtesan, public defamation could be an extremely powerful weapon against her. It could cost a woman her clientele and ability to earn in the future, leaving not only the courtesan destitute, but also those who relied on her, such as family members, her children, and servants. The humiliation could also cost her a valuable reputation, for though courtesans were sex workers, they were considered "*oneste*" or honorable due to their education and cultivation; defaming Angela could reduce her to a lower status and decreased earning power. Of course, there's also the physical trauma and increased chance of contracting a disease that would harm her prospects or could lead to a deadly disease like syphilis. The *trentuno* potentially affected her whole future. Lorenzo, being a nobleman, escaped all punishment. Rossi points out that "The normalization of group rape as a form of social discipline was confirmed by the ambivalence to such crimes by the ruling class" (227).

To go a step further, Daniella Rossi believes that the *trentuno* is a satirical poem, containing gross exaggerations that render it farcical. The poem begins like a classic epic akin to Homer's *Odyssey*, as Lorenzo declares he will "sing / Of [Angela's] history in such a divine style" (qtd. in Rossi 228), and he employs *ottava rima* as one would use for a classic epic. Comic elements are added, such as a bored man "who marks the blows with a piece of coal" as each rapist takes his turn (230). The poem is theatrical in nature, intended to entertain audiences with its incredible extremes (230). Furthermore, the men in the poem sing comic songs and laugh uproariously, creating a comic tone (Quaintance, *Textual* 79). The humor would have appealed to the sensibilities of Renaissance era men (90) and would have reinforced male bonding through the telling of smutty jokes (81). Angela never does take revenge or leave a response, indicating that the whole thing was a sort of inside joke that she went along with (Rossi 233). Lorenzo Venier felt the need to publicly humiliate Angela to put her in her place, and his poem could be as potent as the violent act that he wrote about. The poem itself could also bring Lorenzo literary fame, particularly if it were written with style and humor (Quaintance, *Textual*

82). Whether or not the assault took place, though, is a separate issue at this juncture. Apparently, no doctors examined Angela for her injuries, and no one would be brought to a witness stand or summoned to tell the whole truth. The goal was to remind Angela that men wielded the most power, and Lorenzo employed the best weapon in his arsenal to achieve this end.

Even without the social advantages that a patrician like Lorenzo enjoyed, Angela was a survivor. Though *Il Trentuno* wasn't officially published until 1536, no doubt Lorenzo was vocally defaming Angela around Venice; if the poem is true, Lorenzo had graffitied on Chioggia's and possibly Venice's walls, "How on the sixth of April [1531] Angela Zaffetta / satisfied everyone in a *trentuno*" (qtd. in Rossi 233). But Angela was not so easily broken. If the *trentuno* or some version of it took place in April 1531, by October 1532, Angela was back on top of her game, garnering lavish compensation for her time and talents. According to historian Marin Sanudo's diaries, when powerful Cardinal Ippolito de'Medici visited Venice in 1532, Angela slept with him, arranged with the aid of her friends Titian and Aretino, who often enjoyed Angela's company (Quaintance, *Textual* 82). She was back in business, with a prominent and desirable client. But at the top of Angela's game, Lorenzo felt the need to remind her to watch her back.

Angela's celebrity continued to rise. Books such as the *Tariffa delle puttane di Venegia* (*Rates for Venetian Prostitutes*) in 1535 and the *Catalogo di tutte le principali et piu honorate cortigiane di Venezia* list Angela as one of the city's top courtesans, and she is referred to as Venice's "second highest paid courtesan" (Hale 339). Historian Guido Ruggiero observes that courtesans were often compensated with gifts and services, "that real courtesans usually did not have a set price and much of their income was from 'presents'—in this they acted rather like artists and intellectuals who were given rewards for their service, but not a straight out fee" (Ruggiero, email). In a city with 150 to 200 courtesans out of possibly ten thousand sex workers, Angela faced a lot of competition to maintain her status (Henry 111). Whatever the case, Angela's time and company were coveted. She was not closing the curtains on her bedroom or hiding in the dark as Lorenzo might have hoped.

The painter Titian played a significant role in resurrecting Angela's reputation. Apparently, he adored Angela as a subject. According to Titian's biographer Sheila Hale, he painted at least four canvases featuring Angela. In fact, one of the Italian Renaissance's most famous pieces, known as the *Venus of Urbino*, depicts Angela's face, if not her body (which could be a model). In this brash pose, Angela reclines on her side on a garnet red divan, roses in her right hand, and her left hand resting where it can bring herself pleasure. Her gaze is directed calmly at the viewer, a smile on her lips. Angela's loose golden brown hair lies haphazardly upon her shoulders and pillow, with a band of it braided across her head. Her body is softly rounded, adorned only by a jeweled bracelet, pearl earrings, a pinkie ring, and honeyed light. The carved windows and the hanging drapery, which both match items found in Titian's home in the Biri Grande neighborhood of Cannaregio in northern Venice, indicate that Angela probably posed for the portrait there.

The first of Titian's reclining nudes, some say it may be a marriage painting since the maids are unpacking typical Venetian *cassone* used as dowry trunks. Others say Titian was simply painting a very pretty nude. The painting is referred to as the mythical Venus, goddess of love and patron goddess of Venice, because Titian includes her typical symbols of myrtle and red roses (Hale 341). Since the painting depicts a classical goddess, its stature is elevated. However, it's important to remember that men were the painters, and "the body of the courtesan appears not as a site of self-representation or promotion, but as the instrument of a male author" (Henry 111). In spite of this, for a woman who had been publicly humiliated, Angela was not afraid to allow her image to be glorified on canvas. She sat for and apparently sanctioned this painting and the image it created of her. Scholar Chriscinda Henry even suggests that many courtesans used scandal that might appear ruinous for their own fame instead because "it was an important part of their culture and self-promotion" (116). The more fame, garnered in any fashion, the more clients and income.

Mark Twain, who later saw the painting in Florence's Uffizi Gallery, called it "Titian's beast" and "the foulest, the vilest, the obscenest picture the world possesses" (380). Due to the placement of Angela's hand coupled with her gaze, Twain believed she was dangerously immodest, for "there the Venus lies for anybody to gloat over that wants to; and there she has a right to lie, for she is a work of art, and Art has its privileges" (380). Though Twain was shocked by the position the Venus lies in, with his characteristic insightful wit he acknowledged that all may dare to gaze upon her, and she would gaze unabashedly back. The confident woman in this portrait was not one to be destroyed by a spurned and vengeful lover. In 1881 art critics described the woman's gaze as "not transfigured into ineffable noblesse, but conscious and triumphant without loss of modesty" (qtd. in Hale 341). She was not apologetic nor timid nor cowed. Titian apparently painted this piece in hopes of selling it to Ippolito de'Medici, Angela's former lover, though it still sat in his studio on December 20, 1534, as evidenced by one of Titian's letters, and sat unsold until at least 1538, perhaps because its value had increased beyond most buyers' resources by then. It hangs in the Uffizi now, and its form has been copied dozens of times, most famously by Eduard Manet as *Olimpia* in 1863.

The painting's impact, while certainly a testament to Titian's talent, also expresses the power of a woman—Angela—who audaciously owns her sexuality. Some of that power resides in the singular woman captured by Titian's paintbrush.

Titian captured Angela's likeness three times more. In 1536, the same year *Il Trentuno* appeared in published form, Titian painted *La Bella*, a woman in an elegant, courtly dress with a rosary around her neck. Titian employed costly blue lapis lazuli in *La Bella's* gown. The Duke of Urbino wrote to Titian requesting to buy this beautiful woman in blue. Before selling the portrait, Titian replicated the face and pose in *Woman in a Fur Cloak* where she exposes one breast to the viewer. The similar *Woman in a Feathered Hat* is also believed to feature Angela's visage. As evidenced by Titian's portraits and letters, Angela kept company with Titian and his influential coterie, her star continuously rising. Pietro Aretino implored Titian, "Under dark, transparent veils / one sees here angels from heaven in the flesh. / O Titian, you perfect spirit, paint / their noble semblances, let us feast our eyes on them!" (qtd. in Lawner, epigraph). Titian's hand had the power to direct society's gaze and mind, and though he controlled that image, still he used it to lift Angela from the place Lorenzo Venier had tried to bury her.

Though a courtesan's career could be short-lived due to loss of beauty, disease, or a client's hostility, Angela's career was rather extended. Aretino wrote that Angela "retained her beauty even after she was thirty" (qtd. in Hale 339). Aretino was not a flatterer; he was, rather, a pragmatist who took stock of what life had meted out so he could make the most of it. This may have been a quality he admired in Angela. He consorted with a number of courtesans, but his character's attitude in another of his dialogues seems to fit Angela's demeanor and experience. In "The Best Profession" from Aretino's *Ragionamenti*, when Nanna discusses the courtesan's profession with her friend, Antonia states that a courtesan "is like a soldier, who is paid for doing wrong, and doing it, she is not to be held for so doing, because that is what her shop has to sell, that is what she has to sell" (Aretino 111). These women are not to be condemned for doing what a restrictive society has allowed them to do. It appears that Angela would not be cowed nor silenced but instead took what muck was thrown at her and then ascended above it. Angela earned a sizable income and knew better than to squander it; at one time it was rumored that she planned to purchase the Palazzo Loredan, one of the most imposing Grand Canal palaces (Hale 340). She could add money management to her list of talents as well.

Angela set her sights on something grander. She and a friend named Flaminia traveled south to Rome, the other mecca for courtesans, where the prima donna courtesan Tullia d'Aragona reigned at that time.

One young Roman fondly recalled "the delicate Angela del Moro and Flaminia, who are like two stars" (qtd. in Masson 148). Without Titian to paint her and Aretino to write about her, future readers would only see Lorenzo Venier's ugly portrayal and Angela's humiliation. But she can be remembered as a survivor, a winner, and a beauty. The injury Lorenzo did Angela was grave, but it's said that the greatest revenge is to live well, and by that metric, perhaps Angela won the final round. Through Titian's portrayal and her own triumphant perseverance, Angela remade her image in the likeness she desired and is remembered now as triumphant Venus.

*La Bella* by Titian

# Modesta Pozzo

## The Worth of One Woman

*F*rom the time she was a small girl, Modesta Pozzo amazed others with her photographic memory. After hearing a poem once, for example, she could recite it word for word. She read and wrote voraciously, penning poems that she kept bundled together and took with her everywhere. One day, while traveling in a carriage to her family's estate, the bumpy river crossing caused a basket containing Modesta's poems to spill into the stream. Papers fluttered away from her hands, and ink washed away in the rolling water. Young Modesta was inconsolable at the loss of her writings, crying tears of frustration and desolation. However, the poems were not actually gone forever. In the following days, Modesta reconstructed her poems from memory, astonishing everyone.

Though she was a daughter and not a son in sixteenth century Venice, Modesta was determined to be educated. She would live within the bounds of propriety, but she would not be deprived. As she wrote in Canto 4 of her work *Tredici Canti del Floridoro (Thirteen Cantos of Floridoro),* she believed

> If when a daughter is born the father
> Set her with his son to equivalent tasks,
> She would not be in lofty and fair deeds
> Inferior or unequal to her brother,
> Whether he placed her among the armed squads
> With himself, or set her to learn some liberal art.
> (Fonte, *Floridoro* 145-6)

Her female protagonist Risamante in this epic poem proved herself on the actual battlefield, but Modesta Pozzo chose the liberal arts instead. She went on to compose books in a number of genres that argued for women's education and equal consideration and proved that women could write on par with men.

Her given name, Modesta Pozzo, connotes one who is modest, unassuming, one who de-emphasizes or discounts one's worth, abilities, or achievements. Dictionaries generally include a secondary definition as well, stating that modesty refers to a woman who behaves or speaks in ways to avoid indecency or impropriety. "Modest" comes from the Latin *modestus* meaning to "keep due measure." As a noblewoman, Modesta Pozzo would have been well aware of her society's injunction that women temper their behavior and live a circumscribed life. In fact, her narrator in *Floridoro* editorializes these thoughts in Canto 2, stating, "Every person must be humble / and display benevolence and love, / for humility binds every noble heart / with a sweet and most gentle chain" (Fonte, *Floridoro* 88-9). Modesta's surname Pozzo likewise slides hand-in-glove with her given name, as a *pozzo* is a cistern such as those seen in most Venetian squares. (In Italian, *pozzo* means well, yet in Venice the term specifically refers to the cisterns that gather water rather than wells that pull water up from the ground.) These *pozzi* collect and filter rainwater for locals to use. So a *pozzo* is a reservoir or receptacle, a storage place for others' use, also suggestive of the way women were treated in Venetian society.

However, Modesta Pozzo took for herself a pen name: Moderata Fonte. Clearly, this name echoes her given name with its similar adjective and noun. Yet as Professor Virginia Cox points out, Modesta chose her words carefully to imply quite different connotations ("Introduction" 5). "Moderate" as an adjective means something average, not excessive, though the verb may shed more light on Modesta's decision to take this name. While the noun form implies that she still fits willingly into her restricted role as a patrician woman, the verb implies that she moderates or controls herself, rather than someone else controlling her. For her last name, Modesta chose *fonte* or fountain, a much different water source than a cistern. The Latin *fontanus* means a spring, connoting a source that gives refreshment and life. A fountain is also an ornamental pool, usually decorated with statuary, carvings, or jets of water, a pleasant respite from heat or monotony. Modesta Pozzo's literary identity thus gives insight into her desire to be seen as one who is a source of beauty or even life but who is not controlled by others, one who, as Cox adds, employs reason (5).

Since Modesta published some of her works before her marriage, she was more acutely aware of social pressures to maintain respectability, prompting her to choose a pseudonym. She explained her reasoning herself, in the "Dedicatory Letter" prefacing *Floridoro*. She used this "imagined name," she explained, "since my own true name I have not judged it well to expose to public censure, being a young marriageable woman and, according to the custom of the city, obligated in many respects" (Fonte 49). Modesta felt the anxiety of a watchful society that was ready to condemn anyone who misstepped. She would be careful with her reputation. Many women who had published before her had been married or widowed, which gave them more protection from public criticism since it was assumed that they were under their husband's guidance and safekeeping. Perhaps this is also why the pen name "*Moderata*" fits so well: Modesta at that time had no husband (and no father) to "moderate," shield, or control her. She controlled herself. In sixteenth century Venice, then the European center of the publishing world, Modesta stood out as a woman author, first for being unmarried, and second for not limiting herself to prescribed genres.

Modesta was born in Venice in 1555, on June 15, the feast day of San Vito and San Modesto (and origin of her name), and then she was baptized in the Church of San Samuele. This was the thick of Renaissance Humanism, when women were sometimes allowed to enter into a limited literary life with the men around them, generally within their families and homes. Modesta's father Girolamo (or Hieronimo) was of the *cittadini* class, prosperous professionals accorded certain rights but not members of the aristocracy; Girolamo, in fact, was a lawyer known for his intellectual acuity when he earned his degree at the University of Bologna (Finucci, "Introduction" 3 n6). When Modesta's parents died before she was a year old, her maternal grandmother Cecilia de' Mazzi and her step-grandfather Prospero Saraceni gave Modesta and her older brother a home. Modesta was soon placed at the large, spare convent of Santa Marta where she learned reading and writing, sewing, singing, and rudimentary math. Santa Marta is quite isolated at the far southwestern edge of Venice's Dorsoduro district, but that didn't hinder the nuns there from noticing young Modesta's sharp and quick mind. Modesta probably couldn't wait till prayers and chores were completed so she could meet with the nun who would pull out the books, line up the parchments and quills, and query Modesta on her lessons.

Back with her grandparents after she turned nine, Modesta was still hungry to learn. Each day as her brother Leonardo returned from his tutor, Modesta would accost him after he had barely come through the door. She made him repeat his lessons to her so she might also learn as he did. What new Latin declensions did he have for her? Which speeches from Cicero could he repeat? In this way Modesta taught herself Latin until she could read and write it fluently. Her language skills, keen memory, and quick reasoning were noticed and cultivated by those around her, particularly her step-grandfather and her uncle Giovanni Niccolo Doglioni. This uncle married Prospero Saraceni's daughter, who was Modesta's dear friend, and he invited the orphan to join their household. Giovanni Doglioni took her under his wing as his literary protégé, helping Modesta to publish her own work, and then later writing a biography about her.

Besides reading and writing very rapidly, Modesta excelled at everything she attempted, including math, drawing, playing the harpsichord and lute, singing, needlework, and pattern making. Though she was not involved in the city's academic salons, Modesta was apparently welcomed into the men's literary discussions within her home, which deepened her learning, honed her reasoning skills, and gave her a place to voice ideas and opinions. Gathering in the drawing room, guests were surrounded by sumptuous papered walls and upholstered furniture, with servants bringing trays of cheeses and glasses of wine. One person would propose a topic that all could debate or discuss, punctuated by recitations, improvised poems, or musical performances. Canto 10 of *Floridoro* shows that Modesta knew who the literary lights were in Venice; she praises, among others, Domenico Venier, "a man worthy of every honor and reverence . . . light of the world" (Fonte, *Floridoro* 283). He ran a literary salon in his home and acted as patron to many writers in the city.

Modesta commenced a public literary career in December 1581 by performing for the doge to celebrate the feast day of Santo Stefano; Modesta recited her work "*La Festa*," a dramatic piece with a religious theme, which she later published. She must have looked rather small and fragile in the grand Basilica di San Marco with its echoing vaulted domes and side altars. But this event must have given her some confidence, for following this debut, Modesta published verse narratives entitled *La passione di Christo (The Passion of Christ,* 1582) and then *La Resurrettione di Giesu Christo (The Resurrection of Jesus Christ,* 1592). These works confirm Modesta's lifelong devotion to her faith.

Fortunately, Modesta found a man who valued her mind and supported her writing. She married Filippo Zorzi, a tax lawyer, on February 15, 1583, when she was twenty-seven, relatively late by the day's standards. This might account for their marriage involving more equality than most. Filippo returned a portion of Modesta's dowry to her control, due to his "great love and affection" for her, and he showed his support of her writing by penning a sonnet to preface her verse *The Resurrection of Jesus Christ* (Cox, "Introduction" 37 n19). Being a writer as well as a respectable wife was unique for Modesta's era, a time when women were sequestered from cultural and political life. She enjoyed love as well as intellectual freedom.

In 1581, about the same time that Modesta wrote *The Passion of Christ*, she also began *Thirteen Cantos of Floridoro.* It was quickly published to glorify a Medici family wedding, "these splendid and regal nuptials" (Fonte, *Floridoro*, Canto 13, 379), though the piece was never actually finished as planned. *Floridoro* was a chivalric romance in the predetermined style of Ariosto's epic *Orlando Furioso*, with a female protagonist as the savior knight. Though the epic's title character is Floridoro, this male knight (who is actually quite feminine) is not as central to the story as Risamante, a female warrior. She and her twin sister Biondaura are separated at birth, with Biondaura being bred as a queen and Risamante trained by a wizard as a knight clad in white armor, her symbol a pure lily. Modesta was attempting to give voice to her ideas of gender equality while maintaining a woman's required role as chaste and modest. Moreover, Modesta was making the point that women could excel at any task that men could, if given the opportunity, education, and training. She began Canto 4

> Women in every age were by nature
> Endowed with great judgment and spirit,
> Nor are they born less apt than men to demonstrate
> (with study and care) their wisdom and valor.
> And why, if their bodily form is the same,
> If their substances are not varied,
> If they have the same food and speech, must they
> Have then different courage and wisdom? (*Floridoro* 144)

Here Modesta makes the point that women can be equal to men in all categories.

Typical for the genre, Risamante sets off on adventures that take her to far-flung locales, where she tests herself against other warriors, rescues damsels in distress, and even pits herself against a serpent, using her cunning together with her training to overcome it. In Canto 3, section 15, readers hear that "The greedy beast with mouth open / rushed upon her, and yet it could not catch her. / Rather, incautiously it swallowed the iron of the lance / which the lady wielded against it, and pierced and struck itself" (123). A principal demon that Risamante destroys is the potently symbolic serpent, both phallic and for Christians representing a sinful temptation. According to biographer Valeria Finucci, this scene symbolizes that "women can get what they want only if they themselves pursue their goals" ("Introduction" 176 n12). In the end, Risamante fights to regain a kingdom that rightfully belongs to her, metaphorically pronouncing that women deserve to own the intellectual kingdom just as men do. Further, Professor Stephen Kolsky writes that "Fonte is making a determined effort to rewrite myth; to valorise female achievement in the context of a universal story" (171). Myths may traditionally show men as heroes, but Modesta wasn't satisfied with that trope.

Modesta was a bold pioneer within her chosen genres. A handful of other female authors penned chivalric romances around this time, notably Laura Terracina, Tullia d'Aragona, Margherita Sarrocchi, and Lucrezia Marinella. But Modesta is credited with unique innovations. Finucci writes that Modesta was the first women "to construct (and politicize) history" (336 n1) when she included a long section of Venetian history in Canto 12, "to make known to us from [Venice's] founding / the beautiful successes of an illustrious city" (Fonte, *Floridoro* 337). Later, in Canto 13, Modesta recalled the Battle of Lepanto, "a cruel war, born of a certain incident / between the Turkish Lord and the Venetians" (370). This was groundbreaking as a "first account by a woman writer of a naval battle," states Finucci (372 n8). Besides banquets and balls, in *Floridoro* Modesta described swordfights and jousts, things she never experienced. She had numerous books at her disposal to read and learn about such sports, yet it still required an avid imagination, not to mention a poet's skilled facility with rhyming octaves, to create such an epic story.

In addition to her authentic content, Modesta also wrote with an eye to her craft and to engaging her audience. Plot lines overlapped, "in order not to sing always of one subject," the narrator explains in Canto 5 (Fonte, *Floridoro* 184). Modesta retained readers' interest by cutting off one story line to pick up another, heightening suspense. Such storytelling that presents a female character as strong, able, valorous, and fearless contains much power; it provides a role model for women to follow, a hero to emulate. Risamante even boldly says in Canto 5, "When I find a way / to expose myself to some dangerous undertaking, / I don't draw back; rather I enjoy it more / when it's held for an impossible thing" (187). Men and women alike must have thrilled to hear a warrior pronounce this. But bravery wasn't her only trait. With modesty in Canto 13, Modesta's narrator writes that "I with such beautiful threads adorn and weave / my cloth, which in itself has a rough texture, / that it can indeed seem beautiful; and it can stand near / any other of gold and silver" (368). Though this was the narrator speaking, Modesta occasionally used this character as a chance to insert herself into the story and express her personal thoughts. In this instance, she downplayed the "rough texture" of her writing, but Modesta took the opportunity to show that she still knew its value.

Modesta may have been supported by men and their literary world, but that didn't make her into their replica. At a time when the dialogue genre was most popular, when men such as Baldassare Castiglione in his publication *The Book of the Courtier* were following Plato's example of discussing ideas and displaying reasoning through fictionalized dialogues between predominantly male speakers, Modesta was the innovator. Virginia Cox points out, "Fonte's most striking innovation is, without question, her depiction of a group of exclusively women speakers" (Cox, "Introduction" 18). The work to which Cox refers is Modesta's *Il merito delle donne,* or *The Worth of Women: Wherein Is Clearly Revealed Their Nobility and Their Superiority to Men,* a fictional account of seven noblewomen spending two days together at Leonora's lovely villa in order to argue that women are every bit as capable, intelligent, and valuable as men. "To tell the truth," points out the character Lucretia, "we are only ever really happy when we are alone with other women, and the best thing that can happen to any woman is to be able to live alone, without the company of men" (Fonte, *Worth* 47).

In this conversational and often humorous book (published posthumously in 1600), all but two of the women are married, one quite recently, and one widowed. The unmarried two include Virginia, a naïve young woman, and Corinna, who has decided to renounce marriage in favor of a literary life; certainly not by coincidence, the sixth century Greek poet Corinna bested Pindar in literary competitions. Almost without exception, the women denounce marriage and men in general. Freshly married Helena speaks excitedly about her new husband but later reveals his jealous nature and malicious comments. She tells the others, "I'm not sure I can say yet whether I am happy or not" as she contemplates the new restrictions marriage brings (46). But the young widow Leonora is unequivocal regarding marriage. "I'd rather drown than submit again to a man!" she exclaims. "I have just escaped from servitude and suffering and you're asking me to go back again of my own free will and get tangled up in all that again? God preserve me!" (53). For a time in Book 2, the women recount the merits of particular men for their learning or magnanimity, including even Modesta's uncle Giovanni and her husband Filippo. The women discuss, often punctuated by Corinna's expositions, such wide-ranging topics as the animal kingdom, politics, herbal remedies, law, grammar, poetry, clothing, heraldry, and the cosmic order. Then each of these topics is summarily rounded off by returning to men's inferiorities and failings, be they moral, physical, intellectual, or otherwise. Jaded Leonora quips that she will take on the "onerous" task to speak about men though it is akin to a "vast shoreless and bottomless ocean" to list all their shortcomings (57). Each woman shares her experiences and opinions, with Corinna taking a leading role with her greater store of knowledge.

Modesta presented a rather intimate portrait of noblewomen's cares and concerns when no men are present, a picture that had never yet been painted. Another remarkable feature of *The Worth of Women,* as Cox reveals, is the way it raises so many questions and issues without outlining staid solutions ("Introduction" 19). Modesta's characters banter about men's virtuous and evil attributes. Early on Corinna offers this insight: "And when it's said that women must be subject to men, the phrase should be understood in the same sense as when we say that we are subject to natural disasters, diseases, and all the other accidents of life . . . since they have been given to us by God as a spiritual trial" (Fonte, *Worth* 59). Or, during a discussion on goodness and wickedness, the women point out the double standard that society unfairly sets up for men and women. For example, men may gossip about women's sexual behavior and label women as "whores" and "sluts," Cornelia contends, "And I don't quite know how they've managed to make this law in their favor, or who exactly it was who gave them a greater license to sin than is allowed to us." She continues with a question still asked by women today: "What makes [men] think they can boast of the same thing that in women brings only shame?" (90). The characters describe a double standard that continues to the present day.

While the women in this book seem biased against men and marriage, they also inject examples of honorable men and relationships. At the end of their discussion, the character Lucretia points out, "For we poor women are constantly being assailed and abused, and cheated of our money, our honor, our lives; so it seems better to have one man at least as a friend, to defend us from the others, than to live alone with every man against us" (240). Some men are worthy or can become worthy through a woman's influence, they contend, and this companionship can lead to a life of immeasurable happiness. Modesta's marriage was an example. By employing the seven characters and their diverging opinions, Modesta was able to present a full complexity of women's issues.

Through her characters' voices, Modesta subtly showed readers that she had done her homework: she had read her Aristotle, Ariosto, and Agrippa, her Boccaccio, Castiglione, and Dante, her Petrarca as well as Pliny. Many of her ideas referred to these men's works, showing that a female scholar could be as learned as men, but at the same time imparting this knowledge to her female readers, who had every right, she believed, to know what men know. At one point the character Lucretia states, "It's good for us to learn about these things, so we can look after ourselves, without needing help from men. In fact, it would be a good thing if there were women who knew about medicine as well as men, . . . and we didn't have to be dependent on them" (181). Simply because the ideas in *The Worth of Women* spout from women's mouths, at a time when women were expected to be silent and believed to be intellectually inferior, the ideas have fresh impact.

Furthermore, Modesta injected humor and playfulness into the conversation, making it more intimate and realistic while using a light tone that made her readers question otherwise serious topics or opinions. For example, when Corinna suggests that women should get to keep their dowries to support themselves, Leonora wonders, what if "instead of taking a husband, [women] just bought a nice pig for themselves every Carnival, which would fatten them up and keep them in grease rather than keeping them in grief" (114). Many humorous comments sound spiteful, but not all. At one point Leonora teases the new bride Helena, who has defended her husband, saying, "I'm not sure that her husband has behaved so decently toward her. In fact, I suspect that he has caused her to lose something she had before" (58). Helena blushes at reference to her virginity, and then Corinna adds further jibes against men. As the seven women poke fun at each other, it encourages lively and even irreverent questioning of social mores.

Modesta continually challenged readers to question society's assumptions and strictures. For instance, a key tenet in *The Worth of Women* relates to the cosmic order as laid out in the Bible. Leonora explains, "For all things were created for [men's] benefit and ours, and in fact men themselves were created specifically to help us in life. Additionally, they do their job far worse than trees and other irrational creatures, which never fail in their duties" (168). She later adds, "And yet, as I've said, all the other creatures recognize us as the ruler of the world, just as much as men, if not more" (169). If indeed men and women rank at the top of the natural order, and were created to be helpmates to each other, then men have abused or ignored that divine injunction. Modesta's characters may have debated this, but it was certainly a proposition that she wanted her readers to consider.

Women, however, face some challenges that men never do, such as having babies. During the Renaissance era, roughly ten percent of women died "as a consequence of childbirth" (King, *Women* 5). Modesta gave birth to three children successfully, but while giving birth to her fourth one, a girl, Modesta died on November 2, 1592, at the age of thirty-seven. Women knew that childbirth was a dangerous time, and many of them made out their wills before their child was due. Modesta prepared in a different way: she completed her manuscript. She must have been filled with anxiety as she felt her time drawing near and hastened to put the final words on paper. Her uncle Giovanni Doglioni recorded that she had finished *The Worth of Women* the day before she entered her confinement to have her baby (Doglioni 38). "Her death left all those who had known her devastated, with a sorrow from which few of us will ever recover," he wrote (38). He later named his daughter Modesta in his niece's honor, and that name carried on through successive generations.

Modesta's children were all educated equally, regardless of gender; Giovanni wrote that at the time of their mother's death, the elder children, two boys and a girl aged six, eight, and ten respectively, already knew Latin and could play the viola and sing. They were apparently as bright and quick as their mother. Giovanni Doglioni's biography appeared with the publication of *The Worth of Women*, which also included a dedication by Modesta's daughter Cecilia and two sonnets by her son Pietro. Modesta was buried in the cloisters at the Basilica dei Frari, where her husband was later laid to rest; a plaque originally commemorated this location, but it can no longer be found.

This respectable and modest woman carved a place for her ideas and writings. Modesta attempted to hide in the shadows, "in back where there was little light," she wrote as she surreptitiously described herself in Canto 10 of *Floridoro* (288). "She did not dare come out with the others into the light, / quite ashamed that she, too bold, / aspired to the way which leads to heaven" (288). Like many women of her era, Modesta tried to downplay her talents. She also needed the support of the men around her, yet she was and is a source for new insights and perspectives. Modesta made both her names—her identities—work for her in Venice's strict social hierarchy, and she repeatedly displayed courage and intelligence in her writings. Like her character Risamante in *Floridoro*, she was a knight fighting to regain her rightful kingdom—equality—inspiring many who came after her.

*Venice: Frari Church* by Michele Giovanni Marieschi

# Lucrezia Marinella Vacca

## No Defect, No Mistake

Men "would not be loved by women were it not for our courteous and benign natures, to which it seems discourteous not to love our male admirers a little," wrote Lucrezia Marinella (Marinella, *Nobility* 63). Her indignation must have poured from her quill onto the page as she penned this line, maybe gritting her teeth while her pen could not keep up with her swirling thoughts. Ensconced in her rooms overlooking a small *campo*, Lucrezia had few ways to express her ire except with her mind, her words, and her pen.

Lucrezia was responding to Giuseppe Passi's claim that a woman was a "mutilated male" or a "mistake of nature," in his treatise *I donneschi deffetti* (*On the Defects of Women*). He agreed with San Giovanni Grisostomo that women were a "necessary evil" and wished that men could reproduce without the aid of women at all (qtd. in Panizza, "Introduction," *Nobility* 20). Giuseppe Passi did, however, admit, "But I was led to this only by anger against those women who, caring little for their honor, have been the cause of innumerable ills" (qtd. in Marinella, *Nobility* 126). He blamed women for their own disempowered state.

Understandably, Lucrezia Marinella Vacca was livid at having such demeaning epithets hurled at women. She had prepared herself her whole life to respond. Daughter to physician and philosopher Giovanni Marinelli, she had read her science and philosophy. With access to her father's vast library, she knew her classics—Petrarca, Boccaccio, Plato, Aristotle, Agrippa, Virgil, Homer, Ovid, Dante, Ariosto, and Tasso, to merely skim the cream. Though Lucrezia had led the typical sequestered life of a Venetian upper-class woman, she had practiced her rhetoric and dialectics with her father and brothers and their learned friends. Within the walls of their home, she and the men would sit side by side to pore over books together and discuss classic works, leather-bound books grasped in their hands. Her brother Curzio became a physician, while brother Antonio took orders as a Servite monk; due to their father's early death, it may have been these two who shaped Lucrezia into the scholar she became (Stampino 6). Lucrezia studied alongside her brothers, recalling lessons by heart and reciting Latin passages. As an already published author, Lucrezia had honed her writer's craft and brought female heroines to the forefront.

She was ready.

And she gave her outrage wings.

Lucrezia's polemical book *La nobiltá et eccellenza delle donne—The Nobility and Excellence of Women*—hit the shelves in its first edition in 1600, with expanded versions in 1601 and 1620. "My desire is to make this truth shine forth to everybody," she wrote in her preface, "that the female sex is nobler and more excellent than the male. I hope to demonstrate this with arguments and examples, so that every man, no matter how stubborn, will be compelled to confirm it with his own mouth" (Marinella, *Nobility* 39-40). Lucrezia wanted to silence doubters or squabblers; her tightly reasoned philosophical arguments would have made Socrates proud. One engraving shows off her high forehead, small mouth, fine eyebrows over large eyes, and smooth skin, with small hoops adorning her ears. While her hair falls loose down her back, tiny curls surround her face and are piled up into small horns at the top, the prevailing style shown in many women's portraits. Lace softens the neckline of a simple dress with a laced bodice. Once one knows Lucrezia's thinking after reading her works, it's difficult to shake the feeling that her smile in this portrait has a bit of the smirk to it.

Lucrezia Marinella came from a fairly privileged *cittadini* family where both her father and brother were doctors who fully supported her education. Her father wrote books of his own, including a gynecological guide for doctors and midwives and an edifying health guide for women. Lucrezia's father even prefaced one of his books thus: "I have seen how much valorous men and equally valorous women have esteemed my writings, . . . it has occurred to me to explain something new and something so important that it will give all gentle people material for discussion" (qtd. in Ross 198). In the Humanist tradition of the sixteenth century, Giovanni Marinelli believed women capable of intellectual activity equal to men's, so he didn't pressure his daughter to wed nor force her to enter a convent. Following her literary bent, Lucrezia chose to study and write, producing her first book, *La Colomba Sacra*, on the life of Santa Colomba of Sens, in 1595, when she was quite young. It's unclear just what her age was: most sources cite her birth year as 1571, though Professor Virginia Cox references various other documents that point to 1579, making Lucrezia sixteen years old when she first published (Cox, *Prodigious* 271 n5). Lucrezia published under the name Marinella—notice the final "a," indicating it as feminine, rather than Marinelli as her father was known.

Next, Lucrezia followed her *ottava rima* verse poem on Santa Colomba with a life of San Francesco in 1597. She continued writing on such sacred subjects over a span of twenty-two years, next penning an often-reprinted life of the Virgin Mary, and then the lives of Santa Giustina and Santa Caterina. These pieces reveal her deep religious convictions. But it was when Giuseppe Passi's tract on women's defects hit the scene in 1599 that Lucrezia's ire rankled, and at the request of her publisher, she cranked out *Nobility* in a year. Translator and editor Letizia Panizza explains that no woman had previously written such a "formal debating treatise" ("Introduction to the Translation" 2), and Lucrezia displayed her vast knowledge of classic works, plus her training in rhetoric. She was a warrior heroine, akin to the champions she described in her lives of the saints. Lucrezia also penned an allegory on Cupid and Psyche, in which the arrogant arrow boy is bested by wiser women. A female perspective applied to the standard literary genres in Lucrezia's hands became an inspired work.

At this point, Lucrezia also switched from writing verse to prose, for "Actions that have the qualities of greatness, magnificence, and divinity, and that surpass human attainments, demand a manner of speech that is grand and miraculous," she wrote (qtd. in Cox, *Prodigious* 153). This choice of Italian vernacular made her writing accessible to all literate women, not just university-educated men. Few authors before her had done this. Lucrezia became a role model for women yearning to study, to think, and to grow. They could find a well-lit spot, gather their skirts about them and sit with Lucrezia's tract, smiling at her audacious arguments. Lucrezia put books—and thus power—in women's hands.

Lucrezia employed the rhetoric of philosophy as she outlined her arguments. After Lucrezia began her book with a section on how fabulous women are, she proceeded into a second section that listed men's deficiencies; each section contains numerous examples from classical antiquity. Lucrezia moved on briefly to scripture and the story of God's creation. Even though God created all things, "Different degrees of perfection can be found," she claimed. "Why should not a woman be nobler than man and have a rarer and more excellent purpose than he, as indeed can be manifestly understood from her nature?" (Marinella, *Nobility* 53). According to her interpretation of the Bible, that men are superior is not a given. In fact, she cited Eve's creation from Adam's rib as proof, with a lovely bit of reasoning: Adam was created from earth, a base material, while Eve was created from Adam's rib. If he was already a being with a soul, then she was created from superior materials. Because men are inferior, Lucrezia posited, they feel the need to mask this by attacking women; she wrote in section V, "But in our times there are few women who apply themselves to study of the military arts, since men, fearing to lose their authority and become women's servants, often forbid them even to learn to read or write" (79). These ignoble qualities—the need to defame and oppress others—are proofs of men's inferiority, she reasoned.

But this was merely the beginning of Lucrezia's rebuttal.

Her brashest arguments followed next, as Lucrezia discussed the body and physical beauty. She wrote that beauty was caused by "a grace or splendor proceeding from the soul as well as from the body," (57) taking inspiration from Plato's *Symposium*. Beauty was not purely physical. Men were severely maligned here, though, when Lucrezia wrote, "I say that compared to women all men are ugly" (63). Some men may display some attractiveness, but theirs would never compare to women's. Furthermore, physical beauty was only a manifestation of inner beauty. "If [corporeal beauty] came solely from the body, each body would be beautiful, which it is not. Beauty and majesty of body are, therefore, born of superior reason," she argued (59). Since women, with their temperance and superior morality, had more inner beauty, and thus more physical beauty, it stands to reason that they had overall superiority. Besides, as a little icing here, Lucrezia pointed out that "Nobody honors another person unless they know that the person has some gift or quality that is superior to his own" (69). Since people saw men so often honoring women, then they must believe that women were worthy of that honor and were, in fact, superior to the men who honored them. Lucrezia probably smiled to herself more than once as she expressed her reasoned outrage in these arguments.

Lucrezia initially conceded that men's and women's souls were equal—an idea vastly contrary to Giuseppe Passi's book that claimed women were a different species—but then she went a step further to contend that women's souls were actually superior. How? Because women were morally superior to men, more temperate and even physically "cooler," allowing them to think more rationally. "It is a fact known to everyone that women are continent and temperate," she wrote, "for we never see or read about them getting drunk or spending all day in taverns, as dissolute men do, nor do they give themselves unrestrainedly to other pleasures" (94). Maybe this was because women were locked away in their homes, preparing the pasta, nursing the babies, and washing the linens, not allowed the same freedoms men enjoyed. But remember that Lucrezia was replying in a polemical fashion to Giuseppe Passi's arguments, addressing and disproving them head on. This tennis match style of arguments was the standard of the time, and while it might feel stiff to modern readers, Lucrezia showed that she was able to play a man's game with his rules. In fact, one of her greatest strengths was her vast list of citations from classical literature, showing her breadth of knowledge, especially considering that she was excluded from a university education (Ross 289; Panizza, "Introduction," *Nobility* 2).

While modern readers, who have had the benefit of the Enlightenment, civil and women's rights movements, and, well, four hundred years of progressive thought, Lucrezia's contentions may seem a bit one-sided and mean spirited. She even, disappointingly, judged women's worth by their beauty, an argument many women are still battling today. However, for her time, Lucrezia was a grand thinker, a trained philosopher, in many ways an anomaly and also a trailblazer. Yet to call her an exceptional woman may be a disservice. Writer Satya Datta explains that "exceptional women" in Lucrezia's era were those who displayed "male" qualities of fortitude and erudition and somehow conquered their "female biological nature" (173-74). For her era, how could Lucrezia be fairly praised? The only standards for the work she was producing were those designed to judge men.

Like Modesta Pozzo, her contemporary, Lucrezia Marinella believed that women only suffered an inferior status because men had the power to keep them there. She may have been angry, as her writings show, but she channeled that anger and proposed a cure for women's ills: education. Women should be educated, she contended, writing, "But man does not permit woman to apply herself to such studies, fearing, with reason, that she will surpass him in them" (Marinella, *Nobility* 140). As Datta also points out, "A little over a century later, Montesquieu and Rousseau repeated almost word for word the conclusions Marinella drew with respect for education" (166). She was well ahead of her times. "But if women, as I hope, wake themselves from the long sleep that oppresses them," she wrote, "how meek and humble will those proud and ungrateful men become" (Marinella, *Nobility* 131-32). As a start, she argued for a level playing field, then she expected women to show their true abilities and strengths, not as exceptions to any rule, but as any other scholar would shine once granted the opportunity. Though Lucrezia was indeed exceptional in many respects, as Professor Sarah Ross shows there were actually a large number of women writing at this time; Venice being a center for publishing and the 1500s being a prime time for the *querelle des femmes* or "the woman question," it afforded many women the opportunity to publish (6). Lucrezia, however, was one of the most successful and prolific of her sisterhood, with over ten publications and great renown among her contemporaries.

Although *Nobility* is now Lucrezia's best-known work, perhaps her most original is a heroic epic titled *L'Enrico overo Bisantio acquistato* (*Enrico, or Byzantium Conquered*). In this saga about Venice battling the Turks, Doge Enrico Dandolo leads the Venetian army into the fray in the main plot line, and in the secondary story, friendship between the sexes becomes the ideal. Using Homer's epics and especially Torquato Tasso's *Gerusalemme liberata* as her models, Lucrezia created a fictional fantasy world unlike anything other contemporary women or men had written (Cox, "Fiction" 61). And though she was writing in the epic genre, she veered from its standard format by having the woman walk away after two male characters die as they battle for her. The range of female characters reveals that "In Marinella's epic, women do not need romantic passion, sexual liaisons, or even marriage, to make them happy," Panizza writes; "they are perfectly capable of developing morally and intellectually as men's equals and therefore of cultivating abiding friendship with men without erotic attachments if they so wish" ("Introduction" 14). Sometimes Lucrezia included small, humanizing details that differed from men's epic storytelling, such as when the Greek king "even cries tears of pain for the loss of his men" (Canto 17.80, 288). Moreover, the many sequences depicting battlefield skirmishes, strategy meetings, duels, and hand-to-hand combat showed that Lucrezia was well-versed in the arts of war, and she didn't shy away from including gruesome details, like when a "knight's spear passed through his lips and into his brain" (Canto 8.105, 189). Lucrezia may never have proven her skills on a battlefield herself, but she certainly did her homework in order to generate these vivid scenes.

Lucrezia also included a number of female warriors deep in the action. Meandra is hailed for leading her soldiers into battle and for inspiring them to greatness on the field, for "with her words she strengthened, reinforced, and reassured their disheartened and hesitant spirits" (Canto 12.42, 246). Then there is Claudia, a leading member of the archery corps, fighting alongside men. "Each arrow she threw let loose its anger in the Thessalians' chests," wrote Lucrezia. "Soon the best and most courageous were left lying and slow to go to their weapons because of her" (Canto 19.56, 46-47). These two women eventually battle to the death, proving their valor as would any knight, but without any witnesses, and "Both women liked [the location] for it was hidden" (Canto 24.38, 340). They behaved in contrast to male knights who fought for glory, honor, and praise. Besides these fighters, Lucrezia also developed women characters who embodied complex human emotions of loyalty, anger, courage, grief, and love, written not as cardboard cutouts but as fully-developed people who can elicit sympathy from readers. Moreover, Lucrezia occasionally used first person to directly address her characters, as when she said to the young maiden Idilia, "If only I could make you eternal at least with my song, O unvanquished one, to take you away from blind forgetfulness" (Canto 10.72, 225). With this she developed immediacy and a sense of intimacy in her readers for these characters, something not often seen in other epics from the day. As translator and editor Maria Galli Stampino contends, Lucrezia's "gift for creating women whose behavior goes beyond accepted roles in her time, . . . and her talent in showing her sympathy for these characters and in generating the same in her implied readers characterize *Enrico* throughout, making it an incisive pro-women (or proto-feminist) text" ("Singular" 65).

Surprisingly, Lucrezia's final publication, *Essortationi alle donne et a gli altri* (*Exhortations to Women and to Others*) seemed to contradict her earlier writings, calling for women to live a secluded life highlighted by weaving and running a household. The nine chapters in this early self-help book urged women to show modesty, speak carefully, behave prudently, and live in harmony with their husbands. Most strikingly, Lucrezia recanted her earlier writings in *Nobility* and told women to avoid a life of literature. "As I faithfully love you," she addressed her female readers, "I desire that you put aside your vain passion of literature and thereby escape the damage, distaste, and resentment that always accompanies it" (*Exhortations* 61). Writing at the age of seventy-four, though, Lucrezia seemed to be expressing her bitterness at the ill treatment she had received for being a woman of letters. "You, who believed you could amaze the world with your talent and your writings, are left disappointed, regretful, and almost scorned," she stated, as if addressing herself (57). She suggested that women should forsake writing not because it was not a worthy pursuit but because they would be treated so poorly by their families, men, and even other envious women. Perhaps Lucrezia was worn down from a lifetime of abuse for being a vocal learned woman, and she was trying to save others from a similar fate. By this time, also, liberal Humanism was losing favor in the rising tide of the Counter-Reformation, and society was once again expecting women to be modest and silent rather than educated (Benedetti 18). Ross argues that the examples in *Exhortations* are so extreme and anathema to Lucrezia's own life that she seemed to have been writing a satire modeled on Erasmus' *Praise of Folly* (Ross 297). It's difficult to know Lucrezia's motivation, but in any case the *Exhortations* outlined the stresses women writers endured.

Despite these negative warnings that resulted from attacks that Lucrezia had endured, she was simultaneously praised lavishly by her contemporaries such as Jacopo Sansovino and Lucio Scarano, who called her the "glory of our age" (qtd. in Ross 291). Fellow writer Cristoforo Bronzini lent credibility to his own work when he publicly shared a letter that Lucrezia had sent him. She was also included in biographies listing literary lights. After the great popularity of Lucrezia's *Nobility,* Giuseppe Passi was forced to recant his nasty arguments (which he did haltingly and begrudgingly, tasting sour grapes). Additionally, Lucrezia's vehemence inspired her contemporary Arcangela Tarabotti, who read her works.

Lucrezia may have railed against unjust men, but that didn't mean she hated all men. Comparatively late in life, she married a physician, Girolamo Vacca, and they had two children, Antonio and Paulina, whom Lucrezia mentioned in her will in affectionate terms. Her Humanist husband supported her literary career, a perfect example of what Lucrezia called "a loving partnership with interchangeable roles" (Marinella, *Nobility* 137). Lucrezia stayed home, appropriate for her social position, as she and her husband were not included in the State functions or formal balls that nobles attended. For eighteen years she published nothing, presumably at the time she was raising her children (Benedetti 14). They lived in a house in the Campiello dei Squellini (a name that refers to small bowls produced nearby). It's a cockeyed, almost triangular *campo* featuring grass and trees, a bit of green for Lucrezia to gaze upon from her windows when she paused in her writing. No records have yet surfaced to show that Lucrezia attended any literary salons like other learned women of her times. Hers was a more retired life physically, though clearly not intellectually. However, after their daughter's marriage Lucrezia lived apart from her husband, though it's not clear why.

On October 9, 1653, Lucrezia Marinella Vacca succumbed to something called "quartan fever," a type of malarial infection with fevers that recur every three days. Lucrezia lived a long life—eighty-two years as quoted on a now-missing plaque in the Church of San Pantalon in Venice, where she was apparently buried (many records were lost during renovations). Her tomb lies beneath the enormous vaulted ceiling, with soldiers, citizens, angels, and San Pantalon himself gazing down. Despite the many attacks she endured, Lucrezia had enjoyed a supportive relationship and had the opportunity to publish her thoughts to a world in need of hearing them. She also wrote in a wide variety of genres, from polemical treatises, to the praise of saints, to one of the earliest epic romances by a woman. "Indeed, it is the sheer range of her production, rather than her achievements in any single genre, that deserves recognition," points out her translator and editor Laura Benedetti (2).

Lucrezia was done hurling epithets. Her superior reasoning silenced her detractors and paved the way for Enlightenment thinkers and feminists who followed. Her vehemence turned to vindication once her words could find a place on a page and last forever.

# Sarra Copia Sulam

## Generous to a Fault

*P*apers littered the table around Sarra, books sat opened, and the blotter stood by her hand. Ink staining her fingers, Sarra finished penning her treatise about the soul's immortality. Sarra Copia Sulam (sometimes spelled Sara Copia Sullam) dedicated her *Manifesto* to her departed father, hoping it would "increase [his] joy at seeing perhaps the little renown that accrues to my name," she wrote. "For this reason I think that having brought a woman into the world will be no less dear to you, for the conservation of your name, than having brought a man into it, as you so fervently hoped would happen in this life" (qtd. in Harrán 314). In so many cultures, parents want sons to carry on the family business and name, to bring a sort of immortality to their fathers. Daughters often leave the family and take on another man's name, so while a father may love his daughter, he may not have the same pride in her accomplishments as he would for a son. Sarra wanted to make her father and her larger community proud of her.

A scholar had publicly attacked Sarra as a heretic for supposedly declaring that the soul is not immortal, and though she didn't actively seek to publish her essays or letters, she felt it necessary in this case to defend her reputation from those who could bring her great harm. In 1621, when her treatise was published, the Venetian State Inquisition still prosecuted people for heretical beliefs or for refusing to convert to Christianity, and Sarra, as a female Jewish scholar, had enough public recognition as to endanger her life. She couldn't be an anonymous Jewish scholar in Venice; the community was so small, contained, and scrutinized that anything she wrote would affect all other Jews in the city. The act of writing that she turned to for the joy of composition also must have caused her some apprehension, knowing what weight her words carried.

Sarra's father, Simon Coppia, a very successful maritime insurance broker, educated his three daughters: Sarra, Rachel (Diana), and Esther (Ster) (Harrán 18). Besides being well-versed in Italian and Jewish culture, Sarra also learned Latin and Greek, Spanish, Hebrew, and of course Italian and Venetian. She must have relished learning to put in the many hours it would have taken to master these languages. Sarra lived her whole life in Venice's Ghetto. Jews used to reside in all parts of Venice, but the Venetian State declared in 1516 that they must instead move to the Ghetto Nuovo (spelled as *Getto* or *Gheto* in ancient spellings), a term later adopted by other communities to refer to an enclosed Jewish neighborhood. This island reached by three bridges previously contained the city's iron foundries; *gettare*, in fact, means to cast iron. The foundries were moved out and the Jews moved in—the population peaked during Sarra's lifetime, with roughly 3,500 Jews in 1655. They all had to fit into these confines, so families renovated houses to have lower ceilings and thus more floors. In 1541 the Ghetto expanded to encompass the Gheto Vechio. (A curiosity here: the terms New, *Novo* or *Nuovo*, and Old, *Vechio* or *Vecchio*, refer to the original foundries, not the Jewish communities, so that the Gheto Novo is actually an older Jewish community than the Gheto Vechio.) The Jewish residents had arrived from numerous countries—Germany, Spain, and the eastern parts, Turkey or the Levant. These congregations built their own synagogues, so that at one time there were eight of them within this small area. Five still exist, though no records indicate which one Sarra would have attended. These synagogues were always built on the top floor of a building; people could not live above the place where they worshipped God. The synagogues also each had a women's balcony above the benches where men sat, and in most synagogues, a wooden grill blocked the women from view. Sarra would have attended synagogue each Shabbat and of course on all holy days, always devout in her faith.

Due to scant records, Sarra's birthdate is unclear, though biographer Don Harrán concludes that it was around 1600-1601 (16). In one of the Ghetto's synagogues, lit by hanging oil lamps and surrounded by members of their community, Sarra and Jacob Sulam were married when she was fourteen or fifteen. Sarra would have been veiled, hiding her blond tresses and vibrant, sparkling eyes, both remarked upon by those who knew her, and a delight for Jacob when he removed her veil later. As the exhibit in the Museo Ebraico in Venice's Ghetto points out, during the Qiddushin part of the traditional wedding ceremony, Jacob would have slipped a ring onto Sarra's finger, reciting, "Be sanctified (betrothed) to me with this ring, in accordance with the laws of Moses and Israel." For Jacob Sulam, these laws posed no hindrance to supporting his wife's future literary career.

Sarra was about eighteen or nineteen when she began taking part in a life of letters. To broaden her world, Sarra held a literary salon in their house, inviting scholars of Christian and Jewish faiths to expound on a heady cocktail of philosophy and the humanities. In a century more often marked by prejudice and segregation, Sarra's house offered a haven for those who would rise above such divisions. Scholars Mark R. Cohen and Theodore K. Rabb share evidence that Jews and Christians did mingle for sermons, literary evenings, and other gatherings within the Ghetto (13). The Palazzo Sulam in the Ghetto Vecchio is the last house before the bridge to the Ghetto Nuovo, alongside the Rio del Gheto canal. Four stories high, it has a balcony on the second floor and a large garden out back, where guests could have stepped out for fresh air on still nights. Though it is not confirmed in documents that this is where Sarra lived, it is most likely; Jacob Sulam was a wealthy merchant who could have afforded a fine *palazzo*, and there are few such abodes in the Ghetto, where the norm was to crowd families together within the limited space. Visitors would have passed a mezuzah at the door upon entering the house—a talisman containing a prayer from the Torah that indicated it was a Jewish home—then been surrounded by paintings, velvet wallpaper, upholstered chairs, carved tables, all lit by candles in glass chandeliers.

Many salon attendees belonged to the celebrated and highly-literate Accademia degli Incogniti (The Academy of the Unknowns), and Sarra availed herself of lessons from them in exchange for financial help. Also in attendance would have been Rabbi Leon Modena, a lauded preacher, author of books in both Italian and Hebrew, teacher at the school (which was subsequently named for him), and head of the music academy. He wrote poems honoring Sarra (and later wrote her epitaph), and in fact his wife was related to Sarra's uncle (Adelman & Ravid 212 note m). According to reports, at her salon Sarra often sang, accompanying herself on "some keyboard" (Harrán 397). Alexis Francois-Rio, her contemporary, said that with her singing and poetry she could "immediately express all the feelings that exalted or affected her soul" (qtd. in Harrán 84). Exaltation would have come, at least in part, from her religious faith, while her soul was undoubtedly affected by the ill-treatment she received from some jealous or self-serving colleagues. Sarra was also quite skilled at improvisational "dueling," where two combatants would extemporize poems on a theme in a kind of battle of verses. Chronicler Nahida Ruth Lazarus reports that "people were at a loss which to admire most—her musical talent, her sweet voice, her poetry, or her beauty" (141). Sarra was benevolent and kind, attending to a sick friend, finding someone a place to live, liberally compensating her laundress, helping friends financially, or writing to praise another's work. However, Sarra seems to have been trusting and kind to a fault.

Despite the widespread admiration, many of the men in Sarra's literary circle took advantage of her. Historian Howard Tzvi Adelman points out that "gradually many of these male admirers betrayed her and humiliated her in the way that men of letters often treat talented women" (Adelman). Though she was married, settled, and safe from accusations of promiscuity, many exploited her kindness or harassed her in potentially damaging ways. Perhaps naïve, definitely generous, Sarra was vulnerable to being taken advantage of.

First to abuse Sarra's goodness was Ansaldo Ceba, although their relationship appeared warm from the outside. A monk in Genoa in 1613, Ansaldo had published the play *L'Ester* (or *La Reina Esther*) about the Old Testament heroine Ester who gained a king's favor due to her beauty and reasoning and thus saved the Jewish people from massacre. While Sarra was bedridden, recovering from a miscarriage that must have left her despondent, she read Ansaldo's play (Adelman & Ravid 235 note j). Young Sarra was so taken with the work that she wrote to him with her praise. She admitted to keeping his book under her pillow where she could access it while lying in bed. Thus began a fervid correspondence that lasted four years between this admiring, perhaps guileless girl at the cusp of twenty, with a fifty-three-year-old celibate cleric. Ansaldo Ceba hadn't garnered enthusiastic praise for his play, so when this Jewish girl, so like the protagonist of his play, praised him, he fell in with her enthusiasm. "It is true that out of gratitude for the love this lady professed to bear me," he wrote to their mutual friend Marc'Antonio Doria, "I wanted, in some way, to perpetuate her memory in the present letters" (qtd. in Harrán 116). Ansaldo repeatedly declared himself to be Sarra's "devoted and indebted servant," (118) writing to her even when he was ill, knowing "only how to cough and spit" (260). They corresponded from May 19, 1618, to April 30, 1622, and Ansaldo died just six months later, in October.

The avowals of love and servitude, however, seem, at least in part, specious. All along during their epistolary relationship, Ansaldo Ceba intended to publish his letters. As Harrán points out, Ansaldo knew that correspondence between a Christian monk and a Jewish scholar was a rarity, even more so since she was a woman (40). Ansaldo wrote to Sarra in Letter 31, "Nor should you be surprised at my keeping count of our dialogues, for their novelty is so remarkable as to warrant their memorial through preservation" (220). In all, Ansaldo's volume included fifty-three of his letters and sundry verses, plus five of Sarra's own sonnets. None of her letters. Her voice was, for the most part, silenced, and her letters were lost; Ansaldo knew their value yet didn't keep them for posterity. Although he appears to have cared for Sarra, Ansaldo also seemed to have used this correspondence to further his own gains while not protecting Sarra's rights as an author.

Researchers have nevertheless managed to piece together many of Sarra's thoughts, opinions, and reactions based on Ansaldo's letters. Sarra was often annoyed with Ansaldo, for instance, for his repeated entreaties to convert her to Christianity. "I do not consider your being born a Jew to be a defect in your person," Ansaldo wrote in Letter 33. "But I do believe you have no excuse for not becoming a Christian, for then you would have light to visualize the faith of Christ" (224). Virtually every letter contains such an exhortation. Sarra generally remained firm and patient in response to Ansaldo's cajoling, though at one point she apparently prompted him to respond with this glib reply in Letter 24, "Should I come to Venice to become circumcised or should you come to Genoa to become baptized?" (207). Ansaldo must have been quite peeved to have made this suggestion.

Sarra apparently asked Ansaldo Ceba to desist in his requests, and they nearly broke off their correspondence over it. Yet Sarra knew that Ansaldo intended to publish, and she willingly provided him with continued letters (Harrán 257 n5). Was this perhaps a show of her giving nature to support a friend's literary endeavors? Or her way of showing her love? Or even a desire for literary immortality? In Letter 20 Ansaldo wrote, "How can my friendship serve you if it does not serve to make you immortal? You do not have any need of my verses for this reason, for they cannot do that much. But you are in great need of my faith" (qtd. in Harrán 194). He perhaps arrogantly believed that in one way or another he could bring Sarra immortality in either the literary world or in the afterlife—either by publishing her ideas or convincing her to convert. Sarra showed an almost superhuman patience and kindness to this ambitious and overbearing cleric, but some other glue secured their relationship.

Based on Ansaldo's publication, an ardent love grew between these two. In Ansaldo's "Dedication" he claimed he wanted to "make love to her soul" (116) in an attempt to convert her, and in Letter 1 he professed, "I love you, Signora Sarra, and revere you as much as I am honorably permitted by my law and yours" (118). Sarra wrote a sonnet in response, in the voice of the character Esther, claiming, "She holds the worlds intent on your verses / while feeling her chastest passions unfold" (120). Of course, this language of love is not so unusual in the long-lasting era of idealized Petrarchan love. However, later, Ansaldo played on Sarra's last name Coppia, meaning couple, where he wrote in Letter 17, "At the outset I wished myself luck from your surname, hoping we could make a 'couple' as a Christian and a non-Christian." He then revealed that his pun was unsuccessful because she "no sooner removed a consonant from it, reducing it from Coppia to Copia" (187). Sarra may have loved him and wished to help advance his literary career, but she clearly drew the line. She never wavered in her religious faith or her marital faithfulness, despite Ansaldo's and others' haranguing.

Nearing the end of Sarra's correspondence with Ansaldo, she became embroiled in a literary altercation with another scholar clergyman. Ansaldo was not Sarra's only correspondent; she wrote to a number of people, including Baldassare Bonifaccio, a bishop posted to Venice to teach law, and an attendee at Sarra's salon. An anonymous engraving of him from 1647 shows a serious man with two furrows between long brows below a high forehead. His small mouth is dwarfed by mustaches that turn up at their corners, framing rounded cheekbones. He, like Ansaldo, tirelessly worked to convert Sarra to Christianity. Besides entertainments at her salon such as singing, guests often recited poetry, as Baldassare did when he shared poems he had composed at Sarra's request in praise of Ansaldo's portrait.

At the end of 1619, Baldassare Bonifaccio wrote to Sarra, sending wishes for a good start to the coming new year, and then pondering the passage of years and mortality. Sarra replied on January 10, 1620, returning warm wishes and praise for his sonnets, "for I will not fail to revere your merits on every occasion," she added (274). In response to Baldassare's philosophizing, Sarra then launched into musings of her own, delving into Aristotelian theories regarding matter, generation, and immortality. For instance, she stated, "Therefore I speak of matter and form as two component parts that we see in natural things, and [if] the first of the two lasts eternally and the second vanishes, it will be reasonable to attribute corruptibility to the second" (276). These sorts of cerebral topics were regular fare at Sarra's salon, and she had often proven that she could engage in philosophical discourses with the male scholars; in fact, the question of the soul's immortality was also a topic tackled by other writers, notably Rabbi Leon Modena, which shows that Sarra stayed current with the major topics of her day. Sarra went on to post questions for Baldassare: "But for what reason did the Creator not make man immortal by nature if He intended to have him preserved, why constitute him miraculously into a being in which he did not have to last?" (276-7). The rest of her letter continued in this vein, ending with an apology for her "boldness in having advanced these weak uncertainties from a desire to hear their elucidation, in due time, by Your Lordship" (278). The letters so far appeared to be a playful, scholarly exercise, an opportunity to parry ideas for enjoyment rather than as combat.

Baldassare Bonifaccio's response, unfortunately, arrived with all seriousness. He accused Sarra of denying the immortality of the soul, a doctrine considered sacrosanct by both Jews and Christians, branding her a heretic for such a thought. He published his "Discourse on the Immortality of the Soul" in 1621, publicly tearing apart Sarra's ideas and publishing her letter as well. This move could damage not only Sarra's reputation and standing, but also that of her husband and, by extension, the Venetian Jewish community. As mentioned earlier, heretical thought could lead to imprisonment, torture, even capital punishment. Jews in Venice were tolerated by Christians because they provided much-needed services to the Christian community, such as money lending, which was forbidden in the Bible's New Testament. Thus, Jews often worked as bankers, pawnbrokers, and insurers, like Sarra's father. They were restricted from producing goods, but instead they sold them, being quite adept merchants, or they took in used linens and clothing for resale in a *strazzaria,* a type of pawnshop. Many Jews also worked as doctors and were, in fact, so desired for their skills that they were the only Jews allowed out at night from the gated and locked community. Any Jew venturing beyond the Ghetto was required to don a yellow hat for the men, or a yellow shawl or scarf for the women. Sarra may have worn the rich laces and brocades of other noblewomen, but upon leaving her neighborhood, she would be marked by that yellow scarf for others to know she was not from a Christian patrician family. Hearing of Baldassare's public declamation, Sarra must have quaked with fear for her social standing, reputation, and even safety. What had started naïvely as amicable greetings and musings became, to Sarra's astonishment, attacks on her beliefs and thus, her welfare and that of her whole family.

To make matters worse, when Baldassare's publication reached the public, Sarra was gravely ill. She had mentioned sicknesses in a number of her letters to Ceba, including a miscarriage in 1618. But Sarra rallied quickly this time, gathering her strength, knowing that she must respond before gossip could take hold. In the second line of her *Manifesto*, which she had hastily composed in two days, she resolutely stated her belief in the soul's immortality. "This truth is as certain, infallible, and indisputable for me as it is, I believe, for every Jew and Christian," she wrote (317), quelling any doubts about where she stood. As she had stated in the closing of her original letter to Baldassare, she explained that she wrote, "Solely out of curiosity to hear from [him] some curious and uncommon teaching to provide a solution to my arguments" (318). Sarra listed Baldassare's flawed reasoning but did not resort to countering each of his arguments, "lest I consume my time uselessly," she said (328). His logic was faulty, she contended, adding, "You, by foolishly pretending to prophesy by yourself without any other inspiration than excessive arrogance, have shown, as effects, your totally crass ignorance rather than any marvelous divine virtue" (320). A touch of her impatience and even anger reared up here, in contrast to her usual amicable nature. Sarra composed this treatise so quickly that it indicates she had all these arguments at the tip of her mind, the logic already framed and ready to employ.

Sarra was incensed at this unfair attack and wondered why Bonifaccio would wish to harm her in this way. She chided, "What point is there in challenging a woman, indeed a woman who, though devoted to studies, does not practice such sciences for her profession?" (327). Baldassare must have been trying to make himself look good by taking on someone with supposedly less learning, and she also admonished him for his "vain little ambition" to prove his learning by publishing often (326). "O courageous challenger of women," (328) she sarcastically called him as if Baldassare was a playground bully taking on a smaller child to prove his worth. Baldassare actually replied in a rebuttal and published all three documents in one volume. He also declared that the *Manifesto* couldn't have been written by Sarra, a woman, but must have been penned by another, probably by the scholar Rabbi Leon Modena, who was in reality a teacher and great friend to Sarra. Baldassare's remarks were mostly ignored. Happily, Sarra's reputation survived the attack, and she remained steadfast in her Jewish faith. She had proven her kind spirit and keen mind to her community who supported her throughout this fiasco. After also recovering from an illness, Sarra must have been relieved that this storm had passed.

Unfortunately, still more calumny was in store for Sarra. Her desire for greater learning, coupled with her generous nature, led her to employ Numidio Paluzzi as her teacher and perhaps editor. Originally from Rome, Numidio attended Sarra's literary salon, arriving with recommendations from others for his scholarship. The situation was described thus: "After the lady was enticed by that patina of knowledge that he seemed to show in his lively chatter, she was pleased to make him her teacher" (qtd. in Harrán, *Notices* 356). Sarra found him a place to live nearby the Ghetto with her laundrywoman, Paola Furlana. Sarra also provided Numidio with new clothing, pocket money besides a salary for his teaching position, and even treatments, including steam baths, for the syphilis from which he suffered.

Then Numidio Paluzzi turned on Sarra with stealth and trickery. He enlisted the help of Furlana, his landlady, her three sons, another servant of Sarra's named Mora, and Alessandro Berardelli. Together, they devised numerous ways to fleece Sarra of money and goods. One such elaborate trick involved creating a fictional French Count who admired Sarra and requested her portrait. Alessandro Berardelli painted it, and the group sent it to the Count along with a basket of fine marzipan fruits, all at Sarra's expense of over 100 ducats, which they pocketed. They also fabricated an "aerial spirit," in communion with Mora, which absconded with jewelry and cash from Sarra's house. This continued from 1622 to 1624, "for the total ruin of the luckless gentlewoman" (374). Sarra's friend Giacomo Rosa tipped her off to the treachery, and Sarra brought charges against Numidio and Alessandro to the Signori di Notte al Criminal on July 8, 1625, (though these records have not been found). Sarra admitted in a sonnet, "I later perceived the ways / of a boorish heart" (461). Sadly, Numidio and Alessandro's attacks did not end there. They went on to write a satire titled *Sariede* or the *Satires of Sarra,* lambasting Sarra and accusing her of both stealing and plagiarizing Numidio's writings. In a later sonnet, Sarra wrote, "Afterward, the base, repugnant slander of an odious tongue / Added scorn to the infamous theft" (469). Sarra sounds angry at this point, probably feeling betrayed for her many kindnesses.

However, Sarra took the high road. She did not respond publicly to these slanders. As she wrote in a later sonnet, she did not want "to awaken illustrious fame from a despicable contest" or be drawn into an insult match in a public sphere, only "for the sake of winning an ignoble trophy, dark and common" (463). Five of her sonnets, though, did appear in a work titled *Notices from Parnassus*, a fictional story where Numidio and Alessandro are tried before a court at the mythical Greek Mount Parnassus. The judges include some of the great Italian women writers: Vittoria Colonna, Veronica Gambara, and Isabella Andreini, as well as the Greeks Sappho and Corinna, plus commentary from Pietro Aretino and Baldassare Castiglione. The whole is supposedly collected by Giulia Solinga, but the existence of this person has not been proven, and it's possible that she was fabricated to protect the identities of Sarra's friends and herself. The *Notices* recount the tricks and betrayals by Numidio Paluzzi and his crew, and though by the time this writing appeared Numidio was dead, the author stated that "the sight of piety abused, benefits wasted, a good name sullied, innocence trampled, and this wrong remaining stamped in print through the actions of that contemptible servant was the motivating cause for uncovering the truth to all" (365-6). Legal justice was not full justice in the courts of one's community, so Sarra's friends came forth to defend her. She must have felt vindicated, proud of her friends, and, knowing her nature, humbled by the honor they bestowed in coming to her defense.

While the *Notices from Parnassus* are ostensibly a fictional account following a standard genre of the Parnassan trial, they also gave their authors the opportunity to condemn Numidio, Alessandro, and their cohorts. In Pietro Aretino's voice, they describe Alessandro Berardelli as "the panhandling scullery boy, that filthy ruffian, that contemptuous lawbreaker, . . . that herald of infamy, that witness to lies, that shelter of perfidy, that portrait of impudence!" (392). Numidio Paluzzi fares no better with "that soot-covered mug of his, that voice of a hermaphrodite, that leer of an evildoer" (372). In this story, Numidio turns on Alessandro to blame all evil deeds on him, thereby showing more of his treacherous character. The judges of Parnassus announce their guilty verdict for Numidio and assign a sentence that includes an hour in the public pillory, branding on his forehead, and bells on his knees to warn others that a hooligan is approaching. Then a statue of Alessandro is burned in effigy (450). According to the *Notices*, Sarra had inexpertly employed several lawyers against these criminals, resulting in a sentence less severe than the punishment meted out in the *Notices* by her sympathetic friends.

A number of sonnets are also included in the *Notices*, many by Sarra's friends and a few by Sarra herself. In one of Sarra's sonnets, she lamented, "I do not know what infernal Megaera [Fury] / Would so encumber his soul as to cause me not honor, / But harm, offense, and death" (461). She had merely sought greater learning but reaped abuse instead. In another sonnet she declared that now this "infamous monster" and "its unworthy boastings are known to everyone there / And no veil conceals them" (466). Next she gratefully acknowledged that Numidio had been publicly denounced, using this opportunity to show gratitude to her defenders in another sonnet stating that "Bothersome cares have cropped my beautiful desire's wings / On which song rises and life is renewed" (469). Her words displayed her gracefulness and a feeling of lightened cares. The *Notices* ended with a number of sonnets in Italian and Venetian that each share different responses to Numidio's and Alessandro's crimes. Even the Rabbi Leon Modena may have submitted some poems, saying that Alessandro "with a placid brow and sneering smile, / Stole from [Jacob Sulam] even his underwear" (494). Hopefully Sarra and her husband Jacob were able to laugh with their friends at the close of this noxious chapter of their lives.

So few of Sarra's writings survive: five sonnets in the *Notices from Parnassus*, some sonnets preserved by Ansaldo, her *Manifesto* refuting Baldassare, a couple letters. Writer Nahida Ruth Lazarus laments the loss of Sarra's letters, which Ansaldo Ceba did not preserve or publish. "What a source of encouragement and elevation could these letters have become for the faint-hearted and the wavering in their belief!" (151) she points out, recognizing that Sarra's steadfast faith against Ansaldo's conversion attempts could have provided a strong role model for others. Don Harrán goes further to point out that "One can only speculate on the kinds of themes Copia would have emphasized in her poetry if she had not been pressured on all fronts to explain, justify, and 'fight' for her rights" (71-2). Would she have shared more of her learning and insights? Would the generous, compassionate, and sensitive Sarra have felt safe enough to come forward more than the guarded Sarra needing to defend herself?

The Copia family device on its coat of arms shows a creature that might be a scorpion or an ant; Sarra proved in her *Manifesto* that she, like a small but mighty creature, could do battle with the best of them, "who had both captivated and bested Christian clerics in public" (Adelman). Her feisty words and reasoned responses showed her mettle, yet what is apparently lost is the softer woman beneath: the loving wife, the mother who lost all her own children, the friend who cared for the ill, the woman with unbreakable faith. One sonnet that gives a peek into this Sarra shares her thoughts on the beauteous immortality of the soul, so much greater a gift than corporeal beauty:

> Well do I know that the beauty that pleases the world
> Is an ephemeral flower and abounds in pride;
> But the frail shell that surrounds me,
> However it is, hardly interests my soul. (qtd. in Harrán 330)

Sarra's "frail shell," so long prone to illness, gave out on February 15, 1641, her mother Ricca outliving her by four years. Like others of her faith, as reported in Leon Modena's writings, Sarra would have made a general confession on her deathbed, gathering her loved ones and her rabbi around her (Davis 57 n20).

Sarra is buried in the Jewish cemetery on the Lido of Venice, her tombstone green with moss and small stones placed atop it in remembrance. This cemetery was founded by the Ashkenazi Jews of Venice in 1386 when they were granted land on this deserted isle for this purpose, and generations of Jews are buried there. Leon Modena provided Sarra's epitaph, complimenting her by writing, "Wise was she among women, / A jewel for the miserable, / and of every poor soul / A friend and companion" (qtd. in Harrán *Notices* 521). Those who came after Sarra were kinder to her than some who lived alongside her; numerous scholars, both Christian and Jewish, list her among other illustrious writers, and Rabbi Moritz Abraham Levy called her a "heroine of faith" for her unwavering beliefs (Harrán 79). She is even mentioned in Giorgio Bassani's acclaimed novel *The Garden of the Finzi-Continis* and is included in the Museo Ebraico exhibits in Venice's Ghetto.

After all that controversy about the immortality of the soul, Sarra has lasted, in her own words, as "a living memory of oneself" (qtd. in Harrán 331).

The Palazzo Sulam

# *Arcangela Tarabotti*

## Battling Tyranny

"*A* girl lies prostrate, her lips touching the stone floor. A black cloth is thrown over her, and lighted candles are placed at her feet and at her head," wrote Arcangela Tarabotti in *L'Inferno Monacale.* "All the signs suggest that she is dead. She is a witness at her own funeral" (qtd. in Laven 23). Actually, the girl was professing her vows to become a nun, the bride of Christ.

"You should know that if I did go through the ceremonies of taking the veil," wrote Arcangela, "I did not respond to the voices of the Holy Spirit with the fervor I ought" (*Paradiso* 157). Born February 24, 1604, in the Castello district of Venice to her parents Stefano Tarabotti and Maria Cadena, she was given the name Elena Cassandra. Arcangela was early destined by her father for the nunnery because she was "ugly and maimed in body," as she put it (*Paradiso* 156). She officially entered the convent at age eleven as a boarder seeking an education. Arcangela later angrily denounced fathers who "do not offer as brides of Jesus their most beautiful and virtuous daughters, but the most repulsive and deformed: lame, hunchbacked, crippled, or simple minded" (*Paternal Tyranny* 66). Such fathers seem to blame their daughters for "whatever natural defect they are born with and condemned [them] to lifelong prison" (66). At age sixteen, Arcangela professed her initial religious vows, taking the name Arcangela, and the Benedictine convent of Sant'Anna at the far-eastern edge of the Castello district became her permanent home. Early on she rebelled, refusing to wear the habit or cut her hair as nuns must, so it's a bit perplexing that Arcangela took her final vows at age nineteen in 1623, thus making an indissoluble pact to be Christ's bride for eternity.

To understand her choice, one must understand the Venetian marriage system for the upper classes. Families sought to consolidate their wealth with usually only one of their sons. (Surplus sons often lived bachelor lives or sought political or military careers—and mistresses.) Daughters generally had two choices: "*maritar o monacar*" as the saying went. Marry or become a nun. Exceedingly rare were those Humanist fathers who educated their daughters, and even those few educated daughters were generally expected to marry. But dowries—the money paid to the bridegroom as part of the marriage contract—kept rising, threatening to bankrupt families. By the 1600s, dowries reached into the tens of thousands of ducats, while in comparison a journeyman mason earned fifty ducats a year, according to historian Mary Laven (26-27). It was not unknown for a patrician family to sell off a palace or estate to fund a girl's dowry, so families could only afford for one daughter to marry. In Arcangela's family, only two of the six daughters married. Convent placement was not free, however; fathers still had to pay a small "dowry" to partially pay for a daughter's meals and clothing.

How was any young girl to resist such pressure, such "paternal tyranny?"

Having too many single women in society was unthinkable; it was believed they might dishonor the family or cause social chaos, and the teachings of San Girolamo even favored claustration—confinement in a convent—over marriage. In fact, Giovanni Francesco Loredan, a well-known founder of the Accademia degli Incogniti and correspondent with Arcangela Tarabotti, wrote to his own niece to pressure her into taking vows. By accepting this fate, he told her, "you will wish to console your parents, to bring stability to your lineage, to find security yourself, to give an example to the young, and to make known to your descendants that prudent minds do not allow themselves to be tyrannized by human considerations but by reason" (qtd. in Laven 44). He did not mention a religious calling.

How was any young girl to resist such pressure, such "paternal tyranny?"

So Arcangela took her vows and moved permanently into her convent cell. Sant'Anna's large church, composed of red brick, was rather austere inside, without many gracious marbles or elaborate reliquaries. After the bubonic plague of 1630 to 1631, a separate altar was added, with a large depiction of Christ, the Virgin, San Rocco, Santa Anna, San Sebastiano, and San Lorenzo to give thanks for their intercession to bring the plague to an end. Was it terrifying or soothing to be enclosed in the convent while the dreadful disease killed a third of Venice's citizens?

During Arcangela's thirty-seven years residing at Sant'Anna before her death on February 28, 1652, she spent much of her time writing and revising thoughts about women's forced enclosure, publishing six surviving works. She first wrote *Tirannia paterna* (*Paternal Tyranny*, later published as *Innocence Betrayed*) and *L'Inferno Monacale*, but these works weren't published until after her death. This was for the best, for they seethed with rage and vitriolic contempt for those men in society who would "[bury girls] alive in the cloister for the rest of their lives, bound by indissoluble knots" (*Paternal Tyranny* 60). Not a kind word had Arcangela for such men, whom she termed "liars," (47) "evil sorcerers," (50) "enemies of truth," (51) "blasphemers," (52) "butchers," (57) "tyrants from Hell," (59) "monsters of nature," (59) "Christians in name, and devils in deed," (59) "madmen," (71) "wicked dissimulators," (73) and even "Satan's pimps" (77). Forcing women to make eternal vows before God, vows they didn't truly believe in and could not sincerely keep, condemned their souls for eternal damnation, Arcangela reasoned.

Arcangela's many publications are all the more impressive considering she called herself an autodidact who had been poorly educated in the convent, "a young woman reading books for my own edification," she wrote (152). From age eleven, Arcangela had sat at a bare wooden table, an older nun at her elbow pointing a finger along a line of text. A leather-bound Bible, some lives of saints, and a grammar book or two made up their reading choices. Convent education was so inferior, Arcangela railed, because "You give them as a governess another woman, also unlettered, who can barely instruct [nuns] in the rudiments of reading, to say nothing of anything to do with philosophy, law, and theology. In short, they learn nothing but the ABC, and even then this is poorly taught" (99). She herself had experienced this form of education and could serve as witness, she said, and men had no right to accuse women of being ignorant. Arcangela neatly summed up the problem: "You forbid women to learn so they are incapable of defending themselves against your schemes and then proclaim how stupid they are and how you triumphed over them" (108). Men knew that they could protect their power by keeping women ignorant, and Arcangela seethed at this injustice. She broke out in sarcasm, sneering "that illiteracy is [women's] proper condition" (101). But before her male readers had enough time to smirk, she jabbed them with this: "But you do well . . . to keep us away from intellectual pursuits, since you realize that once knowledge is added to a woman's natural lively disposition, she would usurp the honors and earnings you amass by unlawful means" (101). Men, Arcangela contended, had unjustly kept for themselves the law professions, though women would rule more fairly if they were allowed.

Arcangela Tarabotti had a lot of time on her hands to read scriptures and classic texts, to educate herself, and to perfect her arguments. Education and scriptural reading are built into a Benedictine's day, and she read and wrote extensively, both ecclesiastical and classical literature. Arcangela also kept up a correspondence with members of the literary academy such as Giovanni Loredan and her brother-in-law Giacomo Pighetti. Even though she was enclosed in the cloister, they brought books to her at the grillwork in the convent visiting room and facilitated her participation in the Accademia degli Incogniti (The Unknowns). Like many Humanists of her day, Arcangela published her letters, titled *Lettere Familiari e di Complimento*, which showcased the great thinkers who helped her hone her reasoning and who critiqued her writing. In fact, this volume was dedicated to Giovanni Loredan, immediately granting the publication—and its author—greater clout.

A year later, in 1651, Arcangela published again in conjunction with the writer Francesco Buoninsegni; he had written the polemical treatise *Satira,* attempting to prove women's inferiority, and Arcangela responded with her own *Antisatira* to refute his arguments. Though Arcangela's work railed against Francesco Buoninsegni's writing, a crafty publisher knew that readers would feast on the two works together. That same year another of her polemical works hit the bookstalls: *Che le donne siamo delle specie degli uomini* (*Women Do Belong to the Species Mankind*). It, too, refuted an earlier misogynist work attributed to "Orazio Plata Romano" titled *Women Do Not Belong to the Species Mankind,* according to editor and translator Letizia Panizza ("Introduction" 11). Arcangela's response uncovered Romano's misreadings of scriptures and showcased her superior reasoning skills; she quoted extensively from the Bible, as well as displaying her knowledge of theology, philosophy, rhetoric, and literature, all principally self-taught. Disappointingly, though Arcangela's tone in this treatise was light and her reasoning sound, many of her admirers turned against her, writing denunciations against her ideas or claiming that, because the style of this piece differed from others, Arcangela must not have authored it. She was angry to begin with, and these criticisms must have made her seethe.

Besides her literary life, Arcangela Tarabotti's cloistered days were otherwise filled with prayer, chores, or lace-making and little else. The convent she termed a prison, inferno, and even Hell. Leaving the convent grounds was not an option; in actuality, convent restrictions became so strict that windows and doors facing the outside world were often bricked up, and some nuns weren't even permitted to enter gardens on the grounds (Laven 103). Jacopo de' Barbari's 1500 map shows a low wall running around the convent grounds, with a few small trees and shrubs as well as vegetables in rows, a small bit of green and ground in contrast to stone cells. The convent of Sant'Anna sat alongside the Canal de San Piero with views across the green water to the island of San Piero (or Pietro). Being so near the Arsenale, numerous boats would have skimmed these waters often, with standing rowers or with large triangular sails, though the nuns would never have enjoyed such pretty views. Any respite from dreary, enclosed life was cut off. It's hard to imagine the sense of claustrophobia added to this existence as the Black Death lurked around the convent's perimeters. Today, it's easy to sense the isolation as the buildings still there have bricked up windows.

Arcangela raged against the deadening sameness of this life. In *L'Inferno Monacale,* she wrote, "Oh how wearing it is to find oneself always sitting at the same table with the same food! How tormenting to return every night to the same bed, always to breathe the same air, always to conduct the same conversations and to see the same faces!" (qtd. in Laven 102). The cloister's inner courtyard is only fifteen paces across, twenty in length, too small to offer any sense of enlivening space. With roughly fifty to one hundred nuns living in a convent, and women joining or dying infrequently, Arcangela faced little opportunity for social diversity. As Benedictines, the nuns would have attended group prayers five times each day, starting with vigils upon waking and ending with compline before bedtime, usually observing silence from dinner until breakfast. Benedictines generally spend a third of their time in prayer or reflective contemplation, with little communal interaction outside of mass, meals, and daily work. Instead of complaining, though, Arcangela reasoned that God detested such sameness. He had created a wonderful variety on the earth, and "It is precisely variety and dissimilarity that arouse amazement in our intellect and make divine omnipotence abundantly clear to our eyes" (*Paternal Tyranny* 67). Convent similarity went against God's own design.

Arcangela Tarabotti turned to Scriptures for many of her arguments against forced claustration. She quoted the Book of Genesis to point out that God created woman as "a help like unto himself" to prove the equality of the sexes (50). Giovanni Loredan published his own work in 1640 titled *The Life of Adam* contending that Eve was responsible for humans' fall from grace. But Arcangela countered him, saying that if Adam "had the grace of free will and was superior to Eve, she would not have sinned at all, despite the serpent's promptings and insinuations, for the simple reason that she could not have made the choices without her husband's consent" (51). With this she turned men's arguments back on themselves. Arcangela's position, grounded in scripture, returned time and again to the Humanist precept that God "has granted free will to His creatures, whether male or female, and bestowed on both sexes intellect, memory, and will!" (44). How can men forcefully restrict women's choices and movements? What right do they have to limit women's liberty? she asked.

In fact, free will is one of Arcangela's most frequently recurring themes. A cornerstone to Humanist thought, free will or choice was believed to be "bestowed on men and women alike by the Divine Majesty" (43). The Book of Genesis, itself, sets up men and women to rule equally and freely (44-45). Men show excessive pride and contempt for God's design when they confine women against their will. Arcangela seemed especially incensed that she must spend her day imprisoned by men's infernal logic that took her beloved God's words, which she intoned multiple times a day in chorus with her sister nuns, and used them to deny her freedom. No wonder her rage never cooled.

Arcangela may have been physically restricted to the cloister all her life, but that didn't silence her voice. Writer Letizia Panizza points out that Arcangela Tarabotti's ideas about "liberty, equality and universal education" preceded by 200 years similar writings by Mary Wollstonecraft or John Stuart Mill on women's rights, to say nothing of comparisons to Rousseau on freedom and human rights ("Introduction" 1). Arcangela was a feminist centuries before this concept or term existed. "Tarabotti not only overcame the reticence, so strong in early modern women writers, about revealing deep personal emotions, longings, and opinions, especially when these meant condemning men," writes Panizza, but also "she resisted to a remarkable extent, and in one case overcame, attempts by them to silence her" (1). No other Venetian woman before modern times wrote with so strong a voice. "Once you have lost liberty," Arcangela said, "there remains nothing else to lose" (*Paternal Tyranny* 38). So she spoke. She at times must have felt so angry or so hopeless that she was prepared to say all and risk all.

Still, Arcangela felt she had some explaining to do. Though her early works, *Paternal Tyranny* and *L'Inferno Monacale,* had circulated only in manuscript form, enough people read them to get her into some trouble. Despite being sequestered in a bare cell, Arcangela was accused of heresy along with the worst accusation to be hurled at a woman: impurity. But "without chastity no woman is beautiful and that physical beauty cannot and should not claim a greater adornment than purity of heart," she wrote in *Il Paradiso Monacale* published in 1643 during her lifetime (155-56). Despite her disavowal of forced claustration in this book, Arcangela still believed in Church teachings and adhered to many standard opinions of the day, including attitudes regarding beauty and purity.

Brother Francesco Ricci, a Church consulter brought to Venice to review *Paternal Tyranny*, said Arcangela's work contained "statements that are plainly erroneous in matters of faith, outrageous, misleading, offensive to the ears of the pious, and scandalous" (qtd. in Panizza, "Introduction" 28-9). If her work were widely read, he said, standing tall in ecclesiastical robes and gripping a Bible, it might lead others to question the religious life or the social structure. At a time when Protestant ideas were on the rise, the Catholic Church couldn't allow one of its professed nuns to write such antithetical works. Besides, men in power couldn't countenance a woman who fought so vocally against her oppression. "On my word of honor," she wrote in *Il Paradiso Monacale*, "I testify that I have allowed my words to overflow in defense of my own sex only for the sake of refuting the wicked and false slander written by men over so many centuries to the detriment of women" (157). She couldn't countenance the idea of future women being confined against their will, so she put pen to paper to protect her sisters.

Moreover, Arcangela was unfairly accused of being a libertine, of promoting a life where anyone should be allowed to behave in any fashion. Venetian libertines of the day indulged in drink and gluttony, gambling in the city's *ridotti*, or clandestine affairs in the city's many *casini* or private apartments. Arcangela expressly refuted such ideas, writing, "You should not believe that what I may have exaggerated so far springs from an unwise desire for liberty of conscience or an inclination to live subject to no authority" (*Paternal Tyranny* 128). Far from desiring a life with no guidance, Arcangela even seemed to yearn for a true calling. At one point in her writings, she beseeched the Virgin Mary to look upon her with compassion, to "not regard the poverty of my gifts, but rather gaze upon the ardor of my devotion," and bless her with her "heavenly favors" (126). The religious life for those with a true calling is a great gift, but one she had not received, and for that she suffered. "I bear a holy envy of the religious life of true nuns," she confessed (64). Moreover, Arcangela quoted scriptural evidence, such as Psalms 53:8, to show that God "is indeed well pleased by the voluntary vow of virginity more than all other sacrifices offered up to Him" (41). What one gives freely has more value than a false vow or forced religious profession. Arcangela often felt that she was damned—living a lie to God—all under duress and with no recourse to salvation.

Yet she must still live in her world. Though she published, she did so sometimes using a pseudonym: under the name Galerana Barcitotti she published *Women Do Belong to the Species Mankind*, and later she composed *Innocence Betrayed* using the similar name Galerana Baratotti (Panizza, "Introduction" 2 n1). Some critics accused her of recanting her earlier beliefs by publishing *Il Paradiso Monacale*, whereas Arcangela explained that she was simply professing her admiration of the religious life for women who felt a true calling. "Numberless women, true living flames of the church . . . have chosen for themselves through their own free will and have taught others the true path to eternal salvation . . . ," she noted, "but women forced are little if at all pleasing to Him, and deserve to be banished from His mercy" (qtd. in Panizza, "Introduction" 9). By acknowledging this dichotomy, Arcangela virtually condemned herself since she had already admitted that she lacked a true calling. She didn't write to excuse her own actions but to create a better future for other women.

Arcangela Tarabotti was a contradiction: though she enjoyed less freedom than other women writers, she had the strongest voice of them all. Before feminism existed, she blew the bugle to start the march. Centuries passed before others came to take up the baton, but women can thank this cloistered, angry, self-educated woman for the gift of her voice.

# Cecilia Ferrazzi

## Passion and Pain

*I* turned in anguish from the pain to implore that crucified Christ to clothe me in the love of His Passion and allow me to feel some of His pain, that is, a bit of it. And then I saw something like a fire, divided into five rays like lines from His wounds, detach itself from that crucifix. And standing with my arms extended in the form of a cross, I felt those rays strike my hands, feet, and ribs, and I felt very great pains, which I feel even now most of the time. (Ferrazzi 29)

Cecilia Ferrazzi confessed this vision to a tribunal as she faced trial for supposed "pretense of sanctity" or pretending to be a holy saint. She was probably quaking with fear, being a simple citizen not used to facing robed government officials. Her heart probably raced with anxiety but also exultation as she relived her glorious vision of Christ's love.

*"Putta pericolante"*—a "girl in danger," was a phrase that could describe many girls growing up in early modern Venice (Schutte, "Introduction" 9). More specifically, it referred to unmarried girls who were in danger of being assaulted or seduced, in some way having their chastity dishonorably stolen from them. If girls lived without the protections of families, patrons, or the convent, they could quite easily fall prey to men who didn't fear punishments for rape or adultery, and from there it was a short journey to prostitution. Women were admonished to be chaste, obedient, and modest—but being too pious posed another danger altogether.

Cecilia Corona Ferrazzi lived surrounded by these dangers.

Born into the God-fearing family of Maddalena Polis and Alvise Ferrazzi, a skilled box maker, Cecilia was the eldest daughter of ten children and was expected to marry. On April 20, 1609, she was baptized at the Church of San Lio, a small, dark church decorated now with many *ex votos*—silver hearts thanking the saints for their intervention to heal afflictions. She and her brothers often prayed on their knees and fasted together, sometimes even resorting to self-flagellation; Cecilia records that their mother unsuccessfully tried to moderate their zealous behavior. She seemed to burn with her devotion from an early age. Cecilia was a sickly child who grew "supernumerary teeth"—extra sets of adult teeth—an affliction often attributed to high fevers in infancy (Schutte, "Introduction" 37 n41). She also suffered from convulsions and fainting spells, though no one identified her as being epileptic (well-known and termed the "ugly disease" in Venice at that time) (39 n1). Cecilia endured digestive problems her whole life; she "was born with this infirmity," she said. "I ate when I could but couldn't keep anything in my stomach, and I even vomited clots of blood" (Ferrazzi 23). She must have been thin as an apparition. To comfort her daughter, Cecilia's mother told her tales of the saints, and the life of Santa Caterina of Siena must have resonated with her in particular, as the saint claimed she could not eat and fasted often. Rather than seeing Cecilia's digestive troubles as physical ailments, she gave them a spiritual explanation, through which she found succor her whole life. Religion, prayer, and fasting felt like nests of safety in an otherwise dangerous world. Cecilia was a "girl in danger" for these reasons—death from severe illnesses.

Her childhood maladies continued throughout Cecilia's adolescence, and then in 1630 the bubonic plague swept through Venice, killing a third of the population. Cecilia's parents and all her younger siblings save her sister, Maria, died. "My sister was tended by Frenchmen," Cecilia recorded, "but I refused to be treated by anyone, and so I cured myself by putting herbs on my sores, one of them under my arm and the other on my breast," (Ferrazzi 43) which was reminiscent of San Sebastiano's story. Despite her illnesses, Cecilia tenaciously hung on. She took her cues from saints' suffering, turning hardship into stubbornness and perseverance. Her great piety and devotion compelled her to serve others in her Lord's name, using her gifts for good. Because she had experienced the loss of many family members and her own health, but then had survived through privation, hazards, and uncertainty, Cecilia developed resources and compassion to care for others.

At age twenty Cecilia found herself to be a "girl in danger" in yet another way: she had refused an arranged marriage to a notary, requesting the cloister instead, but now she had no parents to protect her and nowhere to go. It seems that a convent should have taken in such a vulnerable young woman, but apparently Cecilia's persistent illnesses and spiritual visions did more to alarm and scare the convent authorities than to attract them. No one would accept her. In fact, at one point her confessor, Father Giorgio Polacco, brought Cecilia to the convent of Santa Maria Maggiore in Venice's Santa Croce *sestiere*. "I'm putting in a saint," he told the sisters there, "one who lives on communion, one who has the stigmata!" (qtd. in Ferrazzi 61-2). These revelations frightened many of the nuns who lived simpler, more moderate lives in their mostly bare, white cells, in the plain brick convent, their days rounded by prayer. Eventually Cecilia's uncle

Defendi Polis took her in for a while at his home near Campo Sant'Aponal, and later Signora Marietta Cappello, a noblewoman who admired Cecilia's piety, gave her a place in her home. Cecilia needed the safe and honorable refuge these and other patrons provided.

For years Cecilia had been having spiritual visions, including visitations from God, the Virgin Mary, saints, the devil, and others. She fell into trances and ecstasies, sometimes in church but most often alone in her room. She recounted many of these tales in her "inquisitorial autobiography," a document recorded by Friar Antonio da Venezia at Cecilia's request during her later trial for heresy. While living in a house in the San Lorenzo neighborhood and suffering from one of her many illnesses, Cecilia hallucinated that the Baby Jesus visited her, saying, "O daughter, this is the martyrdom God has prepared for you for the salvation of these souls" (Ferrazzi 51). This thought brought her strength and consolation, and Cecilia recorded that she was "filled with a great deal of energy and desire to suffer in order to support and aid those souls with the strength I requested from the Lord, the male and female saints to whom I was devoted, and in particular St. Joseph" (51). She welcomed the illnesses and suffering because the more she suffered, the more she could alleviate the suffering of others as if she were a conduit for divine intervention.

With this in mind, Cecilia often resorted to self-inflicted pain. She told of a holy hermit who taught her self-flagellation to do penance for her shortcomings. She described a hazy week where she was unsure if she ate or drank, though she had "blood running down me in buckets" from her self-abuse (25). In another instance, after miraculously receiving a thrush as an anonymous gift one day as she prepared a meal for a sick nobleman, she wanted to show her devotion and gratitude to God. "I began to flagellate myself," she said, "thanking the Lord and praying" (44). Copying a practice of Santa Caterina of Siena, Cecilia wore a thick chain beneath her clothing for so many years that it "had grown into the skin" (69). Her Jesuit confessor Father Chiaramonte discovered it while he nursed Cecilia through an illness. When he ordered her to remove the chain, she "went into a trance, and three days later she found [herself] with the chain detached from [her] flesh without any pain at all" (69). Painful ulcers remained on her skin, though, and Cecilia suffered humiliation and shame when her self-inflicted wounds were discovered. Nevertheless, Cecilia continued to obey completely the guidance of those around her, tempering her actions as her mentors prescribed.

It's necessary to understand the context of these abuses and privations. As historian Margaret King points out, fasting was practiced by thirty percent of all Italian holy women from the thirteenth through the seventeenth centuries (*Women* 124). Food production and preparation were women's work, one of the few tasks that women had any control over. While men might renounce money or possessions, women gave up food. "If one is powerless in all other regards," writes King, "one still has power in this: not to eat, but to love" (125). Eating the Eucharist brought women closer union to God, and though Cecilia kept down food with great difficulty, taking communion consoled her. After one of her visions, she reported that "as soon as I'd received the Most Holy Communion, I was completely free of all ills" (Ferrazzi 61). She channeled her inability to eat into service to God, empowering herself in the only way she knew how, one of the only ways open to her.

This sort of starvation gave Cecilia an emaciated, asexual body, in keeping with her desire for chastity and suffering. It also brought on or exacerbated her other illnesses. For most of her life, Cecilia suffered from bladder stones, which often result from malnutrition or nutrient deficiencies. Once, her excruciating pain was such that she "broke plates and glasses with my teeth when they gave me food and drink to relieve me" (51). As she writhed in pain, she envisioned the Baby Jesus who "showed me a winding road, full of stones, down from which he wanted me to walk and he later went ahead and broke up those stones with a little hatchet" (50). She apparently saw these stones as the manifestation of a trial sent to her by God, but one which He would assist her to overcome. Despite her many illnesses and the numerous times she was in danger of dying, Cecilia must have been very strong indeed to have survived. In fact, she lived seventy-three years.

Ironically, it was these illnesses that led to one of Cecilia's greatest strengths: her ability to help others. After each tale of suffering, of visions and revelations and prayer, some good came from them. Some instances were fairly benign, like the encounter with a nobleman beggar where Cecilia almost ignored him until she "heard an internal voice saying, 'That's not how your father behaved'" (68). Cecilia reached into the purse she thought was empty and was surprised to find coins there, which she gave to the man. Cecilia foresaw the deaths of some or the recovery of others, all of which she dutifully reported to one of her various confessors. When Cecilia's sister Maria accidentally swallowed a hook-shaped needle, Cecilia prayed fervently for her sister's recovery. An "internal voice" told her to feed some lasagna noodles with greens to her sister, who was able to pass the needle successfully (58). Another time, Cecilia helped care for the mute five-year-old son of Signor Antonio Maffei. After she prayed daily for "God's grace that, if it were good for [the boy's] soul, He deign to give him speech," (55) the boy did indeed begin talking, astonishing his parents. Small wonder that many saw Cecilia as a holy woman.

Many of Cecilia's visions, however, were not so harmless nor did they end so well. She narrated multiple reports of being beaten by the devil, or a group of devils, or someone disguised as the devil. These are very disturbing accounts. In an early vision from her adolescence, when Cecilia still lived at home with her parents, she imagined the devil visiting her, appearing as "a frightening animal or as an ugly man breathing fire from his mouth" (41). This devil beat her repeatedly and urged her to accept the marriage her parents had arranged. Then the devil tried to "make [her] touch it all with [her] hand, and that [she] really should experience the taste of flesh" (42). Cecilia admitted to responding naïvely, not understanding that the devil was trying to do more than force her to eat meat. Later in life, when Cecilia envisioned a visitation by a holy hermit, who instructed her in doing penance with a whip, she realized he was the devil in disguise. "While beating me and dragging me to and fro," she explained, "he grabbed me by the braids and made me hit my head violently on the walls on both sides [of the room], splattering the walls with blood" (26). Her braids—and scalp—came off in the devil's hands, and she remained bald thereafter. Was this wound self-inflicted, divine, or at the hands of someone who should have taken care of her? Was Cecilia sexually or physically abused? For a "girl in danger," the harm could come from a multitude of sources and in a multitude of forms.

The men in Cecilia's life—mostly priests—were expected to protect her mortal self as well as her immortal soul. But Cecilia's reports are full of suspicious encounters. Father Antonio Grandi berated Cecilia for going into a trance in the Church of San Giovanni Elemosinario, yelling, "Wretch, is this the place to go into ecstasy? Get out of this church!" (53). He threw her out bodily into the streets of the Rialto district, telling her not to return. Another priest, whose name Cecilia did not know, shoved her, causing her to "fall backward over a wooden clog, which hurt [her] so badly that [she] had to be put in the care of a barber [surgeon]" (27-8). She mentioned no provocation for this action. Father Giorgio Polacco, who was supposed to be her prime confessor and protector during much of her adult life, routinely berated and humiliated her, then begged her forgiveness. He eventually decided that Cecilia needed to be exorcised, and he brought in three other priests to help. They gathered at the church of San Martino near the Arsenale and used the attached house and courtyard of Dominican friars. Cecilia "was sitting on the knees of the friar from San Giobbe, and all of them whispered in [her] ear that God give [her] patience and exhorted [her] to suffer willingly for the love of God" (71). Cecilia reported experiencing the "greatest consolation" during the exorcism, feeling like she "was in paradise" (72). By modern standards, people might characterize these reports as psychological abuse as well. Where could a woman like Cecilia turn for safety from the dangers all around her?

Perhaps surprisingly, though, during the years of these visions, torments, and revelations, Cecilia was entrusted with the safety of others.

She had begun as a "girl in danger," and then she began to take in young *"putte pericolanti"* as a sort of "social worker." While she was living at a house in San Lorenzo, two girls from Bassano were brought to Cecilia to look after her during one of her illnesses. "And little by little," she reported, "first I was given a small child who was going around begging, then another, then another, and so on, so that when I left there . . . I had one hundred twenty girls" (24). They moved together to larger quarters near San Giovanni Evangelista in the San Polo *sestiere*, then to Cannaregio, and finally into a house bought by the noblemen Francesco Vendramin and Sebastiano Barbarigo. Here Cecilia took in an estimated three hundred girls, many of them beggars or orphaned, and all in danger of falling into prostitution. For a woman who refused marriage and was denied the convent, Cecilia instead fashioned a useful life for herself that provided a valuable social function. Many wealthy nobles came forward to support her financially and otherwise, for, as Cecilia admitted, "I had no money, . . . but rather debts, as one can understand, since unfortunately I've had to spend for the girls, trusting only in God, Who provided as necessary in ways that stunned and amazed me" (74). Cecilia carried on this work for many years, despite her debilitating and sometimes lengthy illnesses.

Cecilia did all this "for the sake of charity," (48) she said, or to save a girl from an unchaste life. In one case, a woman brought her the daughter of a prostitute, hoping that Cecilia could prevent the girl from following in her mother's footsteps. However, the girl, Orsetta, ran away while they were at mass at San Severo. Cecilia had a vision of where to find the girl, and indeed, there she was. Disappointingly, Cecilia gave few details about the homes she provided for these girls. Venice offered a number of such homes of refuge, such as the Zitelle, an institution that took in orphaned girls and taught them trades to make a living. It's unclear if Cecilia focused on teaching the girls how to support themselves, or to save a wedding dowry, or, probably most likely, how to live a religious life. Cecilia explained that some of her charges died or ran away (58). Yet she continued to receive support from patricians and some members of the clergy, so clearly there were many people who valued the social service she provided.

Apparently not all were pleased that Cecilia took in such girls. A "known prostitute" (qtd. in Ferrazzi 31 n28) named Chiara Perini Bacchis, who was trying to get her two daughters and a niece released to her—a demand Cecilia refused—denounced her to the Inquisition. This plus a denunciation from Chiara Garzoni, a woman who had been taken in and raised by Cecilia but who now ran a safe house of her own, led to the Holy Inquisition to summon Cecilia into court. The charge? A form of heresy called "pretense of sanctity." In this era of the Counter-Reformation, when the Catholic Church was trying to bring adherents back into a traditional definition of Catholicism, authorities mistrusted people who claimed to be holy, prejudging them as insincere, writes Anne Jacobson Schutte in her "Introduction" to Cecilia's trial records (16). Furthermore, Schutte points out that while holy people represent positive attributes and are meant to gain praise, "if they appear to pose some challenge or threat to these values . . . they are accorded negative recognition, frequently expressed in exemplary punishment" (Schutte, *Aspiring Saints*). According to historian Ben Schill, "the Church hierarchy wished to both restrict [women's] actions and reaffirm traditional gender roles." Evidently, Cecilia did not fit the prescribed role for a holy person; she was not of the elite, nor was she a consecrated nun. Church authorities apparently believed that controls must be placed on her behavior. For a woman like Cecilia who so valued obedience and humility, she must have felt confused at her treatment.

Italians had multiple words for this type of "pretense of sanctity": *affettata* / assumed; *finta* / feigned; *pretesa* / pretended or claimed; and *simulata santita* / simulated holiness (Schutte, "Introduction" 14). According to Cecilia, Father Giovanni Priuli claimed that she "was playing the holy woman to fool the world and waste poor clerics' time with ecstasies and apparitions" (Ferrazzi 63). She appeared in court, clothed in a black wool dress and silk shawl typical of women of her class, but with her own touch added: a black veil layered over a white veil covering her forehead. Ben Schill points out that most priests at that time came from the patrician class, and they "did not like the idea of the lower classes intruding on their 'domain.'" Rather than nurturing or protecting Cecilia, her confessors most often criticized her of inappropriate behavior, and ultimately the Church authorities completely curtailed her activities.

Similarly, many women also attacked Cecilia. Neighborhood women or even some of the girls in Cecilia's care accused her of secretly having and then killing a baby, turning some of the girls over to prostitutes for money, or dressing ostentatiously so she could be adored. But the worst sin, in the Church's eyes, was the claim that Cecilia gave her girls confession, disguised as a hooded Capuchin friar. It was unthinkable that a woman could fulfill a function granted only to priests. All her visions and ecstasies aside, it was the thought of a woman crossing this boundary that brought about her trial.

Cecilia Ferrazzi wanted nothing more than to be a holy woman, to give her life to God. She said, "I begged them to make me a nun in one of the strictest orders there was so that I'd be more separated from the world" (42). Her illnesses coupled with her calling sent her into spiritual ecstasies and brought her visions. She strove to bring up vulnerable girls and to obey the dictates of her confessors, even testifying, "nor did I know what my own will was, because they ordered everything contrary to my will, and I obeyed" (28). Despite all that, she was denounced for her piety and brought before the court. In Venice, the Inquisition was not the torture-wielding body that is so often depicted; Cecilia was never tortured, nor was she in danger of being put to death. In the wood paneled rooms of the Inquisition, she testified on four separate days, from May 7 to July 8, 1664, other witnesses being questioned in between; the entire trial lasted fifteen months and involved over three hundred witnesses.

Despite her obedience and respect towards her superiors, Cecilia made the unprecedented request to dictate her own autobiography. "Dear Sirs," she began, "do me the favor of sending me either a confessor or anyone you want who'll write down everything I'll dictate to him, and I'll remember better and be less embarrassed" (37-8). Because Cecilia could write no more than her signature, a priest was brought in as a scribe. Thus records include not only Cecilia's four days of testimony, but also her "autobiographical act," (5) as Anne Jacobson Schutte terms the document from which so many details of Cecilia's life come. Readers are fortunate to receive this glimpse into the difficult life of a Venetian woman, though of course Cecilia often censored herself to present the best story to her judges.

Cecilia seems to have modeled her storytelling structure on other saints' lives, first giving a chronological account of her childhood and then recounting experiences with divine encounters and miracles. For instance, when questioned about her visions and supernatural visitations, she replied, "My dear sirs, I beg you not to make me say these things because I have never accepted them and I'd rather suffer than speak about them" (Ferrazzi 37). Cecilia saw herself as a sinner, not a perfect saint, and she also knew she must deny any pretense to holiness or risk imprisonment. Schill adds, "By portraying herself as a sinner and not maintaining any certainty in her abilities, Cecilia attempts to simulate humility and modesty, two traits of the ideal Counter-Reformation woman." Since her dictated autobiography was part of her trial, it is difficult to know her true thoughts or how much she is compelled to say what others expect to hear. She was protecting herself. Few others would do that for her.

Unfortunately, Cecilia's worst fear came true. While her autobiographical dictation was her opportunity to tell her side of the story, it also created opportunities for the judges to follow up on stories she told and to bring in more witnesses. Schutte notes, "Ferrazzi's autobiography facilitated [the Inquisitor's] task by highlighting issues to be pursued in the prosecution of its producer" ("Introduction" 13). While Cecilia was riding in a gondola on the Grand Canal on June 12, a boat pulled up alongside hers, and she was told she was under arrest. Cecilia was brought to the prisons of the Inquisition near San Giovanni in Bragora. She had been sentenced to seven years in prison and was told to desist from speaking about divine visitations. Schill contends, "In essence, her punishment was meant to be an example to others." She was also prohibited from ever taking in "girls in danger," and thus her means of livelihood and cause for respect in the world was taken from her. Her house of refuge was eventually brought under the control of the Provveditori Sopra Monasteri, which regulated female religious institutions. As soon as the trial was over, though, her defense attorneys appealed the ruling. After two years' imprisonment, Cecilia was transferred to a sort of house arrest with the Bishop of Padua, and in 1669 she was released altogether. Many may have accused her of wrongdoing, but Cecilia also apparently had many patrons who supported her, working on her behalf while she sat powerless in prison.

Cecilia Ferrazzi's story is a complex one. A "girl in danger" from many points of view, she still somehow found ways to aid other girls, use her visions for good, obey her superiors' guidance, and let her voice be heard. For one "kicked . . . around like a ball" (Ferrazzi 27) by priests like Giorgio Polacco, she still survived these abuses and illnesses. "Since she was independent, powerful, and a 'little woman' supposedly blessed by God," points out Schill, "Cecilia Ferrazzi did not embody the religious and social values of the time and was condemned as a heretic rather than beatified as a saint." In her social work she displayed compassion and devotion, a willingness to take in others whom the world had cast aside, or to aid those who had lost hope or direction. She turned her privations and sufferings into a tool for good.

Nothing is known of Cecilia's life after her return to Venice, until her death on January 17, 1684, after nine days of fever and lung congestion. Her friends still took care of her, procuring her burial at the Church of San Lio where she was baptized so many years before. Hopefully Cecilia's own heart found peace and rest after her life in danger.

# Barbara Strozzi

## To Risk Is to Find Joy

"*M*ost merciful Love / you never abandon / one who reverently offers you his heart," sang Barbara Strozzi before an intimate gathering at her father's house. The drawing room was filled with poets and philosophers, men in breeches, waistcoats, and wigs, listening to this virtuoso singer who had composed the music for many of the songs she sang. The title of this one was "*Priego ad amore*" or "Prayer to Love," the lyrics written by Barbara's father Giulio Strozzi. "Come, oh come to us," Barbara sang lightly, beseeching Love to enter her life, "bestow your sweet gifts / and for a kind affection / toward my Barbara make fertile my heart" (qtd. in Magner). Did she finish the song with a wink as she sang this last line about herself? No doubt some in the audience laughed with delight, the men slapping their knees, enchanted. The room would have been filled almost exclusively with men, members of a literary academy, taking a break from heavy discussion to enjoy romantic music. Barbara may have felt some trepidation at being outnumbered by men, though her father and other friendly scholars would have been there. Here she was able to share her music, the thing she did best. Barbara's robust charms, tumult of brown curls, and lilting voice filled the room, a place provided by her father to showcase her talents.

However, Giulio was not Barbara's father on record. Her baptismal record was blank on that line. Giulio Strozzi, a librettist and poet, could not provide his daughter with a marriage dowry, but he instead gave her perhaps the best gift of all. He shared his intellectual and artistic world with her, giving her right of entry into the world of singing and composing, so she might develop her talents. Surely this was a way to show her his love and acceptance. Barbara must have been grateful for his help and guidance, particularly since she was in a precarious social position as a woman without a legal father. But she was hardworking and tenacious as well, determined to develop her talents and create a place for herself. Barbara went on to become a renowned singer and the most published composer of her era.

Barbara was baptized at the Church of Santa Sofia, a small church built at an angle to the canal that used to run in front of it; its façade is now blocked by shops and housing, and the canal was filled in to become the busy Strada Nova or New Street. Baptized on August 6, 1619, Barbara was probably born three to six days earlier. Her mother's name, Isabella Griega, appears in the church's records (though in some other books her name is listed as Isabella Griegha, meaning the Greek, or even as Garzoni). But no father is listed at all. Isabella had worked as a servant in the home of Giulio Strozzi, himself a "natural" or illegitimate child of Roberto Strozzi, who later acknowledged Giulio as his son; the Strozzi family were wealthy and well-connected financiers from Florence. Did Barbara face scorn from neighbors and kin for her uncertain status? Did she feel embarrassed or shy? It doesn't appear so, as she moved forcefully forward in her musical career.

Regrettably, Barbara's father Giulio apparently had little income and little facility with money. He dedicated his life to literature. Besides poetry, he also wrote the librettos for composers in a variety of musical genres—mostly operas and cantatas—though he himself was not a musical composer. Giulio's portrait by Tiberio Tinelli reveals a kind, round face, tufts of hair on the top and sides of his head, and a fashionable mustache and goatee the focal point of his face, his eyes being rather small. Giulio and Isabella apparently raised their daughter Barbara together, with one residence in nearby San Felice in the Cannaregio district. They rented a home on Calle de la Racheta from the Pesaro family; this may have been the Palazzo Pesaro-Papafava facing the Canal de la Misericordia, though documentary evidence is unclear (Magner, email). In 1628, when Barbara was yet a child, Giulio wrote up a will naming Isabella as his principal heir. He may not have had much cash to offer, but what he had, he offered to her. (This included his manuscripts plus a portrait of himself by Bernardo Strozzi.) In this will he mentioned Isabella's daughter, listed as Barbara Valle, acknowledging her presence in his life, showing that he was already considering how to include her in his inheritance.

Growing up, little Barbara would have been surrounded by the comings and goings of intellectuals, writers, and musicians—late night discussions of poetry and philosophy, the sound of instruments being tuned, people writing or reading their work, writers dropping by for a glass of wine. Probably on every surface sat a violin, lute, or theorbo, plus piles of books, folios, and broadsides. Around this time, Francesco Cavalli, director of music at the Basilica di San Marco and a preeminent composer of his day, became Barbara's music teacher and one of the most valuable gifts that Giulio could give his daughter. Barbara sang in a light and flexible soprano, able to sing rapidly but also hold a "long legato line," probably accompanying herself on the lute or theorbo, according to biographer Ellen Rosand (183). Other composers and musicians noted her skill as well. When Nicolo Fontei composed a set of songs titled *Bizzarrie Poetiche* (*Poetic Oddities*) for Barbara in 1635, he dedicated it to "principally the most kind and virtuosic damsel, Signora Barbara" (qtd. in Magner). For a young woman without a noble rank and few financial resources, she must have been pragmatic enough to know that music could provide a means for her to make a future for herself.

At this point in her education, Barbara was still but a teenager. Records unearthed by researcher Beth Glixon show that in 1650 Giulio Strozzi moved to the opposite side of the Church of Santa Sofia, to a house he rented on the Calle del Remer at #4765A, a building where he had enough space for an office (Glixon, "New" 313). His wife and daughter had remained with him as a complete family in every way except for the legal marriage papers. Barbara remained in this house for many years, paying the rent even after her father's death. Tax records and other legal documents also show that she was a "savvy investor," earning good interest on her investments and solvent enough to offer loans to others (314).

After her education, the next gift that Giulio presented to his daughter was a salon. Actually, a pair of salons. First, he brought Barbara to sing at the prestigious Accademia degli Incogniti (The Unknowns), founded by Giovanni Francesco Loredan and peopled by the cream of Venetian literary society. This group gathered at the Palazzo Loredan, a vast and imposing white palace in Campo Santa Maria Formosa. Frequented by writers, philosophers, composers, librettists, historians, and even clerics, they met to debate and wrangle with ideas. The Incogniti were also known as libertines, questioning some of society's mores, and believing that the Church didn't always have the best answers. For example, they might ponder the question of women's equality, agreeing with the Humanist approach to educate women. (Loredan also wrote to Arcangela Tarabotti in her convent, supplying her with literature and letters.) Barbara Strozzi began her singing career at the meetings of the Incogniti, and Giovanni Loredan noted in a letter to a friend, "Had she been born in another era . . . [she] would certainly have usurped or enlarged the place of the muses" (qtd. in E. Rosand 173). However, though the Incogniti were seen as liberal thinkers, women were still not listed as official academy members; furthermore, this being the seventeenth century, women who attended these gatherings often had their virtue and chastity questioned or even slandered. Wives did not attend such meetings, only courtesans, singers, and poets (or, quite often, women who were all three). Thus, many people assumed that Barbara must belong to the courtesan set.

Once Barbara had debuted at the Incogniti, her father presented yet another gift—a salon designed specifically to showcase her talents. Dubbed the Accademia degli Unisoni—The Like-Minded—the name was also possibly a pun on the idea of unison in musical compositions.

It was a sort of subset group of the Incogniti, comprised primarily of musicians, composers, librettists, and opera aficionados (E. Rosand 170). The group met in the Strozzi home, though which Strozzi home is unclear. Barbara did much more than just sing; as hostess, she chose the discussion topics for the evening and often refereed the debates. Quite often, the topics turned to love. Standing before a fireplace, glass of wine in hand, a member might ask, "Which is a more powerful tool for love, tears or song?" While tears come naturally, the group reasoned, they couldn't be stronger than song, which uses art to harness the power of nature and make it something greater. Barbara, rising to act as judge, ended the debate with this reasoning: "I do not question your decision, gentlemen, in favor of song; for well do I know that I would not have received the honor of your presence at our last session had I invited you to see me cry rather than to hear me sing" (qtd. in E. Rosand 184). What resounding applause and smiles of approval this response would have garnered. In order to come up with witty responses like this, Barbara had to overcome any anxiety at being a member of this male society.

She also revealed her romantic side. In Barbara's composition "*Canto di Bella Bocca*," she sang, "Lovely, charming voice, / with rapid scales, / allures you, surrounds you, also touches you / and sinks within almost to kiss your heart" (qtd. in Magner). A coquettish glint in her eye, a tilt to her head, and Barbara must have quickened the breathing and flushed the cheeks of her audience. Barbara, with her wit, intelligence, and beauty, played a perfect hostess, though her singing was still the centerpiece that drew them all together. Actually, more documents exist praising her singing than any of her other accomplishments, perhaps because a good voice was an acceptable accomplishment for any refined lady, more so than composing was.

Other male singers of the seventeenth century might sing sacred music, or perform in the theater in operas, the great rage of the era. Nuns or the young women of the *ospedali*, institutions for social welfare, sang in the churches at masses and feast days. These public venues had their benefits and limitations and also signaled one's social class, with the opera being a rather scandalous place for young women, and the *ospedale* being limited to those who needed its refuge. Barbara led a more private life, though, singing at a salon in her home. Her father Giulio probably never had enough money to provide a convent "dowry" to pay for her placement in that type of chaste house, so the next best gift he could offer was a more intimate venue. It must have felt fairly safe and familiar. Music historians Jane Bowers and Judith Tick point out that "Strozzi's formal studies were supplemented by frequent opportunities to exercise her musical talents before audiences of connoisseurs—both apparently part of her father's plan to prepare her specifically for a career in music, possibly even for the profession of composing" (131). This sphere, where the musical world was laid at Barbara's feet, gave her every advantage amongst Venice's musicians and composers and launched her towards composition.

Besides a teacher, a venue, and connections to Venice's musical elite, Giulio next supplied Barbara with texts for her early compositions. She published her first collection of madrigals in 1644, which contained music composed by her and texts written entirely by her father Giulio. Madrigals are secular pieces most often for multiple voices, a popular genre during the Renaissance. In the dedication to Vittoria della Rovere, Duchess of Tuscany, Barbara acknowledged her father's gift, stating, "The choice of the lyric verses will help me somewhat, which are all trifles of he who from my girlhood has given me his surname and material comfort" (qtd. in Magner). While not publicly calling Giulio her father, Barbara noted his gift to her, though, as was typical of the times, she tempered the value of her work to humble herself before the Duchess. Musicians usually dedicated their works to wealthy and well-connected patricians or nobles in the hopes of receiving remuneration, gifts, or even permanent patronage. Each of Barbara's collections is dedicated to a different person, yet unfortunately there is no record that any of them supplied her with income or gifts to sustain her.

After her father Giulio passed away in March 1652, Barbara continued to compose and publish at a prolific pace. Opus 2 came out in 1651, then Opus 3 in 1654. Opus 5 followed in 1655, with Opus 4 sometime between them, now lost. Opus 6 appeared in 1657, and Opus 7 a year later, with Barbara's final collection coming in 1664. Overall, she published 125 pieces of vocal music (that are known), more than any other composer of her day. Florentine composer Francesca Caccini, Marieta Morosina Priuli of Venice, and Isabella Leonarda of Novara were the only other female composers who wrote more than a couple pieces, and Antonia Padoani Bembo followed later, with her principal work completed in Paris. While some cloistered women wrote sacred music, most pieces were not published or preserved. Women also rarely wrote pieces for opera or oratorio—anything for a full orchestra—because there was no acceptable place for a woman to make a career in music or hold a position as a professional musician (E. Rosand 6). Composers Maddalena Casulana and Virginia Vagnoli showed promising musical careers as composers and teachers, but their marriages ended that. These women came closest, and Barbara, by virtue of living in the publishing capital of Europe, had excellent access to models that inspired her plus printers and publishers who could preserve her works. Giulio Strozzi had laid all the groundwork for Barbara to be trained and to enter into this world. Of course, it was her own talent and hard work that resulted in such magnificent accomplishments. She must have spent countless hours with pen in hand, scratching down black notes on lined paper, music filling her head.

Marriage didn't put a stop to Barbara's career as it did for some women writers. She never married. But that doesn't mean that she had no romantic attachments. In the 1640s, Barbara had four children, at least three of whom are assumed to be the children of patrician Giovanni Paolo Vidman (sometimes spelled Widmann), a family name preserved on street signs in Venice's Castello district. The Vidmans were affluent merchants who procured a place in Venice's noble class by their financial contribution of 100,000 ducats to the Venetian State, and their palace and the private altar in the Church of San Canzian attest to their wealth and prestige. Giovanni Paolo Vidman was friend to Giulio Strozzi, who dedicated two of his opera librettos to him. Giovanni Paolo's portrait shows off his handsome visage and dashing style, with a fashionable goatee and curled mustaches framed by wavy black hair and a stole around his shoulders. Because of the differences in class ranking, Giovanni Paolo would have been pressured to never marry Barbara, plus he had already married a noblewoman as a social and economic match. According to researcher Beth Glixon, a story circulated that Giovanni Paolo raped Barbara, initiating the relationship ("More" 136). While this appears heinous, it might actually have been merely a story that was used to protect Barbara's reputation: if the woman had been forced into sexual relations, then she was less at fault and her virtue less suspect (Music Academy Online). Though the couple never lived together, Giovanni Paolo did recognize the children as his own; in fact, the Vidman family paid for Barbara's two daughters, Isabella and Laura, to enter a convent, and they also provided money to Massimo, one of the sons, to become a monk (Glixon, "More" 137-8). The eldest, Giulio Pietro, who was later recognized as Giovanni Paolo's son and took the Vidman name, inherited his mother's estate, such as it was.

Conjecture abounds regarding Barbara's sexual morals: Was she or was she not a courtesan? Did her position as *ridotto* singer and salon hostess indicate promiscuity? Did her choice of musical texts and debate topics centered on love indicate that she must be somehow more versed in the love arts? The first song of Opus 1, "*Sonetto Proemio dell'Opera*" alludes to sexual satisfaction, when she sings, "To delight in joy, to laugh at laughter, / not ever sighing, unless that sigh be / from a death that heals and does not kill" (qtd. in Magner). The most "damning" evidence is the only known portrait of Barbara, painted by Bernardo Strozzi (apparently not a direct relation) and titled *Female Musician with Viola da Gamba* completed in 1639. It depicts Barbara standing at an angle but with her gaze pointedly addressing the viewer as if to offer no apologies or excuses. A rather full-bodied woman with thick chestnut hair and wearing a crimson skirt, her blouse dips down to expose one breast. She is not smiling. She holds her viola da gamba and bow in one hand, and she leans on a table where rests a violin and duet score, as if in invitation to join her in play. The roses in her hair are a typical mark of Flora, the symbolic prostitute in countless paintings. Bernardo Strozzi had painted the portrait of musical luminary Claudio Monteverdi, and also one of Giulio Strozzi; surely a sanctioned painting, the *Female Musician* gives every indication that Barbara was a courtesan. This is coupled with the usual defamations hurled at women who did not stay in their assigned boxes; a satire circulated in 1637 said of Barbara, "It is a fine thing to distribute the flowers after having already surrendered the fruit" (qtd. in E. Rosand 172). Was Barbara humiliated by this? Angry? Or resigned to the fact that her society worked in this way? How much importance should be assigned to these accusations and judgments? Are they simply indications that a creative woman was prey to slander for not fitting the social expectations? And does it have any bearing on her accomplishments as a composer and singer? Biographer Ellen Rosand argues, "It may be unfair to venture an opinion on the morals of Barbara Strozzi on the basis of slanderous (if even jesting) remarks in some anonymous satires against her and the traditional yet general association between courtesans and music-making—unfair and, perhaps irrelevant" (172). Sadly, this is a topic that comes up and needs to be addressed for nearly every notable woman.

Since Barbara left no journals and very few letters, it is difficult to know her personal thoughts and attitudes. Most of her surviving words come from the dedications to each opus. As was the custom for both male and female writers, any address to an equal or a superior took a self-deprecating tone. In Barbara's first dedication, she downplayed the beauty of her music, explaining that "These [songs] will relieve the boredom of anyone who does not remain entirely pleased with the poor harmonies of my songs" (qtd. in Magner). Barbara knew also that her role as a female composer was remarkable, and perhaps choosing a woman, Vittoria delle Rovere, as her hoped-for first patron was one way to appeal for sympathy. "Therefore, I must reverently consecrate this first opus, which I, as a woman, too rashly bring to the light to the most august Name of Your Highness, in order that under an Oak-tree of gold it rests protected from the lightning bolts of slanders prepared for it," she wrote (qtd. in Magner). The oak-tree she referred to was a pun on the name Rovere, meaning oak tree, indicating that she hoped delle Rovere would protect her. "But favored by the protection of her Highness," Barbara continued, "I flatter myself to believe that you will harbor none who vilify these, my works" (qtd. in Magner). By Opus 2, not much had changed, as Barbara wrote in her dedication to Ferdinand III of Austria and Leonora II of Mantua, "The lowly mine of a woman's poor imagination cannot produce metal to forge those richest golden crowns worthy of august rulers" (qtd. in E. Rosand

174). This language was typical of the era, and it indicated that Barbara was playing within the given societal confines.

But by Opus 5, and after Barbara had become a mother and had had to survive without Giulio's protection for three years, her work became much more confident. "Since feminine weaknesses restrain me no more than any indulgence of my sex impels me," she wrote to Anna of Austria, "on lightest leaves do I fly" (qtd. in E. Rosand 174). In another piece, this one dedicated to Giovanni Antonio Forni for a particular cantata in Opus 7, Barbara began the song with a direct address, saying, "I am not afraid of you" (183). It's not clear what there was to fear or what, if any, message Barbara was delivering to Forni, but it is evident that she felt more empowered to speak directly.

Of course, Barbara's strongest "voice" came through in her musical compositions. She wrote primarily cantatas, arias, and madrigals, the arias often strophic, meaning that each stanza is sung to the same music, while the cantatas show more variation in each part. Her intimate music is meant for cozy chambers and informal gatherings—a parlor filled with fifteen or twenty men or women, their bright coats or lavish dresses rustling as they shifted in their seats or reached for lemonade, wine, or warm punch as they listened to the songs. A guitarist might perch upon his chair to strum alongside the singer, or a harpsichordist would accompany her, the keys' tone light and crisp. Barbara's music was about the voice more than the instruments. She wrote for soloists, duets, or groups of up to five singers. Many of the texts that accompany Barbara's songs contain a female narrator addressing a man, one singer addressing another, or even unclear gender references, allowing the possibility of strong female voices. The focus is on the voice, with highs and lows, trills and embellishments that exhibit a singer's virtuosity and control.

Her musical texts were by a variety of writers, some unnamed, but so far there is no proof that Barbara wrote any of them herself. Most of Barbara's songs do not tell stories but instead often showcase the singer's voice, leaving wordless passages that allow the voice to soar and dive, often rapidly and fluidly. "These harmonic notes," she said of Opus 7, "are the language of the soul and instruments of the heart" (qtd. in E. Rosand 185). The music was most often written for a solo soprano voice just like hers, and she chose texts that mostly fit within the love motif. Ellen Rosand describes it as "the suffering caused by unrequited love, sometimes treated highly ironically, even humorously, but more often treated with great seriousness and intensity" (176). Often, her notes climb upward, only to stop their ascent with a minor key that ushers in a melancholy moment. Rather than an exultant high, Barbara's music opts for the minor key, the reigning in, the introspection. Barbara seemed to be a woman of wit and humor and passion, able to navigate a sometimes rocky strait, and growing stronger personally as she developed as a composer.

Barbara Strozzi lived a life of music, not allowing other things to cause her to stray from this course. Some time after May 1677 she left Venice for Padua, where she grew ill and died in November of that year at age fifty-eight (Glixon, "More" 135). She was buried at the Church of the Eremitani, a large brick building that was adorned with vibrant frescoes. She left no will, though her son Giulio Pietro claimed the few belongings that she had left behind. Her father Giulio had left her one other gift, however; his final will made her his main heir and described her as his "*figliuola elettiva*," a euphemism for "legitimate" but that was pragmatically understood to mean he adopted her. He gave her his name and legitimacy, plus his portrait and papers. Barbara proved herself to be a legitimate and prodigious talent, who took Giulio's gifts and enlarged them to create a body of impressive work. She lived outside the bounds of many of society's rules, but as she sang in "*L'Amante Timido Eccitato*," "One who doesn't risk never finds joy" (qtd. in Magner).

*Woman with Theorbo* by Bartholomeus van der Helst

# *Giovanna*

## The Miracle in Corte Nova

$S$uffering surrounded the Corte Nova in the Castello district. The moaning of the sick and the wailing of the bereaved carried over from one neighborhood to the next. Fear like a fever gripped the citizens. Houses were barred to outsiders. Giovanna likely knew more than a few people who had been carted off to the lazaretto for quarantine when they had begun to show signs of this pestilence. First fever, then chills, headaches, muscle aches, a fatigue that felled them to their beds. Then the awful lumps on their necks, in their armpits or groins, lumps as big as a chicken's egg but purple or black as no egg was meant to be. The most terrifying were the excretions from both ends, or blood from the mouth, the nose, the rectum. Some people had black spots on their thighs and arms and torso where blood had congealed under the skin.

The Black Death had visited Venice once again from June 1630 to November 1631.

This was the third major outbreak, after plagues in 1348 and from June 1575 to December 1576. Plague was first carried from the East by armies as they battled Tatars (Lane 19). Venice was a major port, with hundreds of vessels arriving from eastern countries and unsuspectingly transporting rats that carried infectious fleas on their backs. Of course, officials had not yet discerned that the rats carried the fleas that carried the plague. Some thought it was vapors, other said exhalations, while some claimed it was the wrath of God upon sinners, particularly in a city like Venice with its scores of prostitutes, rampant gambling, and ostentatious gluttony for luxury. Doctors, who were forbidden to leave the city, tried to protect themselves with their long robe, hat to cover their hair, spectacles to cover their eyes, and a mask with a long beak packed with aromatic herbs to combat the sickly smells as well as the contagious vapors that they believed transmitted the disease. Giovanna might have seen such doctors scurry past beneath the windows of her home safely tucked into the courtyard of Corte Nova.

What many didn't know at the time, but what later research has revealed, is that the Black Death was not the only killer at this time: three forms of plague—bubonic, septicemic, and pneumonic—were lumped together under the same title. In Venice's plague of 1630 to 1631 that Giovanna lived through, subsequent research shows that a smallpox epidemic also raged through the city at this time. Close study of the city's death records, which were kept meticulously, also reveal a sharp rise in deaths related to wounds received through violence. As plague bred fear, fear bred violence; people turned on others, resulting in a quarter of the city's deaths related to causes other than plague (Ell). More women died than men, and especially pregnant women who appeared to be most susceptible to these diseases. Children, too, died more frequently. Though numbers vary by about ten thousand, approximately 50,000 people, or a third of Venice's population, died during this bout of the Black Death.

Yet it did not reach the inhabitants of the Corte Nova, thanks, it is believed, to its resident Giovanna and her unwavering faith, who "urged her neighbors not to give up hope" (Jonglez & Zoffoli 287). This courtyard is long and narrow, so narrow that the neighbors could call out to one another across its width. Everyone would have seen each other's laundry hanging out on wash day and known who was having fish or liver for dinner. They must have watched each other warily for signs of the plague being brought into their secluded refuge. Giovanna watched, too, but instead of inciting suspicion and fear, she promoted calm. She brought together her neighbors in prayer and community to spark hope.

Giovanna was a young girl living in the Corte Nova or "new court" in the *sestiere* of Castello, about a ten-minute walk east of Piazza San Marco. When she saw what the terrible plague was doing to those in other neighborhoods, she decided to do something to protect herself and her neighbors. Giovanna painted a canvas depicting the Virgin Mary surrounded by other saints. Mary, of course, was the Queen of Heaven, sharing her divine mercy with those who asked for her intercession. Beside Mary stood San Lorenzo, known for helping the poor, widows, and virgins, and also seen as a protector against epidemics. San Sebastiano, while a patron of athletes and soldiers, was closely linked to plague iconography; though most often shown shot with arrows, Sebastiano, in Renaissance depictions, appears to suffer little. After years of recurring plagues, many people began to see San Sebastiano's arrows as representing the plague; though he was wounded, God's mercy protected him from suffering. San Rocco, especially, was seen as a great protector against this disease. While on a pilgrimage to Rome, Rocco healed many plague victims he met before he too was stricken by the disease. Water from a miraculous spring and food brought by a helpful dog allowed him to recover. Renaissance paintings often show him displaying a plague sore on his thigh. San Rocco was a survivor, victorious over the plague that was ravaging so many in Giovanna's city. His body was laid to rest across town in the church named after him.

Giovanna included these four powerful figures in her painting and hung it in the long, dark *sotoportego,* the covered walkway that led into the Corte Nova. She and her neighbors gathered there daily to offer up prayers for intercession to these saints, asking that their lives be spared. They brought candles to illuminate the gloomy corridor and help them kindle their hope for survival. "The ravages of the plague continued but did not extend beyond the painting," write historians Thomas Jonglez and Paola Zoffoli, "thus the inhabitants of the courtyard were spared" (287). Giovanna had unwavering faith in God and His mercy and encouraged those who gathered with her to remain steadfast and trusting during those dreadful times.

In fact, Giovanna was not the only person to believe that a painting could bring salvation. Common from the times of epidemics in the 1300s, such "plague votives" like Giovanna's were believed to ward off the disease. These paintings depicted saints as mediators between God and His suffering people. A painting, usually completed by one person but commissioned by a community, was meant to represent a request for atonement for their sins. No records indicate if Giovanna conceived the idea for this painting on her own or if her neighbors urged her to create it. But she is the one who took action. Furthermore, people saw the saints' suffering, which mirrored their own current suffering, linking them to God and His benevolent mercy. These paintings helped city inhabitants feel that they were doing something to protect themselves in a world that felt increasingly unsafe. "Rather than a society depressed and resigned to repeated epidemics, these votives represent people taking positive steps to regain control over their environment," (39) writes researcher Megan Webb. Besides Giovanna's faith giving her neighbors hope, the painting provided them a nearby locale where they could meet to share their faith and quell their fears together.

Giovanna's painting apparently worked. The Black Death never advanced into the Corte Nova; no one there contracted the disease. Their daily prayers and the intercession of the saints in the painting seemed to work a miracle.

Little is known about Giovanna, the miracle painter. But thanks to the work of historian Monica Chojnacka, modern readers do have a picture of daily life in a neighborhood like the Corte Nova. A *contrada* or neighborhood such as Sant'Antonin where the Corte Nova is located, mostly consisted of the *popolani,* working class people, mostly married couples with children. The 1633 census reveals that eighty-five percent of Venice's population consisted of the *popolani,* rather than the merchant or noble classes (Weiner 47). According to census and Inquisition records, most courtyards and small alleys were inhabited by a majority of women, be they widows or unmarried women or those separated from their husbands. Quite often, these women formed "a crucial barrier between the individual and disaster in moments of personal difficulty" (M. Chojnacka 54). While this housing arrangement and lifestyle was seldom an option for women of the upper classes, it was the norm for *popolani* like Giovanna. People relied on their neighbors for commerce, childcare, and socializing. "The parish community, made up primarily of women, provided an economic and emotional support," states Chojnacka, "by offering opportunities for socializing, work, and offering comfort in times of distress" (73). Giovanna protected her neighbors with a plague votive, a natural gesture for a Venetian inhabitant who lived in such close quarters with her neighbors, though one that merited recognition.

No one knows what happened to Giovanna's original painting. But the sentiment was not forgotten. To this day, a *capitello* or neighborhood shrine is maintained in the Sotoportego e Corte Nova. It consists of two shrines, actually, one on either wall of the passageway. In each hangs a portrait of the Virgin Mary, alone without the accompanying saints that Giovanna had provided. Artificial flowers and a candle usually sit on a mantel before the framed picture, all within a stone frame or mounting. The *sotoportego's* ceiling has been decorated with embossed tiles, and to offer illumination, a yellow lantern hangs from the ceiling, rather than the candles that Giovanna would have used.

On the ground, a square of red Verona marble has been laid, demarcating the place where the Black Death could not pass by. Some say it is good luck to step on this stone, while others claim the opposite. Apparently school children today debate this ritual's ability to help them pass their exams. Certainly, many who came after Giovanna believed that this site was holy. Over the entrance to the *sotoportego* is embedded an arched tablet detailing the location's history. It implores the Virgin, "Oh Mary of good health who numerous times you preserved the inhabitants of Corte Nova . . . please accept their grateful vows of this parish and we pray to you to expand your protection onto all those devoted to thee" (translation by Claudia Mandelli). Besides listing the plague years of 1630 to 1631, the plaque also lists 1848 to 1855, though no record seems to exist to detail what happened then. Also posted are the years 1917 to 1918 when prayers for the Virgin Mary's intervention protected the Corte Nova residents from enemy bombs during World War I. This is indeed a special place.

Over 500 *capitelli* grace walls, corners, and passages throughout Venice ("The Sacred on the Streets"). Giovanna's painting may have had remarkable powers, but many citizens built similar shrines, either to ask for help or to commemorate help that was granted. Usually a portrait or icon will be placed in a small niche upon the wall, eye-level or higher, sometimes protected behind glass or a metal grill. Many are decorated with flowers, lace, ribbon, even curtains, as well as candles, real or electrical. People in the neighborhood, mostly women, tend these shrines, bringing the sacred into public spaces. In fact, way back in 1450 the Venetian State declared that local patricians had a duty to maintain neighborhood *capitelli*. Such sacred spaces illuminated dark corners but also promoted religion, which authorities believed promoted a stable society. Sometimes business contracts were signed in front of *capitelli* to encourage people's honesty. For Giovanna and her neighbors, the *capitello* brought protection and hope.

The Black Death finally began to abate in December 1631, with no one from the Corte Nova having fallen ill. Giovanna and her neighbors were not the only ones to turn to the Virgin Mary for relief, however. The doge himself, Nicolo Contarini, vowed to erect a church in Mary's honor for her power to end this plague. He laid the cornerstone for the Church of Santa Maria della Salute, Saint Mary of Health, on October 22, 1630, one week before he died and well before the disease had been eradicated. Perhaps Mary's grace granted an earlier salvation, or perhaps it was the measures taken by the State. Venice had instituted quarantines for years, sequestering all people entering the city from suspicious locations in the belief that the plague was passed between people. Also realizing that cleanliness was linked to disease, Venice was one of the first cities to increase efforts at sanitation and open a public health office. Quite effective was the use of the Lazzaretto, a hospital on a separate island where the infected were brought to keep them away from the general population. Though these separate islands must have been horrifying places to work and to die in, filled with suffering and stench, they did much to limit the spread of the disease. The Lazzaretto Vecchio, where skeletons of thousands of plague victims have been unearthed, is believed to be the first such quarantine lazaretto in Europe, and its model was copied by many other cities.

The Church of the Salute was completed and consecrated in 1687. It is one of Venice's largest, with 1,156,650 oak poles forming its foundation. Built on plans by Baldassarre Longhena, it is unusual with its octagonal layout, but those who venerate the Virgin Mary would understand. Mary's crown has eight points, and this number figures often in the church's design. In the middle of the magnificent mosaic floor lays Mary's crown, and a sculpture depicts Mary vanquishing the plague. The frieze outside features the Sanskrit swastika signifying health, and the elevated stairs are said to further replicate Mary's crown. November 21 has for centuries been the day when Venetians venerate the Virgin Mary, again thanking her for her grace to end the plague of 1630 to 1631. Residents arrive either by crossing a bridge on the Grand Canal, erected especially for that day, or by boat, symbolizing the boats returning to the city after the plague's end. Inhabitants in and around the Corte Nova still celebrate as well, with a local festival on that day, commemorating the events from nearly 400 years earlier. Giovanna would probably be surprised to know that her painting and her prayers set in motion events remembered so long after her passing.

Tablet over the *sotoportego* at the Corte Nova

# Antonia Padoani Bembo

## To Feed One's Soul

*T*he musicians sat in gilt chairs with tapestry cushions, lightly holding their instruments: a viola da gamba, a guitar, and a theorbo. A harpsichord stood to the side, with a man at its keys. They all wore the height of fashion, with their lace collars and cuffs, the men in slim waistcoats and the women in tight bodices. A young soprano stood at their center, facing the audience, as her voice trilled in concord with the song's notes, embellishing and enhancing the instrumentation with her graceful voice. They were performing music composed by Antonia Padoani Bembo, music that provided entertainment for the audience but a saving grace for its composer.

Music expresses emotions in ways words cannot, and it gives voice in ways metaphorical and subliminal. For most of history in medieval and early modern times, this outlet was open to men more than women. Outside of their private homes, few women had opportunities to sing, to play music, and particularly to compose. Antonia Padoani Bembo was one woman, however, who found her voice through music. She composed an opera and a number of pieces of chamber music that not only exalted her benefactors, but also elevated women's identities, emotions, and bodies.

But Antonia faced some obstacles as well as advantages. Some women were blessed to have men in their lives who fed their souls, while others suffered men who devoured them. Antonia Padoani Bembo had both. Though her husband was destructive, Antonia was fortunate to have a devoted and supportive father, plus the patronage of the Sun King himself—Louis XIV. And she had the talent to create pieces that delighted nobles and monarchs so that she received patronage that changed her life. Antonia was quite grateful for these gifts, even though she must have lived with some fear for her precarious situation in later years away from Venice.

After the birth of their only child Antonia around 1640, Antonia's father, the doctor Giacomo Padoani, and her mother Diana Paresco, recognized and developed their daughter's talents early on. In his will of March 13, 1662, her father wrote of "the many efforts of my poor wife in raising my . . . daughter and in giving her tutors, and my own for (one would almost say) having fed her soul, in order to make her succeed, in *virtù*, to the astonishment of the world" (qtd. in Fontijn 20). According to Professor Claire Fontijn, he wanted to develop both Antonia's moral and artistic virtues (20). To this end he hired tutors in wigs and waistcoats who schooled Antonia in grammar (Latin and Greek), as she sat ensconced at a book-strewn table by a bright window. While her contemporaries read only lives of saints or sacred texts, dreaming of prayer or penance, Antonia read more widely in the classics (Manetti 16). She apparently lapped up learning in both literature and music.

Her parents placed Antonia, still a young child, with the highly esteemed Francesco Cavalli, organist and *maestro di cappella* at the Basilica di San Marco and the foremost composer of his epoch in Venice. His neatly trimmed beard, pointed mustache, and intense gaze hint at his being an exacting teacher. Francesco Cavalli collaborated on artistic productions at the small Teatro Sant'Aponal from 1651 to 1660, and it's likely that Antonia attended some of these performances that were near her family's home (Manetti 33). Francesco had schooled Barbara Strozzi a couple decades earlier, as well as taught other young men and women gifted in musical abilities. In fact, Francesco lived in the same neighborhood as the Padoani family, in the Palazzo Balbi on the Grand Canal, with its bright white exterior, stucco embellishments, and imposing four-story façade, though he lived at the back. Like other prodigies, Antonia was seen as a curiosity and a showpiece. She even appears to have been one of the factors considered in her father's bid to secure a post as court physician, as evidenced by Giacomo Padoani's correspondence with Giulio Cesare Gonzaga, a courtier to the Duke of Mantua. In their letters, Antonia is referred to as "the girl who sings" (qtd. in Fontijn 21). Fontijn writes, "Antonia's prodigious vocal talent apparently caused the duke to seek her out, in keeping with the tradition of the northern Italian courts to employ such marvels as marks of distinction and prestige" (21). For better or worse, the negotiations were never completed. Was Antonia disappointed or content with this outcome?

Antonia was apparently a strong-willed child. Giacomo's earlier testament from 1651 hints that his daughter could be disobedient and that in the event of her father's death, Antonia "should obey her mother." If Antonia disobeys and displeases her mother, Giacomo wrote, "Signora Diana can deprive her of everything that [he is] leaving her" (qtd. in Fontijn 16). These threats never came to pass, though Antonia did clash with her father later.

The year 1659 precipitated this disharmony. Antonia's parents arranged for her a prestigious marriage match, despite their status as *cittadini*, the professional class of citizens. The suitor, Lorenzo Bembo, came from the highest stratum of society, his father Andrea Bembo having held a position as treasurer in Padua. But when Andrea died, it was time for the son to marry. It's unclear where the two families would have crossed paths to lead to this marriage—possibly as Giacomo Padoani treated patients in the area of Padua where both families had residences—but it became a social step up for Antonia to become a Venetian noblewoman. She must have felt quite proud.

Giacomo Padoani organized a marriage dowry of 3,000 ducats worth of cash and goods, plus two years of housing with the Padoanis in Salizzada San Pantalon (Fontijn 27). "And for the love that the said Nobleman Lorenzo Bembo holds for the aforementioned illustrious Signora his wife," stated the wedding contract, "to the above [goods] he liberally adds to the dowry from his own goods as a counterdowry, or wedding gift . . . 3,000 ducats" (qtd. in Fontijn 28). At a time when someone with an annual income of 5,000 to 10,000 ducats was considered wealthy, Antonia and Lorenzo began their married life with a comfortable nest egg (Manetti 27). They married at the grand Church of the Redentore on Giudecca on August 20, 1659. Antonia's wedding outfit alone cost 300 ducats, (Fontijn 29) and she must have looked resplendent on the high steps of the Redentore, her dress flashing in the sunlight with pearls, jewels, and gold or silver thread. Her wedding day would have fulfilled any girl's fantasies. At the wedding party, the bride would have opened the dancing with a minuet, and the chamber orchestra would have continued playing into the wee hours. But all this splendor and wealth never hinted at the calamities to come.

Initially, documents such as letters between Antonia's father and the Mantuan court mentioned "the girl who sings" and praised her talents. But later notarized documents complain of strife within the family. Within about six months of Antonia's marriage to Lorenzo and their residence with her parents, relations turned sour. At his wit's end, Giacomo Padoani wrote, "The improper ways in which you, Nobleman Lorenzo Bembo, . . . continually disturb my peace of mind and the tranquility of my house, necessitates me to resolve . . . that I cannot keep you any longer in my . . . house" (qtd. in Fontijn 30). The tone of this letter seems to be through clenched teeth as Giacomo attempts to courteously eject the newlyweds. Though she must have felt bewildered by the rapid turn of events, Antonia took the side of her husband, who denied any wrongdoing and who actually tried to claim money as restitution for the housing he would no longer receive. Furthermore, "Due to the little respect and lack of kindness that both have shown me and my wife," Giacomo wrote in another note, he threatened to leave the couple with nothing except for two religious paintings of the Redentore and San Antonio of Padua (31). Antonia stayed faithful to her new husband.

Antonia and Lorenzo had their first baby, a girl they named Diana, early in the 1660s. She was born at Giacomo Padoani's other residence in Padua, indicating that the father-daughter relationship had been somewhat repaired. In February 1665, Antonia gave birth to a son, Andrea, born at the Padoani home on the Borgo dei Vignali in Padua. Records tell of Antonia's mother, the midwife, a neighbor, and two maids assisting at the birth, shuttling back and forth with hot water and clean cloths. Antonia sipped at a broth given to new mothers to sustain them after the fatigue of childbirth (Manetti 38). Then in November 1666 baby Giacomo was born, just months after his namesake grandfather's death in May of that year. After her father's death, the couple's relations with Antonia's mother Diana deteriorated again, and the couple took housing near Ponte Corvo in Padua (39). Giacomo Padoani's troubles with his son-in-law were at an end, but that didn't mean that Antonia was free from Lorenzo's covetousness, promiscuity, and financial idiocy. With young babies to care for, she needed her husband's support and must have felt dejected to instead suffer through the adversity he brought into their lives.

Lorenzo was not home long with his babies. When the war with the Turks at Candia (Crete) broke out, Lorenzo left to fight in it, taking a position on a battleship. Thankfully, Antonia retained power of attorney over their finances in his absence. Lorenzo was terribly wounded, nearly losing his leg and his life. But he recovered and soon took a job posting near Crema. Antonia tried to collect rents on some of Lorenzo's Bembo family properties, but with three small children to raise on her own, she just didn't have the means to get by. She eventually ran out of patience and stamina. In the autumn of 1672, Antonia filed for divorce on the grounds "that the aforementioned nobleman had been away from his said wife for five years, and for most of that time has left her without money for food, with three children to support" (qtd. in Fontijn 37). In this document, Antonia further accuses Lorenzo of having had sex with other women in their household and also while he was in the army, and he "treated the noblewoman Antonia his wife badly many times, having f***ed her even more than once while she was pregnant" (37). Though a legal document, it employed the vulgar term *"fotendola."* Lorenzo appended denials to this document, but it presaged his lifelong behavior of money mismanagement that became outright theft of other's goods, as he "took the household belongings of said noblewoman—such as food, clothes, and jewels—in order to spend them for his own enjoyment" (37). The couple separated, with Antonia moving to a house in the Santa Fosca neighborhood. Biographer Annarosa Manetti contends that Lorenzo's recent heroics at the war tipped the scales in his favor, and coupled with a lack of hard evidence, Antonia's request for divorce was ultimately denied (44). The couple never shared a roof again, and Antonia's belongings were not returned to her. She probably felt a measure of relief, though life was far from easy.

Antonia's two sons grew into adults and found their own work and marriages. But in order to protect her daughter Diana, Antonia placed her in a convent, first one on Murano and then one in Malamocco. Antonia left many of her remaining jewels and linens there in the hands of the nuns, ostensibly as payment for Diana's upkeep, but also to keep these goods out of Lorenzo's grasp. Antonia later wrote to Abbess Campana requesting that "you absolutely must not allow my belongings to leave your safekeeping until I give you new instructions" (qtd. in Fontijn 45). One can hear the fear in this request, fear of losing her patrimony. The long list of items includes numerous earrings, bracelets, chains, and medals made of gold or silver, inlaid with emeralds, pearls, and diamonds. One pendant of rubies and a pearl was valued at 240 ducats alone, a small fortune. Some particularly Venetian items are listed as well: a *goletta* or ruffled lace collar encrusted with pearls and emeralds; *capete*, which are gold nuggets shaped like conch shells; and a *pistoletta*, a sort of gilded silver knife (Fontijn 48-9). These represented the Padoani family jewels—really, their remaining wealth and all Antonia had to subsist on. Apparently Lorenzo had tried to get his hands on them, or Antonia would not have had to resort to such lengths to protect her valuables.

It is providential that Antonia took this precaution. Lorenzo eventually took a job as a customs official at the Fontego dei Tedeschi, where in September 1690 he was accused of "[taking] large sums of money several times from particular clients . . . keeping the receipts instead of putting them in the public cash box," and "thereby using public money as his own and wreaking havoc with the treasury itself" (qtd. in Fontijn 68). Lorenzo was arrested and imprisoned in the cells adjoining the Palazzo Ducale, moved between cells, sometimes to solitary confinement and sometimes in those that let in more light. Antonia's former pride must have turned to mortification. It was here where Lorenzo died thirteen years later.

Long before then, however, Antonia had decided to take care of herself and had escaped Lorenzo's grip.

It's not clear how or exactly when or with whom, but somehow Antonia got herself to Paris. Biographer Claire Fontijn has gathered evidence that Antonia may have fled Venice during the long Carnevale or opera season in order to wear a mask to avoid detection, probably in December 1676 (41). Bandits and ex-soldiers marauded along treacherous roads, and a woman could not have safely traveled alone. Antonia's most likely escort was Francesco Corbetta, a renowned guitarist whom Antonia knew in Venice and who had connections in the City of Light (40). He had traveled there before and knew members of the Comèdie Italienne.

Francesco Corbetta almost single-handedly popularized the guitar in Europe. A certain Count Grammont in his memoirs wrote, "he had a genius for music, and he was the only man who could make anything of the guitar: his style of play was so full of grace and tenderness, that he would have given harmony to the most discordant instruments" (qtd. in Fontijn 55). Most likely Francesco introduced Antonia at the court of King Louis XIV where he was also a performer.

Perhaps Antonia sang before the king, though no record of this has surfaced. It is clear that she so impressed King Louis that in 1682 he granted her *lettres patentes*, an official order, that provided her a monetary pension and housing (Fontijn 57). The Sun King was known to lavishly maintain artists who struck his fancy (Manetti 51). In fact, in the dedication to her first work, Antonia acknowledged "learning that I had been abandoned by the person who took me away from Venice, Your Majesty was so kind as to reward me with a pension" (qtd. in Fontijn 3). Antonia's original escort had apparently deserted her, but by good fortune she had found a savior. Because no records indicate that Antonia lived a public life of performing or attending court functions, Fontijn believes that Antonia's presence was being kept secret to protect her. Lorenzo was still alive at this point, and the couple was still legally married, so it was safer if no one knew where Antonia was (Fontijn, interview). Though Antonia must have begun writing music earlier in her life, it was after this time that she had the patronage, security, and means to devote herself to composing. She could begin to breathe freely again.

Records confirm that Antonia took up residence first at the Petite Union Chrètienne in the neighborhood of Notre Dame de Bonne Nouvelle. The Petite Union was a housing complex for laywomen, under the jurisdiction of the Church of Notre Dame de Bonne Nouvelle. Between ten and forty women resided at the Petite Union, living a quiet life that followed the monastic hours but that also included music, singing, and drawing. The older residents or outside teachers taught younger women on the harpsichord or ran their voices through the scales as part of their singing lessons (Manetti 68). Antonia would have dressed modestly, minus her gorgeous jewelry, as it was prohibited at religious services. After her life as a Venetian nobleman's wife, this new lifestyle must have felt spare indeed, but perhaps that was more welcome than living in fear.

In Paris, Antonia first associated with the Italian expatriate or theater and music community there, to which Francesco Corbetta could easily have introduced her. From Paris, Antonia corresponded with two different nuns at her daughter Diana's convent back in Venice, in order to pay for Diana's upkeep and because the convent was holding Antonia's jewels in safekeeping; her handwriting on these 1682 documents shows pointed lettering and an enlarged "A" for Antonia. Sister Maria Giordana

Gozzi of the San Bernardo convent on Murano became an important ally for Antonia back in Venice after her mother had passed away, and later when she lived in Paris.

Conveying her gratitude, Antonia was not about to forget the favor granted by the illustrious Sun King. She wrote that his name had been "instilled in my heart since childhood," (qtd. in Fontijn 3) and she went on to dedicate multiple works to him. In the collection of forty-one pieces of chamber music, known as *Produzioni armoniche* (*Harmonic Productions*), the opening song praises King Louis, saying that "the world has not enough glory to bestow on you; heaven has not enough stars to crown you" (95). King Louis XIV wore bright colors, ribbons and laces, fabrics embroidered with gold thread, and his court was peopled by his followers in swirling dresses, heeled shoes, and elaborate ruffles, all multiplied by the best Venetian mirrors, a monarch worthy of honor and praise. Antonia's musical homage came at the height of his acclaim.

Antonia also composed two *Te Deum* settings, a hymn expressing thanksgiving to God for the royal family. It's unclear who wrote the poems for the *Produzioni armoniche*; three were by Aurelia Fedeli, an Italian actress and poet resident in Paris, while others are unsigned. Some may have been penned by Marc'Antonio Romagnesi, one of Antonia's acquaintances in the Comèdie Italienne and Aurelia Fedeli's son (103). Most pieces in *Produzioni armoniche* are in Italian, though a few are either French or Latin. What is clear is that Antonia could write a broad range of secular and sacred music, mostly prepared for a soprano voice like hers, accompanied by basso continuo, the harmonies and bass line usually played on harpsichord or deeper-ranged stringed instruments such as bass or violoncello. The high, clear female voice builds and falls, lilting then thrusting through dynamic changes—high to low, soft to strident, quiet to forceful. Though women of this era were expected to be silent and passive, Antonia overcame these strictures to create expressive melodies. She also gave voice to female characters within her composition; for example, two cantatas in this collection are sung in the Virgin Mary's voice, a highly unusual perspective to take (109). The voice cycles through grief and anger, seeming to rail against injustice one moment and then request pity in the next. The viewpoint places a woman at the forefront and allows her emotions to be revealed and expressed. From somewhere Antonia had found her voice again after the years of married strife, and she now wrote pieces that empowered women characters with strong voices and presences.

Antonia continued to compose, next writing a full-length *Te Deum* for three voices and accompaniment to honor Marie-Adélaïde of Savoy, the Duchess of Burgundy, when she gave birth in 1704 to a son, the first Duke of Brittany. To accompany the *Te Deum*, Antonia composed a five-voice

*Divertimento*. Antonia wrote in the dedication to the book containing these works, "All of this [is intended] as an unquestionable token of the humble zeal with which I present my profound respect, and with which I entrust myself to the lofty patronage of your Royal Highness and of all the royal family" (qtd. in Fontijn 134). The music is often joyful and exuberant, and it shows a complexity that would require skillful musicians to play it (Fontijn 154). The composer of such pieces would have to be adept at such instrumentation herself. At the outset of the *Divertimento*, the singers proclaim,

> Let the sweet sound
> of the musical lyre
> resound through the air
> let the palms be interwoven,
> let the trophies be raised,
> and with festive voice
> let France and Spain proclaim:
> "long live the child, Duke of Brittany,
> the bright splendor of both kingdoms!" (qtd. in Fontijn 151)

In this and other sections, the song emphasizes how Duchess Marie-Adélaïde is a peacemaker, her marriage and her child as agents that can bring together quarreling factions and end strife in her region. It's unknown who wrote this libretto, and it may have been Antonia herself, but in any case she chose texts that underscore a woman's body as potent and generative, and her role as valuable, traits not found often in the music of that day (Fontijn 178).

Moving into a new sphere of composition, in 1707 Antonia wrote and arranged the music for the opera *L'Ercole Amante*, or *Hercules as Lover*. This opera libretto was written by Abbé Francesco Buti and had previously been set to music by Francesco Cavalli, Antonia's early teacher. Fontijn tells that "Bembo's opera presents a hybrid not only for the bridging of musical tastes but also of styles spanning two centuries" (248). The choice of text sets Hercules's story in comparison to King Louis, who is shown to be like a demi-god come to earth, a hero who brings peace to his land. Text and music combine to create scenes of thunderstorms and later of whispering brooks, and pauses make silence sometimes as powerful as the music itself, such as the scene when love has ended (252). The opera spans a huge range of emotional landscapes, from outrage to tenderness to delight. The vocal parts reveal a complexity that probably mirrored Antonia's singing skills, with high trills, full ranges, and waterfalls of notes. Antonia, as a woman composer who had to overcome the injunction that women be silent, employed the power of silence within her musical compositions at times for reflection or to create a more powerful juxtaposition (252). Nevertheless, the opera score also shows some problems in execution. It is the only large-scale orchestral piece that Antonia composed, and some of the instrumentation doesn't work together smoothly. But it is important to remember that women at this time had no opportunities to ever work with a large orchestra, only with smaller chamber groups, so Antonia simply had no practice in this genre (Fontijn, interview).

In 1708, Antonia returned to dedicating her work to King Louis XIV. She wrote that "[she] who gives as much as [she] can, gives what [she] owes," (qtd. in Fontijn 181) referring to her desire to honor this king who had so honored and supported her. Again, she penned a laudatory *Te Deum* and added an *Exaudiat,* taken from the Bible, as she "[made] so bold as to dedicate the third product of [her] weak efforts to your sacred Majesty" (181). These texts are in Latin, a language that Antonia had studied and that was shared by both Italian and French cultures, showing that Antonia was bridging the gap between her first and second homes. Antonia's works as a whole showed her multilingual and bicultural abilities, as she used texts in multiple languages and employed musical traits that were sometimes Italian in style, sometimes French, easily moving between the two. No proof remains to show where Antonia heard musical concerts or where her own music was performed, but by studying her compositional style, analysts can deduce that she probably heard the contemporary music performed at the royal courts in Paris, or local churches, and in royal residences in nearby hamlets. Though Antonia continued to live at the semi-cloistered Petite Union Chrètienne, she likely was invited to hear music in other locales (Fontijn 194). This type of chamber music was intended for more intimate gatherings in smaller chambers rather than vast halls, the chairs set for an audience to view the musicians at their stringed instruments and keyboards. Though Antonia lived in a simple habitation, music filled her thoughts and her time.

Antonia also knew what was fashionable in the musical world around her, such as setting psalms to music. As her final work, published in 1710, Antonia composed music to accompany Biblical psalms, titled *Les sept Pseaumes de David*, set to a translation by another woman, Élisabeth-Sophie Chéron, a painter, poet, and musician herself. Also dedicating this piece to King Louis, Antonia wrote that "I have spent more than half of my life, Sire, praying God that he may unceasingly give glory and happiness to your Majesty . . . and use what is left of my time to work in music, having in mind in all of the airs that I compose, to produce some that could be felicitous enough to have the glory to please your Majesty" (qtd. in Fontijn 213-14). These musical compositions seem to have more French components to them, such as use of a minor-key trio, and Fontijn points out that this work "represent[s] a major contribution to the French tradition of *cantiques spirituels* in the twilight years of Louis XIV's reign" (239). Soprano and baritone voices sometimes converge and sometimes follow each other, echoing phrases and producing harmonies. Bound in red Moroccan leather with the King's stamp embossed on the cover, this manuscript was kept in the King's own library. From celebratory to spiritual music, Antonia composed in a range of styles, uniting voices with violin, viola da gamba, harpsichord, theorbo, organ, and more.

Antonia Padoani Bembo lived another decade after her last composition, dying in Paris around 1720. Her father had been the first to feed her soul, and King Louis XIV provided this nourishment in her later decades with his patronage. Because she had a secure pension, Antonia enjoyed the freedom to compose music without having to worry about procuring individual commissions or earning an income. And she spent many productive years free from fears of her husband's treachery. So many Venetian women became silent when they had to perform the duties of wife and mother. Sadly, it took Antonia's choice to flee Venice to escape her cruel husband's neglect and avarice so she could find her voice, albeit so far from home and her children. Throughout her life, Antonia signed her name "Antonia Bembo, Noble Venetian." Though her musical productions now live in the Bibliothèque nationale de France, she never shed this aspect of her identity, and she retained her connection to the city of her birth.

Palazzo Balbi

# Elena Cornaro Piscopia

## Without Precedent

$H$undreds of leather-bound tomes lined the walls, many of them embellished with tooled red or brown leather. A ladder leaned against the shelves to provide access to the higher sections. Wan and watery light seeped in through the windows made of circular glass set into metal frames. Professor Carlo Rinaldini from the University of Padua had arrived to peruse the comprehensive and brimming Cornaro library. As he leafed through a math book by Archimedes that was reverently displayed on a large wooden stand, he saw a girl standing before him. She was dressed simply in a white tunic and flat slippers, her blond hair in braids. "Suddenly there appeared a very young girl, quite beautiful, her head majestic, her features well-proportioned, with delicate coloring and very dignified in manner," he later recounted. "She began to explain [Archimedes'] theorem. I was dumbfounded and lost my words" (qtd. in Guernsey 52). Carlo Rinaldini had just met Elena Cornaro Piscopia, the girl who would become the first woman in the world to earn a university degree.

This child reveled in learning, devouring languages, philosophy, math, sciences, and literature. She hoped to bring pride to her noble family with her hours of study and proof of her learning. But by the time she was in her thirties, these toils had taken their toll. "With the joy of my studies, the salubrity of the air, and the diligent care of the physicians, I feel much stronger; therefore, I hope that in the future I may resume my studies and thus rescue the name of our House from extinction and oblivion" (qtd. in Guernsey 169). Elena Lucrezia Cornaro Piscopia revealed her contradictory desires in this 1680 letter to her father, just four years before she died. A linguist, mathematician, philosopher, musician, composer, lecturer, jurist, and more, she began her unprecedented education at age seven, eventually surpassing most of her male contemporaries. She created a new role for women and set a precedent for their learning. But at what cost?

Born June 5, 1646, at the Cornaro Piscopia Palace, now referred to as the Palazzo Loredan Corner, Elena had nearly every advantage that a patrician family could offer. The four-story palace, near the Ponte di Rialto and Venice's crossroads, is an imposing structure that seems to stretch itself into a taller stance. The second floor balcony looks out to the Grand Canal's commerce and society, while an inner courtyard gave the family privacy and grandeur. Their *palazzo* housed probably the best private library in Venice, with rare Greek and Latin texts, books on math, astronomy, and philosophy, plus globes, maps, and astronomical instruments. Elena came from a lineage that boasted four doges, three popes, nine cardinals, a Queen of Cyprus, and her father, Gianbattista Cornaro Piscopia, the current Procurator of San Marco, who oversaw the State treasury and library. That was a lot of weighty tradition for Elena's slim shoulders to carry.

Unfortunately, the Cornaro Piscopia wealth was tainted by some family scandal: former Doge Giovanni Cornaro's children attempted fraud and assassination to further their own careers, besmirching the family name. Gianbattista himself added another dark mark when he married Zanetta, his mistress and mother of his six children. Zanetta Boni had been a mere servant, and this marriage forever marred Gianbattista's aspirations to carry the family's prestigious Order of the Sword. Though he did attain the position as Procurator, Venice's most powerful official after the doge, it took him three tries and nearly 150,000 ducats, an unheard of sum. When he realized that his prodigy daughter might become the crane that would lift the Cornaros out of the mire, he left no opportunity untried, regardless of his daughter's desires. Even at a young age, Elena bought into this scenario and developed an acute sense of obligation to help.

Elena was a pious child. When she could yet barely walk or talk, she would toddle with her nurse Lorenza, known as Nonnina, to the rose-colored Church of San Luca near their home. Elena wouldn't have been moved by the gilded cornices but perhaps instead by the ceiling fresco where heaven's door opened and beckoned. Little Elena would mumble nonsense words pretending to pray with the congregants, with light streaming down from the dome skylights onto the cool gray marble below. When she was older and saw elaborate renovations being made to the family palace, she implored, "Father, Sir, wouldn't it be better to give this money to the poor and with the alms build ourselves a palace in heaven?" (qtd. in Guernsey 32). Childhood friends aren't mentioned in her biographies; instead, her closest friends appeared to be priests and nuns. Initially, her family enrolled her in a convent school, but they had chosen poorly, merely pulling a name from an urn, and then discovered that Elena was surrounded not by pious religious but by more frivolous and irreverent noblewomen pushed into convent life. This was not for Elena, who, all her life, aspired to a truer calling and longed for the simplicity and chastity of the monastic life. As a matter of fact, at age eleven she went to her confessor Abbot Cornelius Codanini at San Giorgio Maggiore and secretly took orders to become a Benedictine oblate, one who is not a nun but who vows to live a life after San Benedetto's rule of chastity, scholarship, and charitable works. This was her greatest desire.

Yet it was at the Church of San Luca that Monsignor Giovanni Battista Fabris noticed her devoutness and then her intelligence. Being an Aristotelian scholar himself, he would test young Elena by having her memorize long Greek passages. The priest approached her father and convinced Gianbattista to educate Elena. Sitting for hours at the table in the Cornaro Piscopia palace, she began with languages, Greek and Latin at age seven, which she studied with Father Fabris, who soon added grammar, literature, and philosophy. A year later, native-speaking tutors arrived to teach Elena Spanish and French, which she lapped up like a kitten at her milk. A Jesuit was employed to begin her education in the sciences, and soon she was devouring Homer, Plato, Herodotus, Xenophon, Livy, Virgil, Horace, Caesar, Cicero, and her favorite, the Christian Scriptures. Elena's father brought her to the city's museums and noble families' galleries to educate her in the arts, each of them dressed in their best brocades and Murano laces as emissaries of family virtue.

Father Fabris passed away and was replaced as her prime educational advisor by the British Professor Alexander Anderson, who then taught her English, a very unusual language for someone in her time and place. Being a language prodigy, Elena next took up Hebrew and Aramaic so she might study ancient scriptures in their original, and then they tossed in Arabic to round things off. Music was not left out; Elena could masterfully play the harpsichord, violin, lute, and harp and sing in a lovely soprano, often improvising and embellishing as was the Baroque fashion of the day. At a May 1677 gathering at her family's *palazzo*, Elena entertained the gathering by singing in six languages, with "virtue, joy, and modesty" (qtd. in Labalme, *Women's Roles* 141). She also composed music, though none of these pieces have survived. This she accomplished by her mid-teens.

"I admire, undoubtedly as miraculous gifts from Heaven, the Glorious Talents of Your Very Illustrious Lady," Carlo Grossi penned in his dedication to Elena of a cantata, "*Sacre ariose cantata*" in 1663. She would have appreciated the sentiment that her intellectual gifts were from God. Though she reveled in her education and gladly spent countless hours in study, she wanted no personal praise or recognition for her accomplishments. Yet her father often invited family and later the wealthy and well-connected to their home to hear Elena sing, play, recite, or improvise long discourses on astronomy, geography, math, and the arts. She would stand on the terrazzo floor to perform in their luxurious salon, surrounded by hand-carved furniture and oil portraits with frescoed ceilings and stucco putti in each corner. Wishing to shrink from the limelight, she instead endured it to be her father's dutiful daughter, as she said, "to rescue the name of our house from extinction and oblivion" (qtd. in Guernsey 169).

However, to one of her father's requests Elena remained staunchly opposed. "I would rather elect being treated as a slave and be kept for all my life, like a dog to a chain, than to squander the treasure of my virginity," she declared when Gianbattista Cornaro Piscopia announced that he had chosen Elena's husband (9). He sprang this surprise on his daughter the night of Venice's elaborate 1665 Ascension Day festival, where Elena's erudition had been singularly honored in the processions and at the feast. When her father and Doge Contarini called forth her intended (whose name was not recorded but who biographer Jane Howard Guernsey believes was the doge's nephew, Naval Captain Marco Contarini), Elena instead replied, "Father, Sir, although I were asked by the greatest sovereign on earth, I will never consent to it" (27). She was obedient about nearly all aspects of her life, but not about this request.

Elena sent a note to the Church of San Giorgio Maggiore and her confessor there, Abbot Codanini, who came to see her the following morning. "Save me, Father," she pleaded. "Save me from a freedom that I have never demanded and that I do not wish to accept" (27). He was the one who had granted Elena her wish to be ordained as a Benedictine oblate of the Third Order, allowing her to always wear a monk's habit and scapular beneath her formal gowns. Fancy clothes were "the instruments of her martyrdom," wrote P. Massimiliano Deza in his biography (qtd. in Guernsey 162). Though Abbot Codanini reasoned with her that her family desired this match and that marriage was a holy sacrament, Elena was unmoved, replying, "I don't deny that, but virginity is more pleasing to God; and at the moment of death, the devil doesn't have the power over virgins that he has over everybody else" (28). Gianbattista, generally so arrogant and bossy, relented but began to fashion other schemes for his daughter's—and his family's—glory.

Gianbattista had somehow discovered Elena's secret vow of chastity, yet he apparently didn't know all her secrets. Or if he did, he chose to let her alone. "In other things I will always live a slave to your commands and will die if necessary a holocaust to my reverence for you," Elena told her father, and in this she hardly exaggerated (29). To atone for her accolades and to purify her spirit, Elena turned to the disciplines: flagellation, starvation, penance. She denied herself sleep as she would kneel in her private chapel all night, clothed in a hair shirt, her arms roped to her sides, until she collapsed on the cold stones. Whenever her parents weren't looking, she gave her meals to servants or had her food sent to street beggars. Martyred saints were her heroes. Her friend and correspondent Father Gian Paolo Oliva sent her holy relics, including the skull of Santa Faustina. But Elena had promised her father that she would obey his other commands, and she relentlessly kept on with her studies.

Rudolph Bell of Rutgers University later termed this disease "holy anorexia," what biographer Guernsey describes as the "desire to attain mastery over and suppress such bodily functions as hunger in the belief that this would empower the spirit" (71). These were nearly the only means of control that Elena had left over her own life. Present day research reveals that girls—for it is most often girls—who suffer from anorexia often feel worthless and come from families with an oppressive, authoritative father, much like in Elena's situation. Despite her acclaim and her father's approbation, Elena claimed she had "foul imperfections" (132). Though she was denied her request to live the cloistered life of a nun, she tried to make up for it by serving her own penance. For a number of years, she also escaped the family cage to do biannual retreats at the island convent of Santa Maria della Grazia. Abbess Maria Felice comforted and counseled Elena, saying she should "shine amidst the darkness of the world as a great beacon of evangelical perfection" (79). The pressures on Elena from all sides must have been excruciating.

As would be expected considering these self-imposed privations, Elena suffered numerous illnesses. In her twenties she contracted nephritis, an inflammation of the kidneys, often caused by malnutrition and infection. As much as Elena loved studying and learning, and as much as she revered her father, she also was happy to seek sanctuary. She retreated to the springs outside Padua to take the waters for a cure and there passed three kidney stones. At age twenty-five she suffered from several weeks of dysentery followed by "red fever," probably either scarlet or rheumatic fever (Guernsey 111). Often when Elena was overtaken by illness, her father sent her to their summer home, the Cornaro Odeon in Padua, where the climate was more favorable than damp Venice. Usually her mother Zanetta and companion Maddalena accompanied her with their servants. Elena's relative Luigi Cornaro had built the complex in 1524 to the designs of Giovanni Falconetto, with the Loggia and Odeon buildings meant for light entertainments. The original mansion is gone now, and all that remains are the theater arcade and the music rooms with their elaborate and colorfully painted walls featuring fantastical figures such as hairy-legged satyrs, turbaned swamis, and big-lipped purple sea serpents. These wildly embellished rooms were Elena's refuge during her convalescence. Elena was there to recuperate, not attend the entertainments, and she was probably consoled that the Basilica di Sant'Antonio was so close at hand, containing the body of such a powerful saint.

Elena continued with her studies despite her illnesses. After rising early and attending mass, she spent the morning hours in prayer and the afternoon in rigorous study. Somehow she made time to visit Venice's *scuole* or hospices in order to feed abandoned babies and read to the elderly. When reprimanded that a noblewoman like her shouldn't wait on her own servants, Elena replied, "Who am I more than you, dear sisters?" (qtd. in Guernsey 126). To her academic load was added rhetoric, physics, dialectics, linguistics, and logic, all taught by the best tutors to be found. In 1668 Carlo Rinaldini published a book outlining problems in geometry meant for Elena; he called her Minerva, *Dea del Sapere*, or Goddess of Knowledge. She joined numerous scholarly academies, de rigueur for the times, becoming president of the Accademia dei Pacifici (The Peaceful) in 1670, where she was given the nickname The Unalterable.

Besides presenting and discussing at such events, Elena also spoke publicly about political and social problems plaguing Venice. More than other contemporary women, Elena began to use her voice. Her patrician parents expected her to keep a public presence, at least standing at her *palazzo* balcony when Carnevale processions passed, though Elena considered these spectacles as but "nothing-things" (108). When Elena entreated her family and confessor Carlo Boselli that she be allowed to join the convent of the Vergini di Castiglione near Brescia, Boselli reminded her how it would hurt her parents. But when other suitors came to ask for her hand, including a German Prince, Elena remained resolute in her refusals. And then when her parents insisted on having her portrait painted, Elena claimed, "Saints should have their features handed down to future generations and not sinners like myself" (133). She was The Unalterable. Her faith never wavered.

In 1672 Elena began living exclusively in Padua because by this time Carlo Rinaldini had convinced Elena's father Gianbattista that she should earn a university degree for her erudition. In his quest for family glory, Gianbattista wholeheartedly endorsed the idea. Though the education he had been providing for his daughter was unprecedented, "Being a Cornaro shielded him" from harmful criticism, and "having a fortune clearly helped" (Guernsey 50). The University of Padua was the second oldest in Europe, after Bologna, and it only awarded a doctorate degree at that time. To obtain this, Elena would need to master the seven classic fields of grammar, rhetoric, dialectic, arithmetic, geometry, music, and astronomy, all in the classic languages. She would also need to display advanced knowledge of philosophy and theology, this last being her favorite subject. For six years she focused on this goal, as her health allowed, though she apparently didn't attend any actual classes at the university. Women weren't allowed. Yet most scholars who knew her agreed that she was more learned than virtually all her male contemporaries.

Gianbattista Cornaro and Carlo Rinaldini petitioned the university to grant Elena the opportunity for a doctorate in theology. The hour-long examination would require her to answer numerous unrehearsed questions from the university's masters, which she would respond to in Latin without reference materials. Nevertheless, things were not so simple. When the Bishop of Padua, Gregorio Cardinal Barbarigo, heard the request, he fumed, "What? Never! Woman is made for motherhood, not for learning" (qtd. in Guernsey 130). Church authorities in Rome decreed that a woman must not be allowed a doctorate in theology because it would entitle her to teach, and, as Barbarigo claimed, women had little theological background and might misinterpret the texts. (Clearly, he didn't know with whom he was dealing.) Elena, shrinking from the recognition this degree would afford, claimed, "I cannot do this because, after all, I am only a maiden" (141). Despite her vast learning, she lacked solid self-confidence. Gianbattista and Carlo persisted, however, and eventually the Bishop relented. "If the Procurator of San Marco insists," he said, "I am willing to modify the point and let his daughter become a Doctor in Philosophy" (130). He compromised as long as Elena would take the philosophy degree rather than theology, which she agreed to, albeit with disappointment.

The ceremony was set for June 13, 1678, but Elena objected since it would take away from the feast day celebration of Padua's renowned Sant'Antonio. Instead they pushed back to June 25, soon realizing that the university meeting hall they had planned to use would be too small to hold the expected crowds. On that hot morning, Elena nearly fainted. She retreated to a cool stone side chapel and spent an hour in prayer, reviving her spirits and her energy. Soon Elena entered the vast, airy, white space of the Basilica of the Blessed Virgin, also known as the Duomo, and stood before the multitudes to be questioned by the professors. Paduans, proud and curious, packed the room. Elena so awed her examiners with her fluent responses that they decided to forego the usual secret ballot process and instead declare her a Master by unanimous acclaim, an unprecedented move. Elena's shoulders were then draped in an ermine stole called a *mozzetta*; she was crowned with laurels and given a heavy gold ring and philosophy book. (This scene is recreated in a glorious stained glass window in the Thompson Memorial Library of Vassar College in the United States.) Padua, Venice, and surrounding cities all celebrated her remarkable achievement. Her father was suitably proud. Did her modesty and humility allow her to feel proud of herself as well?

After this event, Gianbattista continued to bring dignitaries, scholars, and foreigners to his daughter so she could display her great abilities to them. She also began giving mathematics lectures at the University of Padua and settling disputes as a jurist. While bedridden with illness, Elena heard witnesses and lawyers on a case between a wealthy man and a poorer one. When she ultimately awarded the suit in favor of the less prosperous man, she replied, "It is not a question of comparing people with people but reason with reason and right with right," a decision lauded by all (174). Too sick to attend to those in the hospices herself, Elena had food and clothing sent to them in her stead. Then when an elderly family servant named Angela Codevia contracted smallpox, Elena was the only person who would tend to her. "We are bound to help our neighbors as ourselves," she said (127). Certainly Elena's learning was important to her, but so too was her compassion for others.

Doctors then discovered an enormous tumor between Elena's shoulder blades. Enveloped in linens in her soft bed, Elena had a vision that the Virgin Mary visited her. Though she asked to be allowed to die "in humility" in straw on the floor, Elena, at her mother's insistence, died in bed on July 26, 1684 (178). People in the streets cried out, "The saint is dead!" and Venice's shops closed. Her simple coffin was fashioned from the cypress tree that had been planted in Padua to celebrate her birth thirty-eight years earlier. Controversy ensued about where to lay her to rest, but her own wish was actually honored. Elena was buried in the Chapel of San Luca in the Church of Santa Giustina, Padua, formerly the burial site of San Luca himself but now a place where her Benedictine brothers were laid to rest. In 1978, to honor the tercentenary of her degree, this chapel was renamed the Cappella Cornaro in her honor. It's tucked downstairs at the right side of the church, a simple room, just as Elena would have wanted.

"I shall lead a short life, Blessed be God," Elena had said during one illness (176). She didn't fear death. Before her passing, she had requested that bequests be given to those who had served her and that her writings, and also her devices for penance, be destroyed. Normally faithful, her companion Maddalena instead displayed the hair shirt and chains so others would know how Elena had suffered. Gianbattista and others at the university collected and published what writings they could find—a few letters, three elegies, an *Ode al Crocifisso*, and Elena's translation from Spanish of Lanspergio's *Colloquy of Christ*. Quite possibly the quotes attributed to her, culled from various biographies by P. Massimiliano Deza, Benedetto Bacchini, Mathilde Pynsent, Nicola Fusco, Francesco Maschietto, and Jane Howard Guernsey may be apocryphal, yet they are the only indication of what she may have felt in her core.

Venice, Padua, and even much of Europe mourned the passing of this scholar, "*Unico Exemplo*" or "Without Precedent" as the 1686 statue by Bernardo Tabacco declares her to be (207). Gianbattista Cornaro, wanting his daughter to remain the only such honored woman, helped to oppose a petition from Carla Gabriella Patin, who later applied for the doctorate exam and was refused. Over fifty years later, Maria Caterina Laura Bassi was allowed to earn her Doctorate in Philosophy in 1732 in Bologna, with the first American woman to earn a degree, Helen Magill in

1877 at Boston University, not coming until 200 years after Elena.

But then Elena passed into obscurity for decades. Some remembered and revived her name, organizing an international tercentenary celebration, with forums, speeches, and dedications. Her statue was placed in the University of Padua's famed Palazzo Bo, its walls and ceiling cluttered by medallions and plaques naming the illustrious professors. Organizers had minted a replica of the 1685 medallion cast in Elena's honor, showing her in profile, crowned in the laurel wreath and draped in her ermine stole, with the motto "*Non sine Foenore*," "Not Without Reward." Elena Cornaro Piscopia's commendations and rewards were great, yet they certainly were not without cost.

Elena Cornaro Piscopia

# Rosalba Carriera

## An Abundance

"*When* I was sightless I cared for nothing, now I want to see everything," wrote Rosalba Carriera, one of Europe's most influential artists during the seventeenth century Rococo movement (qtd. in Blashfield 487). An artist must suffer a particular degree of torture when she loses ocher and umber, indigo, vermillion, and emerald, the glittering diamonds of light on Venetian canals, or the towering, blushing clouds in a cerulean sky. In her seventies, Rosalba still had the energy and vigor to draw with pastels, but she was tragically and rapidly losing her sight. As this quote implies, she had gone blind but had some sight restored briefly only to lose it again completely.

Rosalba was born on the island of Chioggia just to the south of Venice's archipelago. Her family home faced the Church of San Francesco delle Muneghette on the Corso del Popolo and Calle Rosalba Carriera (Lorenzetti 852). Coincidentally, this was later the home of playwright Carlo Goldoni, and a plaque commemorates both of them. Many sources list Rosalba's birthdate as October 7, 1675, though historian Neil Jeffares asserts that she was actually born in 1673. Rosalba had a sister born in 1675 who was given the same name as her but was called Giovanna; many scholars confuse the two, further confusing the birth dates as well. A third sister, Angela, followed in 1677.

Preparing her daughter for self-sufficiency, Rosalba's mother Alba Foresti trained Rosalba in the art of Burano lace pattern making, which was how she contributed money to the household as she grew up. However, the industry declined in this period, so Rosalba began looking for alternative sources of income. Sources barely mention her father Andrea's presence in her life, except that he was a clerk, and certainly Rosalba's mother must have worried over the futures of her three daughters, not only their daily sustenance but also their later wedding dowries. Rosalba's father did apparently care deeply for the family, though, as demonstrated in a 1701 letter. When he was away from home and learned that Giovanna was ill, he wrote, "I vow to do penance for my mortal sins in order to effect Giovanna's recovery from her serious illness . . . . Don't fail to send me weekly bulletins of her condition, including her diet" (Carriera, letter #301). Family was of greatest importance to Rosalba, and she remained close to them her whole life.

Rosalba had begun her art training by learning drawing at age fourteen, apparently with Giuseppe Diamentini because she copied some of his paintings, a typical method for an apprentice to learn the basics. Evidence also points to Antonio Balestra as another teacher whose work Rosalba copied, and her other teachers may have included Antonio Lazzari and Federico Bencovich (Jeffares 1). Besides painting portraits, much of her early work was allegorical, such as a portrait of a woman named *America* or her vastly popular set of the four seasons, which fetched 240 *zecchini*, a handsome price. These symbolic, often voluptuous subjects infused women with characteristics greater than a single self. For instance, the mythical character Flora usually tucked flowers in her hair, diagonally draping fabric to reveal one luscious breast. This was not merely a woman adorned with daisies but one that represented an abundance, a source of fertility. These allegorical images showed up continuously throughout Rosalba's career. Rosalba infused many of her characters with joy that emanated from within, one she must have felt in order to replicate it in vibrant color.

Apparently her caring father supported Rosalba's budding career as an artist. His friend, the canon Felice Ramelli, is believed to have taught her to paint miniatures (Blashfield 393). Popular at this time were snuffboxes, not merely to hold a gentleman's snuff, but as an object d'arte wherein he would keep a miniature portrait, often of his lover. Giacomo Casanova's memoirs, for example, reveal that he collected snuffboxes as part of his wealth and to remember his different paramours. Typically, the portraits were painted on vellum on the box's inside cover; yet Rosalba improved upon this practice by using tempera paint on ivory for sharper, longer-lasting images. Rosalba painted a miniature of Jesus for her friend Sister Beatrice Daria, who wrote in 1731, "It is so beautiful that it seems alive and looks as though it were in Paradise" (qtd. in Blashfield 473). Devout herself, Rosalba was able to depict religious fervor in her subjects, too. Many artists then followed Rosalba's miniature techniques. Besides snuffboxes, Rosalba also painted miniatures on lockets, brooches, bracelets, and even hairpins.

By 1700, though, Rosalba found a new medium: pastels. She began composing full-sized portraits, the standard pose being bust-length, with the subject's body turned slightly away but the face turned towards the viewer. Besides painting allegorical figures, Rosalba began taking numerous commissions for portraits. Her fame steadily increased. As the eighteenth century blossomed in Venice, society's tenor became increasingly light and frivolous. This was the era of pale blue skies, pink cheeks, white dresses, and yellow bonnets. Frothy dresses, lace trims, fabrics seemingly lighter than air barely concealed bosoms and flirtatious smiles. The Rococo was born, and many art historians credit Rosalba Carriera with playing a major role in its aesthetics (*Encyclopedia Britannica*).

Rosalba's soft pastels, rather than the heavy chiaroscuro oil paints of her predecessors, became the fashion of the day. Pastels allowed Rosalba to work quickly and to keep costs down, which made her work that much more accessible. Rosalba first sketched in the outline so her subject could take a break, to relax and chat with friends, returning later so Rosalba could finalize the portrait. Biographer Evangeline Blashfield maintains that Rosalba's soft and light touch caused her to excel at painting women and children (402). In fact, oil painters began to adopt lighter tones after the popularity of pastels. Rosalba was especially skilled at capturing textures in fabrics: lace, braids, fur, jewels, and even her subjects' hair and skin. One technique she employed was to drag the flat side of the pastel crayon over another color to create a texture, which resulted in more of a "sense" of fabric than an accurate and realistic depiction. Jeffares contends that "Colour and texture outweigh the deficiencies of drawing and characterization of which she was guilty" (1).

In her day no one seemed to be accusing Rosalba of having any deficiencies. Commissions poured in. By 1705, Rosalba was inducted as a member of Florence's academy and then into the Accademia di San Luca in Rome as an *"accademico di merito."* In 1706, the court members in Dusseldorf invited her to come and paint them. By 1708, nobles flocked to her Venice studio for sittings. In 1713 she painted King Augustus III of Poland, who went on to collect over 150 of her pastels, the greatest collection of her work. In 1719, the "Father of Rococo," painter Antoine Watteau, even requested a portrait. In 1720, her fame had grown such that she was named an honorary member of the painting academies in both Bologna and Paris. She sometimes turned down commissions due to lack of time. Her brief diary notes from 1721 remark, "Declined to execute two portraits for Messers Roland. Declined portrait order for Mr. Prussan" (Carriera). Her life was productive and busy and satisfying. Modest and unassuming, Rosalba did what she did best—capture people's likenesses.

In 1704 Rosalba's sister Angela married the painter Giovanni Pellegrini, and he later received a commission from the famous investor John Law to paint the hall of Paris' Royal Bank. The millionaire patron Pierre Crozat, a great admirer of Rosalba's work, convinced the rest of the family to come along to Paris and make their home in his mansion. Rosalba's longtime friend Antonio Maria Zanetti escorted them on their journey and helped with so many details, his presence indispensable since Rosalba's father had passed away the previous year. For eighteen months from 1720 to 1721, Rosalba enjoyed a desire and a demand for her work.

Aristocrats commissioned thirty-six portraits, including a request to paint King Louis XV as a child. After Rosalba had departed Paris, Pierre Crozat wrote to her on August 11, 1721, about the eleven-year-old king's dire fever. "If you had decided to remain in Paris, your presence here would not have passed unnoticed," he noted, "as many people are aware of your strong affections for our young Monarch" (Carriera 57). Pierre so admired Rosalba and desired her company, and this letter shows that others did, too.

The family returned to Venice, but not for long. In 1723 they lived in the court of Modena so Rosalba could paint the trio of young princesses to help procure them husbands. Apparently court life was dull and full of tiresome gossip. Rosalba wrote her thinly disguised sarcasm to sister Angela, "Blessed be a thousand times these princesses and their father, who think of nothing but pleasing me, and therefore are letting us go home, sooner than they wish" (qtd. in Blashfield 455). Though she was well-cared for and adored, Rosalba was ready to leave. In 1730 she journeyed to Vienna to paint for Charles VI, the Holy Roman Emperor, and to take on his wife as a pupil (one of the only pupils Rosalba ever taught). She also completed the opera librettist Pietro Metastasio's portrait while there.

Rosalba's fame and influence spread across Europe like silver threads embellishing the palaces and courts. Rather remarkable for a female painter of this time (and rather remarkable to even be a female painter at this time), she had a wide-reaching influence on many of her male counterparts. Those who followed her lead made an international list: Maurice-Quentin De la Tour, Jean-Etienne Liotard, Perroneau, Rafael Mengs, and John Russell. Rosalba kept a close friendship with the painter Antoine Watteau. At his untimely death in 1721, his friend made engravings of his works and sent them to Rosalba Carriera; she returned her thanks, writing, "As I have always included myself among the group of admirers of this singular genius, I was proud to be the recipient of this book" (Carriera, letter #21). Also swayed by her technique were the French painters Adelaide Labille-Guiard and Elisabeth Louise Vigee-LeBrun, as well as later Venetian pastelists Marianna Carlevarijs, Margherita Terzi, Felicita and Angioletta Sartori, and Antoinette Legru.

Rosalba's sister Giovanna, known in the family as Nanetta, worked at Rosalba's side as her assistant, probably helping to prepare materials. Though Rosalba used pastels from Flanders, Rome, and her hometown Venice, she preferred those from Paris. She also experimented with using "tailor's chalk or ground shells to bind her pigments rather than the more common gum" (Jeffares 1). Back in Venice, Rosalba had so much work that she and Nanetta couldn't keep up. Nanetta often prepared the pastels and filled in draperies and backgrounds, but still the commissions became overwhelming. Rosalba took on young female assistants, first Felicita and

Angioletta Sartori, and also Luisa Bergalli, who later traded paintbrush for pen and gained her own fame as a writer and translator. The two remained lifelong friends and buoyed each other's spirits when depression or desperation overwhelmed them.

When Nanetta died of consumption in 1738, it had a devastating effect on Rosalba. Historian Alberto Toso Fei describes her as "inclined to introversion and needy of the affection of her family," (29) so her sister's death must have been severely traumatic. In one letter, Rosalba Carriera wrote, "I am beside myself, the prey of deepest melancholy, unalleviated by the fact that my mother and my other sister are in good health" (qtd. in Blashfield 476). She did no work for months. Hints of her melancholy had shown up in her Paris diaries from 1720 to 1721: on October 14 she had written, with no further explanation, "A sad day for me" (qtd. in Ricorda 110). Though her paintings most often depict lightness and joy, ease and calm, anything concerning family held the utmost importance for her.

Though she seemed to have many male friends and admirers, Rosalba never married—a footnote barely mentioned in her letters. Scholar Anna Kleinman's research into Rosalba's letters explores the speculation that Rosalba was in love with her friend Zanetti, though their mutual friend Malamani dismissed this conjecture as "pure rubbish" (qtd. in Carriera 14). One tantalizing tidbit tells that her love letter was found slipped behind the frame of her portrait of Humphrey Prideaux (*Wikipedia*), though his name appears nowhere in her letters. Rosalba's artistic talent supported her family financially; she didn't need a man for the reasons that were typical of her era: financial security or protection. But is that why Rosalba never married? She received more than one proposal, one from a suitor twenty-nine years her junior, brought to her by his friend. Rosalba replied to her suitor in a letter, "You surprised me very much . . . . He spoke so well for you that he would have persuaded me if I had been less far from any inclination to change my manner of life. My profession that occupies me so constantly, and a rather cold disposition, have hitherto kept me from thoughts of love and wedlock." Rosalba was then forty-six years old, and added, "I should certainly make everybody laugh heartily if now that my youth is past I should marry" (qtd. in Blashfield 431).

Rosalba's family was enough for her. She even wrote, "Giovanna, who has always had the same intention of keeping herself free from any bond or engagement knows this [offer] but will not speak of it" (431). Rosalba's life was filled with painting, family, church, friendships, the theater, and the thousand daily pleasures of a satisfying domestic tranquility. Rosalba was no rebel to established norms; she simply lived her life on her own terms and was fortunate to have the means to do so. As her biographer Evangeline Blashfield points out, women painters such as Rosalba "were not obliged to become martyrs or fighters, so that they took their tasks and their accomplishments as simply and naturally as professional men would have done" (433). Rosalba didn't fight for equal rights; she sketched and colored, brought light to faces and fabrics, was acknowledged for this talent, and left a legacy of important artwork.

Many writers contend that one of the great attributes of Rosalba's portraits is their introspective quality. Rosalba was able to capture and depict the personality and even psychology of her subjects. There is Anna Sofia Enrichetta of Modena looking imperious and showing off her frothy yet corseted bosom to potential suitors. Or Irish nobleman Gustavus Hamilton sporting a typical Venetian tricorn hat and white *volto* mask, barely cocking one eyebrow as if to ask, "Do you have a problem with me attending the Carnevale?" This is not just a duke or princess sitting for a painting; the viewer feels a sympathy as the duke or princess's inner thoughts show in their eyes, the hint of smile, the placement of hands. Rosalba's pastels have a luminous quality, more common in oil paintings, as she highlighted the edges of lace or the textures of a braid or the glint of an eye. She captured more than merely a likeness.

Yet where is the real Rosalba in all this? She doesn't divulge her interior life in her diaries and only intermittently in her letters. However, she does reveal something of herself elsewhere: in her self-portraits. Though she didn't date many of her paintings, let alone her self-portraits, they show a succession of moods throughout her life. The best-known painting of her, where she holds a portrait of her sister Giovanna, came from earlier in her career; Rosalba has a look of loving tenderness, and the glossy fabrics of her creamy satin dress match the many curls in her hair. Flowers and lace adorn her, and with a paintbrush in her hand, she seems infused with a gentle nature. Her *Self Portrait as Winter* from 1731 shows her face framed by white snow leopard fur trimming a rich cornflower blue dress and cap. Her gentle, closed-mouth smile implies a knowingness and security.

But then a change occurs. The next two self-portraits, possibly in the 1740s, show her wearing deep russet, a hint of a sheer fichu at her throat, and muted adornments—simple drop earrings and a tiny, dark-jeweled tiara that almost disappears into the background. She barely smiles and has almost a suspicious or judgmental cast to her eyes. In this portrait as in the next, which also has a similar coloring and even fewer adornments, Rosalba looks off to the side rather than at the viewer. She looks grimmer here. (These were also after her mother's death and the loss of her sister Giovanna.) Is she detaching herself from the viewer and those around her? Is she lacking love in her life now? These portraits are how she chose to show herself to others, so, though she leaves an unsatisfying diary, the diary of her face displays emotions without the accompanying explanatory story. One final undated self-portrait shows her with merrier black eyes and playful blue ribbons in her white hair, so perhaps not all days felt so somber.

By 1746, Rosalba's sight was failing. In an August 23, 1749, letter to her friend Mariette, Rosalba confessed about the preceding depressing three years of blindness, but that an operation had restored dim sight to her eyes. She wrote, "Now I want to see everything, and I am forbidden to do so until March when I am to undergo a second operation" (qtd. in Blashfield 487). Rosalba underwent unsuccessful cataract surgeries and became completely blind by 1751. She lived six more years, though, to age eighty-one, unable to continue creating the beautiful things that had colored her life. Most reports say she spent her final years severely depressed, accepting visits only from Chioggia family members and a few very close friends. Her home was packed with beautiful objects: a violin and gilded harpsichord, fine china, silver candelabra, porcelain figurines, snuffboxes of gold and lapis lazuli, a commendation medal—objects she might touch but no longer gaze upon (Blashfield 489). Rosalba died on April 15, 1757, just four months after she had written in her will that she thanked God "who has made [my] life rich through [my] painting" (qtd. in Blashfield 491). Unable to enjoy the Grand Canal view of gondolas rowed by men in striped livery, *puperini* boats overflowing with baskets of green and yellow peppers, red tomatoes, deep purple eggplants, Rosalba at least had her sister Angela at her side.

While Rosalba had lost all these colors, these same luminous pastels adorned drawing rooms and salons throughout Europe as the portraits she created to delight others. Rosalba's house, the Ca' Biondetti on the Grand Canal next to the Guggenheim Palazzo dei Leoni, has a tiny, nearly illegible plaque on its façade, marking it as the place she "lived and died," this artist who "took pastel painting to the greatest height" (author's translation). At the land entrance to the house, passers-by can now see singular sculptures, one of a chubby cherub's face set high up into the wall, another of a reclining child swathed in a cloth. The nearby Church of San Vio, where both Rosalba and Giovanna were buried, was demolished after the fall of the Venetian Republic; in 1862 Gaspare Biondetti bought the church ruins and on its site erected a small chapel dedicated to saints Vito and Modesto. Set in the wall used to be a small stone under a cross with the words "Rosalba Carriera, Pittrice 1757." But that is now gone as well. Rosalba Carriera's greatest monuments are her own pastel portraits around Europe and in Venice's Galleria dell'Accademia and especially Ca' Rezzonico, which dedicates most of one room to Rosalba's work. Carved, gilded frames and rich golden wallpaper embossed with blue velvet flourishes showcase a child, a nobleman, a nun, a singing diva, and others, all captured in soft yet brilliant pastel by Rosalba's swift hand.

# Anna Maria dal Violin

## The Hummingbird's Violinist

$\mathcal{A}$ hummingbird's flight captured in black circles and lines. Train tracks populated with notes. A dense thicket of horizontals and verticals and dots. Pages more black than beige, black with flights of notes for violin. All seventy-eight folios bound within tooled leather dyed Venetian red, and embossed with gold leaf calligraphy, inscribed with the recipient's name.

A gift for Anna Maria dal Violin. A challenge.

These pages containing violin concertos belonged to the violinist Anna Maria, virtuoso at the Ospedale Santa Maria della Piéta, a home for abandoned children. She was left there by her mother soon after her birth and never knew her parents. But this humble beginning didn't presage the glory in store for Anna Maria. Antonio Vivaldi, the famous red-haired priest, concert master, and teacher at the Piéta and best-known for his concerto *The Four Seasons*, composed thirty-seven violin concertos for Anna Maria, plus two for the viola d'amore (or at least that's how many have survived to today). This partbook also contains pieces penned expressly for Anna Maria by composers Giuseppe Tartini, Andrea Bernasconi, Giovanni Brusa, Mauro d'Alaij, and Carlo Tessarini. Exceptionally challenging pieces, thick with double-stops and double chords, these pages reveal that Anna Maria must have been tremendously talented to have mastered these concertos.

In the *Violin Concerto in D Minor RV 248 III "Allegro Non Ma Molto,"* the piece opens with a pensive calm, not serene but rather tethered. Then suddenly the hare is off, the race is on, and the bow darts across the strings with a ferocity spawned by release and exhilaration. Is this Vivaldi's joy? Or is his imagination fired by Anna Maria's circumstances as a secluded young woman bursting with a passion to break free? What vivacity comes across in that attack on the violin that Vivaldi wrote for Anna Maria, knowing she would relish it! Her virtuosity inspired composers to create new heights for her to ascend—and to delight listeners from around Europe. In fact, Baron Karl Ludwig von Pollnitz called Anna Maria "the premier violinist of Europe" (qtd. in Baldauf-Berdes 135). Her talent was foremost, but an anonymous poem also praises her beauty, describing her as having blond locks, cheeks of rose, and eyes of fire. In 1739 French visitor Charles de Brosses compared Anna Maria's performance to that of the acclaimed male violinist Giuseppe Tartini. Upon hearing Anna Maria play, de Brosses declared that "It is also the first for the perfection of the symphonies. What strictness of execution! It is only there, [at the Piéta] that one hears the first attack of the bow, so falsely vaunted at the Paris Opera" (qtd. in Stevens).

Anna Maria's red partbook, which contains only her parts rather than the parts for the whole orchestra, is now housed at the Fondo Esposti of the Conservatorio di Musica "Benedetto Marcello" at Campo Santo Stefano in Venice, not far from where Anna Maria lived her entire life. Astoundingly, one third of these concertos have yet to be published or performed since Anna Maria's day, mainly because they are only the first violin part. They were written as gifts and challenges for Anna Maria, yet think of the juicy challenge they pose for modern musicians. Recordings of a number of them are now available so modern listeners can marvel at both Vivaldi's and Anna Maria's achievements. This young woman, orphaned by her parents, would probably marvel at the world that has not forgotten her.

Like all Piéta inhabitants, Anna Maria's last name was subject to change: Anna Maria dal Violin, Anna Maria dal Cello, Anna Maria dal Mandolin, or Oboe, Luta, or Theorbo (a narrow, long-necked stringed instrument). She also played the harpsichord and viola d'amore, her last name changing as needed (and her name was penned onto the pieces written for her so that the other musicians wouldn't fight over who got to play them). This naming was standard practice at the Ospedale della Piéta, a home for foundlings and unwanted babies taken in by the Venetian State, where part of the doge's oath of office included a promise to be their titular father. Some time after July 1696 or in 1697, Anna Maria was deposited there in the *scaffetta*, a hole in the wall the size of a large letter box, covered by a grill, where babies could be left anonymously, on the Riva degli Schiavoni; in fact, the original *scaffetta* still exists, within the wall of what is now the Hotel Metropole's bar.

As part of the routine procedure, Anna Maria would have been numbered, baptized, given a first name, and branded with a "P" for Piéta on her left foot. Children were thus marked on their foot or upper arm to prevent "the widespread practice of foster parents' substituting live children for the state's wards who died," writes historian Jane L. Baldauf-Berdes (140). Anna Maria's clothing and any belongings would have been catalogued at the time of her entry; the *Libro della scaffetta* containing Anna Maria's registration is missing, so the specific details of her rescue are lost, according to researcher Mickey White who has combed the archives and has researched Anna Maria's life in detail (White, "Scenes" 4). Some children were dressed in rags, "*revolta in strace*," while some were clothed more expensively. Maestra Antonia, who was the "*scrivana*" or scribe on record when Anna Maria was deposited like so much laundry, would have spied the mother leaving her baby from the passageway that connects the two buildings and would have hurried down to retrieve her (3). The foundlings were fed and put to bed, separated from the other children at first as a sort of quarantine in case they carried disease (3).

Some children were given to a foster family with a wet nurse or *neon*, and they remained there up to age ten when they were returned to the Piéta for an education and training. Some babies were found with a half a medallion, coin, or card, in the hopes that their mother could one day reappear with the other half to claim her baby. But as the years passed, no one returned to claim Anna Maria. Due to circumstantial evidence—comparing Anna Maria to other similar foundlings—White believes that Anna Maria may have come from a mother who was not poor but rather had had an illegitimate child and needed to provide a different home for her (White, "Scenes" 4). Some babies were orphans; some were one too many mouths to feed, or their mothers had no milk to suckle them, or they were begotten unwanted. The women at the Piéta took them all in, kept them dry, and filled their bellies, then provided these innocents with remarkable choices not open to many children. Though Anna Maria must have wondered about her parents more than once, she was actually quite fortunate in her living circumstances.

Both boys and girls were left at the Piéta, and all received a basic schooling in reading, writing, arithmetic, and scripture. The boys were taught trade skills such as shoe-making, weaving, or stone-cutting until age sixteen, when they left the Piéta to begin more independent lives. Girls, while also being taught practical skills such as cooking, sewing, embroidery, lacemaking, and weaving, usually working on the third floor where the light was better, were also examined for their musical or singing skills. If they showed promise, as did approximately ten percent, they trained to become members of the *figlie del coro* performers group like Anna Maria, rather than the *figlie del commun* who performed the everyday tasks that kept the Piéta running and brought in income from practical pursuits. The 1717 census, when Anna Maria was roughly twenty-one, shows 772 people residing at the Piéta, 242 of them being women over age eighteen, the "*putte grande*" (White, "Scenes" 12). The residents must have raised quite a ruckus as they climbed the spiral staircase from the first to the second floor dormitories. Some women were even trained as surgeons and pharmacists, such as Pellegrina who appears in Piéta records in the 1720s, so that the Piéta could save money and provide all necessary services in-house. Within the walls of this building, women were empowered with quite a lot of agency and capacity.

The Ospedale della Piéta was not simply a big hospital where people slept then came and went at will. The *ospedale* of Venice—and there were a number of them that took in the destitute, ill, widowed, or unprotected virgins—were charitable institutions that cared for those who needed the aid. In the Piéta, these children and women were considered wards of the State to be cared for, but also servants of the State who provided important services to Venice to further her glory. While inhabitants needed to bring in some income to supplement the donations that paid for their keep, they also ran a sensational and renowned musical program. Their instrumental and choral concerts provided sacred music, often sung at masses for benefactors, or presented on feast days to glorify the Church and the Venetian State. "They play like angels in disguise," croons an anonymous poem from the newspaper of the times, *Pallade Veneta* (author's translation).

Antonio Vivaldi even wrote sacred music for Anna Maria for the Feast of the Assumption and the Christmas Eve service. She would have stood in the Basilica di San Marco, the sweet strains of her violin glorifying God. The musical productions at the Piéta, as well as those at three other *ospedale* in Venice, brought pilgrims and travelers on the Grand Tour into these institutions to bring fame—and ducats—to Venice. It was a timely marriage: no other state had provided such welfare for its fatherless, ill, or destitute citizens, and Venice's practice coincided with a rise in music as an industry. The Ospedale's concerts such as these filled a gap, between sacred and profane musical concerts, particularly during Lent when opera houses were closed. Everyone wanted to hear the Piéta's singers and musicians and to see them—though this was impossible since the women were hidden behind grillwork that protected their chastity (while adding to their mysterious allure). She may have been abandoned by her parents, but Anna Maria always knew she was safe.

The Ospedale helped people to help themselves. The women at the Piéta were actually paid to study, to work, and to perform. They saved for their dowries or learned to manage their own finances at the Piéta's credit bank, earning an unprecedented eight percent interest on their savings. The women there had three choices, rather than the two open to most Venetian women: they could marry, using the handsome 200 ducat dowry the Piéta provided; they could become nuns and serve God at a convent; or they could continue as Piéta musicians, going on to teach and take other management roles, receiving a healthy retirement and living out their years there. This was the path Anna Maria chose. Was it her love of music that triumphed over a life of religious devotion or conjugal love?

After playing in the *coro* or chorus for many years, Anna Maria began teaching others and in 1737 became the principal violin instructor or *maestra di violino*. Unusually, she was simultaneously installed as the *maestra di coro,* indicating her superlative abilities, particularly since no other woman was even recommended for the post at this time, and no other musician was granted this honor, before or since. As Mickey White stated, "There were many brilliant musicians here, but Anna Maria was out of the ordinary" (interview). Anna Maria would have received her own room then, too, with a fireplace and necessities to cook her own meals if she wished. She had earned her privacy and independence. Dedicating herself to long hours of toil, Anna Maria continued playing and teaching, also working as a copyist, concert mistress, and orchestra conductor. The two *maestre di coro* also had to confirm that Antonio Vivaldi had discharged his duties satisfactorily. (Such records containing Anna Maria's signature live in the archives.) He wrote dozens of concertos while employed at the Piéta: solo pieces for various musicians, including Anna Maria, concertos for multiple instruments, and uncounted pieces of sacred music, many of which were undoubtedly lost.

The *figlie del coro* were early modern rock stars. Privileges for these girls included special foods, private rooms away from the *figlie del commun,* a higher social status, and eventually the title Signora, usually reserved only for married women. They were also exempt from non-musical duties. Both musicians and singers could earn extra pay by taking on students, income they were allowed to keep. There were only fourteen of these from the *coro,* with the title of *Figlie Privilegiate* (White, email). Star soloists like Anna Maria also had partbooks created for them, though rarely with such an illustrious composer as Vivaldi. While fulfilling her duties as a musician, Anna Maria still had enough freedom to revel in these challenging compositions, probably pouring extra hours into practice.

Besides this virtuoso instrumentalist, the Piéta also produced at least two composers: Anna Bon and Vincenta Da Ponte, girls not orphaned but placed in the Piéta by their parents for a span in order to receive a superlative musical education. Anna Bon began as a *figlia in educazione* but showed such remarkable abilities that she was taught to play and even compose music, also soloing on the flute. The Piéta produced remarkable singers, too. Since no male performers were allowed, women sang all the parts, including bass and tenor, normally male ranges. The documentary *Vivaldi's Women* follows the modern-day Oxford Girls Choir, who train and then travel to Venice's Piéta to prove that women's voices can achieve these sounds. One of their violinists even plays some of the pieces written for Anna Maria, learning what virtuoso skill she possessed.

As previously mentioned, Anna Maria received gifts, such as the many concertos written for her, all preserved in her lovely red leather book in the same careful hand, possibly her own or that of the appointed copyist, a woman named Meneghina during Anna Maria's time. Vivaldi himself bought her a new violin when she was only sixteen, one he paid twenty ducats for as part of his duty as *maestro di violin*. For girls without family to bring them gifts on name days or Christmas, Anna Maria must have been thrilled. This was clearly an expensive and special gift, especially when compared to the twelve-ducat violin he bought for the violinist Bernardina at the same time. In fact, this record for July 12, 1712, is the first document to confirm Anna Maria's existence (White, "Scenes" 7). In 1720, she was given another new violin, which may indicate that she had become the principal violinist in the *coro* (7).

Also in 1712, in order to lighten the mood of a serious event, Anna Maria and three other Piéta women were invited to perform at a Christian doctrine exam called the Third Order of Saint Francis, held at the Church of San Francesco della Vigna in the Castello district (White, email). Audience members would have been sumptuously attired for the event, in contrast to the simple red dresses donned by *coro* musicians. Pearls and jewels sparkled in the candlelight, and women fluttered fans before their faces as they sat attended by their obsequious men. These contrasts of wealth in the pews and simplicity in the chorus were heightened as the dulcet tones of string and wind floated across the church. This visit was one of the few times Anna Maria was allowed to leave the Piéta. It must have stood out as a special memory, a day filled with exciting sights and new faces, and she was one of the day's stars.

Normally, life as a *coro* member, even with its few privileges, was not extravagant or luxurious. Rules were strict. Inhabitants were housed according to age and gender, and they could receive no outside visitors. They prayed aloud while dressing. Their letters were read by the Prioress and even censored or perhaps never delivered at all. Furthermore, everyone attended multiple daily masses—in the morning, both before and after breakfast, and at vespers, plus attending all performances and rehearsals. Even the prioress herself couldn't leave the building without written permission from the institution's governors, a group of appointed Venetian Senators, and any visiting priest must be accompanied by two escorts. Those who broke these rules faced confiscation of their savings and solitary confinement in the Ospedale's "prison," (a small room that is now used for the Hotel Metropole's ironing). Though Piéta women had some agency and often made suggestions for improvements or policies, they were still strictly governed by men in power. Anna Maria had more privileges than many of her sisters, but that didn't mean she was free.

However, *figlie* performers did receive one vacation to the countryside each year, of a rather ascetic nature, though occasionally a few *coro* members might be treated to a chaperoned trip at a benefactor's villa. These sumptuous properties on the mainland featured sunny rooms, lush gardens, and rich meals, so unlike the austere life in the Ospedale. Records indicate that Anna Maria visited Isabella Corner Pisani's villa in Stra in 1729 and 1730 to "take the airs" when she was suffering from stomach and kidney ailments (White, "Scenes" 8). Anna Maria even received a special diet (chicken was added to courses of bread, rice, wine, and often beef or eggs) to improve her health. What a treat, one she must have felt so grateful to receive.

Those who chose to live their life at the Piéta, as did Anna Maria, were expected to train as musicians for ten years then stay for another ten as teachers and performers. For those who chose marriage, they had to train two replacements before leaving and then promise to never again perform in public. Stories abound about wealthy and privileged families who left their children at the Piéta to be so highly trained, but these constraints were designed to discourage this practice, and the number of such boarders was limited to fourteen. Anna Maria would have begun her musical training with senior members of the *figlie di coro*, though it's likely that she trained closely with Antonio Vivaldi himself; his tenure at the Piéta coincides with Anna Maria's years as a principal violinist, from 1703 to 1740 (with a few periods when Vivaldi worked elsewhere before returning). Based on the compositions that resulted from their interaction, the relationship between violinist and composer must have been dynamic and exciting, spurring them both on to greater accomplishments and artistry.

Antonio Vivaldi wrote the bulk of his sacred music while at the Piéta. Besides being inspired by Anna Maria, he must also have been stimulated by the place and the many other dedicated, talented musicians around him. "I believe that what he wrote here picks up on the vulnerability of all these kids, all these mothers," states Mickey White. "There's an innocence, an 'otherness' you feel when you walk through the doors and leave the vulgar, brash, commercial world of Venice behind" (qtd. in Michael White). Even with these restrictions, a Piéta bride was a desirable catch, with her excellent musical training and healthy dowry, especially to other musicians who came looking for a wife. When Jean Jacques Rousseau visited the Piéta, he was so taken with the choir's singing that he thought he was "in love." He couldn't actually see the women, however, who were hidden behind an iron grill, only their voices slipping through the gaps. He begged his friend, who was a member of the Piéta's administration, to allow him to see the performers. At their shared meal, Rousseau was alarmed to find that, in his estimation, the women were ugly or disfigured, though he admitted that they still had a certain "grace" to them. His feelings of love returned, though more tempered, causing him to question the precepts of beauty and love (Baldauf-Berdes 135-6). Overall, though, the Piéta could be a refuge for women away from men's judgment, as well as a safe place to grow into adulthood and to showcase their talents.

The Piéta women lived a full and meaningful life. Most stayed and some even returned later in life. Interestingly, alumnae were generally discouraged from returning to the Piéta because they might "corrupt the innocence of those who had remained" (White, "Scenes" 11); for example, when a certain Giacinta returned to the Piéta as an elderly widow, Anna Maria generously offered to share her room with her, though the *ospedale* authorities decided against it. Anna Maria herself lived a long life, to age eighty-six, finally succumbing to consumption. The *Libro dei Morti* entry announcing her passing early on the morning of August 10, 1782, was printed in unusually large type, an indication of her high status, and she would have been buried the following morning (13). Upon their death, after a service lit by candles, Piéta inhabitants were buried beneath the church under thick, unmarked marble slabs. As researcher Mickey White points out, the *figlie* have never left the Piéta (*Vivaldi's Women*). The church itself has changed since Anna Maria's time: the current building was erected in 1761, during the last part of Anna Maria's tenure there, decades after Antonio Vivaldi's death. In fact, the Hotel Metropole's bar and lobby take the place of the former church, where Anna Maria and her sister musicians once performed. From the hotel's rear garden, visitors can gaze up to the windows of rooms where performances were once held, while later they played and sang in the current Piéta church after its completion.

In a city where women had little power, minimal choices, and virtually no voice, the Piéta provided an extraordinary exception. Yes, it might be faulted for its strictures; from the outside, it appeared to be a veritable prison, all under the control of men. Yet Signora Lucieta Organo, Signora Pelegrina Oboe, Signora Prudenza Violin, and especially Signora Anna Maria dal Violin, among others, showed that women were worthy of an education, that women could be just as talented as men, that women could organize and operate a highly successful large institution, that women could contribute things of great value to their church and society. As Jane Baldauf-Berdes explains, "Women excelled as bearers of a music-centered tradition unique to the Venetian civilization" (149). Due to her close association with Antonio Vivaldi, Anna Maria also became one of the most "important agent[s] in the transmission of Vivaldi's music and performing style," (White, "Scenes" 7) and a great contributor to musical development and history.

At a time when women were so often cloistered, silenced, and devalued, the women of the Piéta created harmonious music. They may have been abandoned by their parents and lived a spare, frugal, and devout life, but that didn't mean it wasn't also rich in soaring joy, lofty ambition, and vibrant music. Mickey White points out that the Piéta women "all shared the same emotional scars," (interview) but perhaps those wounds became wells of emotion and inspiration. "Here comes the beautiful Anna

Maria / True idea of good, of beauty," reads the opening stanza of an anonymous poem praising her. "Within all the world, / she doesn't have an equal—female or male" (author's translation). Anna Maria represents the best of the generations of Piéta musicians, her red leather partbook a testament to her dedication, hard work, and extraordinary talent.

The Ospedale della Pietà

# *Luisa Bergalli Gozzi*

## So They Would Not Be Forgotten

$I$s the best gift something of material value, like a diamond ring or a yacht? Something rare—a one-of-a-kind painting? Something hand-fashioned, such as a song or a lace handkerchief?

Or perhaps a place in history?

Luisa Bergalli Gozzi gave this last, quite precious gift, to 250 Italian women writers. In 1726 she published *Componenti poetici delle piu illustri Rimatrici d'ogni secolo* (*Poetic Compositions of the Most Famous Women Poets of all Ages*), a poetry anthology in two volumes. Throughout her writing life and much of her marriage, Luisa was maligned and mistreated, sometimes by her own family members. Perhaps she wished to buoy the lives of other female poets, making sure they received their fair due and recognition for their work, even if that was not to be the case for her. As shown in an anonymous engraving of her, Luisa was a petite woman with a wide forehead, small chin, full lips on a small mouth, and large, sympathetic eyes. Her throat and chest are bare and vulnerable above a simple white blouse. Here Luisa looks serene and hopeful, not as beleaguered as her biography suggests.

Before Luisa's poetry publication, two other similar collections had been assembled, but she holds the distinct accomplishment of being the first woman to design and produce an anthology of women writers. Furthermore, hers encompasses a greater breadth and diversity of poets than anything produced contemporaneously (Curran 268). According to researcher Adriana Chemello, Luisa sought to trace a "geography" and "genealogy" of these poets so they would not be forgotten (137). The Republic of Letters, overwhelmingly populated by men, needed to provide a place for its female inhabitants, and Luisa's collection would rectify this omission. Another woman would not collate such an anthology until Jolanda De Blasi, two hundred years later in 1930.

Luisa's sister predecessors often argued that women were just as capable as men when it came to learning and a life in letters; however, Luisa sought to prove it with this large collection of writing (137). Of course, she included such lights as Modesta Pozzo, Lucrezia Marinella, Elena

Cornaro Piscopia, Gaspara Stampa, Sarra Copia, Veronica Franco, and Isabella Andreini, a woman born in Venice but whose work as an actress, playwright, and improviser took her away to other cities. Fortunately, these writers' works have been preserved, but Luisa incorporated so many others who might otherwise be forgotten: Isicratea Monte, Gentile Dotta, Pia Bichi, and many with charming names, like Vittoria Telea Noci or Diamante Dolfi. A number of poems name no author and are only marked as "*incerta*" or "uncertain," yet these women's words were collected and shared here. Professor Stuart Curran analyzed the other anthologies available during Luisa's creation period and contends that she must have felt "a commitment to absolute breadth" (268) in her search for the poems that she included in this anthology. Contemporary works contained very few poems by women writers, so Luisa must have consulted unpublished manuscripts, private libraries, and church documents. She also seems to feel responsible to include poems of many genres—not just devotional or religious poetry, but also poems on love, locations, noble families, and even politics (275). In her "Preface" Luisa wrote, "I address my words to those few right-thinking men who conduct themselves like many others in the past and deign, when appropriate, to appreciate and honour us Women" (qtd. in Stewart 54).

One such man in Luisa's life was her father, Jacopo Bergalli, not a nobleman, but one who valued learning and letters. Originally from Piedmont, he married Diana Bianchini and they settled in Venice. Luisa was born there on April 15, 1703, and was introduced by her father not only to French and Latin but also to poetry, philosophy, and arithmetic. The fire was lit, one that would burn without ceasing for Luisa's lifetime.

Early on, friendship became the most valuable gift Luisa would receive. As Luisa began writing some of her own poetry, Apostolo Zeno noticed her and gave her access to his grand library. Luisa could pull volume after volume of leather-clad books from Apostolo's ample shelves and immerse herself in the classic literature. Young Luisa must have toiled happily through her reading, consulting French dictionaries, turning to the speeches of Cicero, familiarizing herself with Aristotle's arguments. Apostolo guided her faithfully through this wealth of learning, and their letters show the important role he played as her mentor. Her Latin and Italian teacher Antonio Sforza also shared the riches of the enormous Soranzo library with her, which he had access to through the well-heeled Soranzo family. These scholars' generosity was repeated by Alvise Mocenigo, who gave Luisa access to Venice's Biblioteca Marciana; what a gift, to spend studious hours in this grand library, surrounded by books and globes, like a playground for the intellectually curious. With brown, black, and white geometric mosaics underfoot and painted ceilings overhead, the dim natural light of the Marciana was supplanted by Luisa's growing spark of knowledge.

These learned men and patricians gave this commoner a leg up into Arcadia, the Greek Republic of Letters, where Luisa became known as Irminda Partenide. She was even invited to join the Arcadian Academy in Rome, as well as being invited to join honorary court positions (Ward 185 n8). During her teens and twenties, Luisa attended literary gatherings at the palaces throughout Venice; she does not seem to have been pressured to prove her chastity nor to marry early, like many of her predecessors. This must have been a heady time for her, reveling in a life of letters, engaging in spirited discussions, doing battle with words, testing her arguments against fine minds.

During these years, Luisa spent her time producing masses of writing, from wedding congratulations, to poems marking a nun's vows, to celebrating important people, including her patrons like Antonio Sforza and Apostolo Zeno. Luisa put her language skills to work by translating French plays into Italian. Beginning with two volumes of comedies by Terence that she translated in 1735 and 1736, she swiftly followed by tackling works by Jean Racine in 1736. In 1745 Luisa turned to translating plays from J. F. Duche, Houdar de la Motte, and Marie Anne Du Boccage. This was an enormous output in a short time.

Luisa didn't just translate plays. She wrote them as well. In 1725 when she was but twenty-two, she wrote *Agide, re di Sparta* (*Agis, King of Sparta*), her first play, with the encouragement of Apostolo Zeno. Following the story line from Giraldi Cinthio's *Hecatommithi*, Luisa enhances aspects of the plot to accentuate the generosity of two female characters, Antianira and Timocla. In her summary, Luisa notes these women's "marvelous courage and ingenuity . . . when they put their mind to succeeding in an important enterprise" (qtd. in Stewart 51). Biographer Pamela D. Stewart believes that Luisa's characterization brings "emotional complexity" to the story (51). Luisa, in line with the era's mores towards theatrical reform and under the influence of Apostolo Zeno's own revision, worked towards improving playwriting with simplicity, clear tone, and forthright messages. *Agis, King of Sparta* debuted at the Teatro San Moise with the music of Giovanni Porta. This theater, with its ceiling frescoes and over 800 seats, was one of Venice's most popular haunts, where patrons dressed lavishly to attend in style, procuring a theater box to view the play while also socializing with their illustrious neighbors. Operas by Francesco Cavalli, Antonio Vivaldi, and Gioacchino Rossini premiered here, as did plays by Baldassare Galuppi and Carlo Goldoni, homegrown Venetian talents like Luisa. Her works were in good company.

Following *Agis's* success, Luisa continued to write dramas. Her tragic play titled *Teba* (1728) tells of the havoc wrought by hiding the truth from others as Teba, a dutiful wife, is condemned to death by her tyrannical husband. Two years later, Luisa produced *Elenia*, a complicated drama that tracks three couples and their machinations, including hidden identities, dissimulation, and even poison. *Elenia* featured Tommaso Albinoni's music and premiered at the Teatro Sant'Angelo. This theater facing the Grand Canal is now a hotel, though in its day plays and operas, both serious and comic, ran here.

But it wasn't all to be about tragedies. Luisa next wrote the comic play *Le avventure del poeta* (*The Adventures of a Poet*), also published in 1730. Her future father-in-law, Count Jacopo Gozzi, urged her towards this work that in some ways mirrors her own experiences, particularly her interactions with the Gozzi family. In her dedication to the Count she noted that she was "looking around myself in a certain way" (qtd. in Stewart 53, author's translation), possibly gathering material to include in the play. The play follows a family where the son Orazio seeks honor and patronage for his poetry from an aristocratic but miserly couple. However, poetry doesn't put food on the table, and it is his sister Camilla who provides for the family with her seamstress skills; her name, ironically, echoes the famous Greek orator and poet of antiquity. At one point Camilla jokes that "The poet's art is too damned that always drinks from the fountain of Helicon and never eats" (qtd. in Ward 72, translation by Claudia Mandelli). The mythical fount of Helicon provided the water of poetic inspiration—seemingly sufficient for a poet, but not enough to sustain a body. Luisa developed Camilla as the more practical, resourceful, and intelligent character, with her foil being Orazio, whose head remains stuck in the lyrical clouds until the play's resolution.

This satire offers layers of irony, especially foreshadowing Luisa's future. In 1738 she married Count Gasparo Gozzi. Carlo Gozzi, often caustic in his comments, wrote in his *Memorie Inutili* (*Useless Memoirs*), "My brother Gasparo had taken a wife in a fit of genial poetical abstraction. Even poetry has its dangers" (Gozzi 22). Luisa was the practical one, and Gasparo the distracted dreamer. Luisa and Gasparo's relationship had unfolded over seven years in Venice's literary salon life, which seemed like it would promise a complimentary liaison. She was ten years his senior, and perhaps she was looking for a partner to bring her life stability as well as a like-minded writer to share her literary aspirations. Gasparo Gozzi was a noted playwright, and the couple collaborated on a number of plays and other publications. At one point, they signed the lease for the Teatro Sant'Angelo from 1747 to 1748, and Luisa "was to play the part of controller, purse-holder, and stage manager for the troupe at Venice and on the mainland," explained Carlo Gozzi (84). In theaters at that time, an acting troupe worked at a particular theater and under a particular manager, a job Luisa took on. Sadly, this venture would fail, only one of the disappointments that Luisa would face in her marriage.

After having five children and some work failures, the couple found that it was Luisa's prolific literary output that provided the family's meat and bread. Carlo admitted that his brother could not handle finances, "for in his hands money found wings and flew away" (93). Luisa was like her protagonist Camilla, whose pragmatism and hard work sustained the family, although Luisa managed to do this with her poetry and writing, like her character Orazio. At one point, Camilla tells the family, "Leave me, so I can finish this hat in peace, if you will, so we will eat today" (qtd. in Ward 174, author's translation). Replace "hat" with "writing" and it could be Luisa shushing her own husband. Furthermore, in *Adventures* Luisa looked at Venice's obsolete socio-economic hierarchies, with a patrician class that could no longer continue as wealthy patrons to artists, and a rising bourgeoisie whose industry and income routinely sustained the city's economy (Ward 169). Luisa came from this latter class, while her husband's family was from the former, and the foibles of Orazio and Camilla bring these troubles into stark relief. While her husband Gasparo occasionally dabbled in the family upkeep, Luisa threw her energy into trying to earn enough to sustain them. Instead of being appreciated, however, nearly every member of the family maligned her efforts, calling her controlling and shrewish. Not even Luisa's work ethic nor their shared literary lives were enough to make up for a mismatched relationship between herself and Gasparo. What disappointment, what exasperation, she must have felt.

The Palazzo Gozzi, which sits in the Santa Croce *sestiere* in Campo Santa Maria Mater Domini at house number 2268-2269, symbolizes the family fortunes—or misfortunes. A bit gray and unkempt now, it probably looked nearly the same in the eighteenth century due to the Gozzi family's impoverishment. Carlo Gozzi explained that "The stone floors were worn into holes and fissures, which spread in all directions like a cancer. The broken window panes let blasts from every point of the compass play freely to and fro within the draughty chambers. The hangings on the walls were ragged, smirched with smoke and dust, fluttering in tatters" (Gozzi 59). This was the noble family that Luisa had married into, an irony also not lost on her, and perhaps incorporated into her own works. She had moved up Venice's social ladder, but into what? A drafty, decrepit heap peopled by a family that could no longer sustain itself or its home. Frustration and disillusionment must have become her constant companions.

While the play *Adventures* lampoons the conventional gender roles for men's and women's occupations, Luisa showed that a female writer could overcome those barriers and earn honor along with the bread. A sonnet she penned in 1752 sums up her views: "Good reason have I to bless the day / That womanly occupations held I in disdain; / Thus can I follow the thrust of my daring mind, / And perchance from someone win acclaim" (qtd. in Stewart 54). She certainly garnered support and notice from important patrons such as Zeno, Sforza, and Mocenigo. Unfortunately, along with pursuing her literary life, Luisa still had to run a household and take care of her children, her mother-in-law, and other family members; she refused to give up one for the other, even without any extra support. Though Luisa was respected by some scholars in her day, she had to wait two hundred years until more recent scholarship in women's writing has given her proper acclaim.

Undaunted, Luisa continued to write throughout her lifetime. She was nothing if not persistent. She collected the poems of Antonio Sforza in 1736 after his death, as a way to honor her great mentor, even confiding to her friend Rosalba Carriera that her "heart will break" (68) in sadness at this loss. Luisa also took the collection that Cassandra Stampa had made of Gaspara Stampa's poems and published this in 1738, putting Gaspara back on the literary map after years of being forgotten. Luisa produced a couple other collections, plus more plays, some anonymous but attributed to her (Stewart 56). Biographer Pamela Stewart contends that Luisa's substantial output "overshadowed her early works, which deserve attention and for which she is above all worthy of being remembered" (54). Researcher Adrienne Ward, moreover, points out that some of Luisa's dramatic conventions presaged her successors; for instance, her use of everyday objects on stage, such as aprons, brooms, and common foods, "anticipates [Carlo] Goldoni's theatrical reforms by several decades" (184 n2). Could Carlo Goldoni, who knew Luisa's work, have been, in fact, inspired by her ideas? Luisa had to write to support her family, and she wrote to honor and promote women writers, but she also wrote for pure joy and to please herself; in one poem from her collection *Componimenti Poetici* she admits, "I cherish my peace and therefore I do not bend my heart to crazy lovers, but I am proud of my spirits that awake at the sound of glory, and not with thirst for gold" (Bergalli Gozzi, Vol. 2, trans. by C. Mandelli). She was moved by a complex tangle of need and desire.

Luisa may not have faced some of the same barriers and expectations that other women writers faced in previous centuries, such as slander against her chastity, but that does not mean that her career was without tribulations. Of all the places this could have emanated, the attacks came from her own family. Her brother-in-law Carlo Gozzi, also a playwright, was the worst offender. In his memoirs, he first praised Luisa's "fervent and soaring imagination, which fitted her for high poetic flights," (Gozzi 23) but which threw the house into more disorder as she and the mother attempted to regulate the family's finances. Though Carlo acknowledged that Luisa tried her best, and he couched his complaints in gentler language, he also said that "Thirsting with soul passion after an ideal realm, she found herself the sovereign of a state in decadence. . . . Yet she accomplished nothing beyond involving every one, and herself to boot, in the meshes of still greater misfortune" (23). Carlo never acknowledged that it was Luisa's labor—her writing—that fed this impoverished noble family.

Gasparo, Luisa's husband, wasn't much better. While siring five children and living off his wife's income, he would periodically disappear or even take up residence elsewhere, leaving Luisa with the children and the house to run, and of course her own work as a writer. According to Carlo, Luisa described her husband as "indolent, torpid, drowned in fruitless studies . . . and wholly averse from thoughts or cares about domestic matters" (65). She is unfairly characterized as the typical scold. After all her toil and hours of writing, such ill treatment must have been a bitter pill for her. Gasparo did write to Luisa with concern at one point, noting that she had suffered a miscarriage, without the help of any doctors (Sama, "Luisa Bergalli" 63). Gasparo eventually moved in with a seamstress, whom he married after Luisa's death. Upon hearing from their son Francesco that Luisa had died, Gasparo at least proclaimed that she had been so good that he hoped she had a place in Paradise (Stewart 51).

Sadly, these men's negative comments were picked up by later critics and historians, notably Niccolo Tommaseo and Pompeo Molmenti, demeaning Luisa's work, disregarding her strained finances, and applying worn-out stereotypes against women writers. To be fair, Tommaseo praised *Adventures* as "most witty indeed" (qtd. in Stewart 55), but he then appended that Gasparo must have helped to write it. Molmenti even wrote, "instead of tending to her children and her house, [she] set herself to translate Madame du Boccage's 'Amazons,' sitting wrapped up in a thick cloak with her husband's periwig on her head for warmth" (Molmenti, Part III, Vol. 2, 128). What petty observations. Not every literary man, of course, attacked Luisa; Carlo Goldoni, Venice's best-known playwright, proclaimed that Luisa's translations and poems "do honour to the female sex and our country," (qtd. in Stewart 55) though he neglected to comment on her plays.

Despite her matrimonial and familial woes, Luisa was buoyed by other friendships and colleagues. A true gift in Luisa's life, the painter Rosalba Carriera and her family appreciated Luisa's friendship and talents. Luisa actually studied painting technique in Rosalba's studio in 1724, where she also became close friends with Rosalba's sisters Angela and Giovanna. In fact, Luisa included Giovanna's sonnets in her anthology of Italian women writers. Luisa dedicated her play *I due fratelli* (*The Two Brothers*) to Rosalba and called the Carriera family a model for the feminine sex, with a mother who educated and nurtured her daughters (Sama, "Luisa Bergalli" 67). These sisters "confirm that our sex is as good as men for intellectual work," wrote Luisa (qtd. in Sama, 67, author's translation). Further, Luisa honored the three sisters in a 1726 poem, where she challenged those who believe that women cannot excel in the arts as men do, to "Come and admire the works / Of Angela, Rosalba, and Giovanna; / And further say if heaven condemns us women / To working just with needle and with thread" (Bergalli Gozzi, Vol. 2, translation by Gregory Dowling). The sisters' work inspired Luisa and gave her a model to present to any who doubted women's abilities.

A few letters between Luisa and Rosalba have survived, and they paint a picture of collaboration and care. For example, Luisa requested that Felicita Sartori, a promising young painter studying under Rosalba, provide the portrait for the frontispiece of her collection of Antonio Sforza's poems, and later portraits of Gaspara Stampa and Collaltino di Collalto for another publication. The women's collaboration could bring "much honor" and more work to both their households (qtd. in Sama, "Luisa Bergalli" 70, author's translation). Luisa also sent missives of consolation after Rosalba's sister Giovanna died; "I dare to send her a sonnet [on Giovanna's death] made by me," she modestly wrote (70). The Carriera home provided a refuge, the women able to sit together, taking a cup of hot chocolate while they discussed the next portrait commission, how a translation was coming, or ideas for a new play. Laced into tight corsets, swathed in yards of fabric, these friends nevertheless still enjoyed a freedom in each other's company, free from restrictive social expectations. Considering the obligations Luisa had to meet, with little familial assistance, the Carriera family's friendship must have been very emotionally valuable, plus it gave her a sense of being a professional artist working with others of similar aspirations.

Luisa Bergalli Gozzi offered many gifts—of friendship, love, motherhood, collaboration, and honor. She added to the growing literary canon more work by women writers, proving women's abilities to compose in multiple genres. In the "Dedicatory Letter" to her anthology of women writers, Luisa said to Cardinal Pietro Ottoboni, "I trust you will accept this offering which, at the kind prompting of others and of my own instinct, I venture to send you . . . knowing that with your erudition and profound wisdom you are free of that almost universal preconception that we women have no ability to make our mark in the arts" (qtd. in Chemello 135). How could the cardinal deny such an appeal, if not for its truth than at least for its flattery?

Luisa focused on women as contributors and producers, rather than on their beauty, modesty, or chastity, a step forward in women's equality and a gift to future generations. Stuart Curran comments that "if we are ever to restore those silenced voices" of the many women who wrote and created, then "it should be undertaken by all of us in a sense of humble partnership with the young woman, yet just an adult, who began this process with such faith in its value in 1726" (280). Perhaps future scholars can give a posthumous gift to Luisa by providing analysis and translations so that more readers have access to her wit and brilliance. She compiled the anthology that preserved the names and words of 250 women. More scholars owe her the same honor.

Palazzo Gozzi

# Caterina Dolfin Tron

## No Fenced in Kingdom

State Inquisition guards first politely knocked at the door to Caterina's private rooms, but once inside, they were not so deferential. They pulled books from her shelves, riffled through her papers, and questioned her regarding her reading habits. Caterina Dolfin Tron, usually not cowed by any interloper, must have felt some trepidation at the entrance of these men looking for evidence to convict her of treason. Or perhaps she just grew angry. She was not one used to being questioned.

Venice's State Inquisition in the eighteenth century did not employ the rack or thumbscrews or the iron maiden. But it did employ spies on its own people, and it did attempt to control Venetian citizens—what they watched in the theater, who they had sex with, what they wore, and what they read. Thanks to the Aldine Press and other great publishers, Venice was a publishing mecca, but it was also prey to censorship. Even Giacomo Casanova, the famed lover, had his rooms searched by the Inquisition and was jailed partly for the books found there.

Caterina Dolfin Tron, a noblewoman of high rank and some renown as a poet, salonniere, and lover-then-wife of one of the most powerful men in Venice, experienced a similar episode as she came under the Inquisition's scrutiny. Historian Pompeo Molmenti called her "The true daughter of Venice and of this century," (Part III, Vol. 2, 125) but status was not always enough to shield one from prying and censure, especially not if one owned books by Jean-Jacques Rousseau, Voltaire, and Helvetius. In 1772, as rebellion fulminated next door in France, such books were specifically banned from sales and circulation (Gambier). The Venetian Republic may have been in economic and social decline, but if the Inquisition had any influence left, it was not about to allow a Venetian revolution akin to France's, particularly one endorsed by a woman.

The Inquisition also forcibly closed Caterina's *casino,* the small apartment where she held a literary salon. Caterina and her salon guests often discussed concepts of social revolution and the rights of man (Molmenti, Part III, Vol. 2, 146). Though the morally dissolute Venice of the eighteenth century allowed for a hedonistic life and more relaxed sexual mores than in previous centuries, its government was not yet ready for rule by its people. "You gentlemen who are subjects of great sovereigns miss one essential emotion, that of patriotism," Caterina wrote in a September 27, 1783, letter to her friend Duke Gian Galeazzo Serbelloni. "We Republicans think otherwise, for we both rule and obey at one and the same time" (qtd. in Molmenti, Part III, Vol. 2, 131). She espoused ideas of giving power to the people.

Caterina's Monday night salon in the San Giuliano neighborhood attracted a wide variety of patrons, including merchants and nobles like Angelo Querini and Giorgio Pisani. Artists and poets also attended, such as Angelo Barbaro, Melchior Cesarotti, and Simone Stratico, plus the Venetian playwright Carlo Goldoni. Caterina was especially close with the brothers Gasparo and Carlo Gozzi, both playwrights as well, who attended her salon but extended their friendship beyond it. At these gatherings, a gondolier announced each new arrival, while conversation must have raged, ideas batted back and forth like so many balls in the air. Caterina reigned as the queen in her elegant gown of flowing silk, her hair piled up and decorated with flowers. Molmenti recorded, "No one of any name failed to attend these assemblies, and all of them took away with them pleasant memories of the amiable lady" (Part III, Vol. 2, 145). But despite Caterina's friendly demeanor, her conversation topics were spicy ones, and historian Joanne Ferraro refers to Caterina's salon as "a perceived hotbed of radical ideas from France," (194) which sealed its doom.

Since she was a girl, Caterina's father had raised her to pursue knowledge. Born in Venice on May 8, 1736, to Antonio Giovanni Dolfin and Donata Salamon in the parish of Santa Maria del Carmelo, Caterina grew up in her family house at San Marcuola (Molmenti, Part III, Vol. 2, 125 n2). Caterina's family enjoyed rank and privilege, though apparently Antonio Dolfin had to borrow money to maintain their lifestyle (Gambier). Caterina was given a convent education, but little is known about the details of her schooling. In the preface to a book of her own sonnets, Caterina disclosed that her father, a judge and lawyer, taught her arts, letters, and sciences, a broad education that she was grateful for (Dolfino Tiepolo, xii). "Who will ever dare to deny that a good education is not the most dear legacy left by a loving father?" she asked. "As well, I recall that he did want to limit my imagination to the creation of infinite nowhere, that he would not fence my Kingdom among charms, beauty, and graces; nor above the tears, and to the sighs of others establish my reputation" (ix-x, translated by Giovanni Distefano). From her beginnings, Caterina was not one to be fenced in.

After Caterina's father died in 1753, leaving them with little money, Caterina's mother realized that their only option was for Caterina to make a good marriage. A suitable match was found—Marcantonio Tiepolo, himself from one of Venice's most noble lines. The couple married in 1755, when Caterina was still an adolescent, and she quickly felt like great walls had closed around her and her home had become her prison (P. Di Stefano). As a woman hungering for more of the learning for which her father had primed her, Caterina was not ready to submit to the circumscribed life usually expected of women of her rank.

Considering that Caterina had received a liberating education and that she aspired to be a writer, it's small wonder that these restrictions felt so stultifying. Like many men—and a few women—of her era, Caterina took on a pen name—Dorina Nonacrina—as part of her role within Arcadia, the idealized land created by members of academia as a pastoral paradise for poets and philosophers. One way she rebelled against her narrow marriage was to write poems. The death of her father inspired Caterina to pen a series of twenty sonnets in his honor. "I grieve the death, oh God! Of my Father," she wrote in Sonnet I, "I grieve the light days now turned dark, / I grieve, miserable daughter, the good, which I lost / of the first flowering of my green age" (Dolfino Tiepolo xiii, trans. by G. Distefano). Caterina felt the loss keenly since her father had championed her education, and his death came at a time when she particularly needed his support to continue her intellectual life. "I had the misfortune to remain without him when I was only fourteen, / thus he had not the time to educate me, as he had just begun," she lamented (x, trans. G. Distefano). Caterina also acknowledged her father's influence in shaping her as a woman ruled not only by her heart; in Sonnet XX she stated, "Rich I am not, but nothing I desired. / Since the burning passions of the heart / I learned to quench from my Father" (xxxii, trans. G. Distefano). Caterina published her book of poems, which contained sonnets by other male and female poets too, in 1767, first under a pen name and then under her first married name, Tiepolo. But she was already rebelling against her constricting status as a noble Venetian wife by participating in a life of letters.

Whenever possible, Caterina attended functions outside her home. At one of these she met the politician Andrea Tron, one of Venice's most influential and affluent bachelors. Besides her lively wit and passion for learning, petite Caterina also possessed long blond hair, large blue eyes, and "the lilies and roses of her complexion" according to her friend Carlo Gozzi (qtd. in Molmenti, Part III, Vol. 2, 125). Andrea Tron was smitten. Caterina was still married to Marcantonio Tiepolo, but in the rather relaxed mores of eighteenth century Venice, when many women had a male companion called a *cicisbeo*, she simultaneously became Andrea's companion and lover. Finally, after seventeen years of married life, Caterina had her marriage annulled on April 10, 1772. She and Andrea then married later that same year. Andrea Tron's political career had steadily risen, and a stable marriage rather than a long-time love affair would help his chances at accession to a higher position. Where Caterina had previously addressed Andrea as "Your Excellency," she now began saluting him as "*mon cher ami*" or "my dear friend" (Gambier). Caterina was feisty, writing to Andrea as they were soon to marry that her salad days were not "all over." She flirted, saying, "rouged, combed, and with my ready wit I'll undertake to rout all the girls" (qtd. in Molmenti, Part III, Vol. 2, 131). Andrea Tron had lain before Caterina a table spread with all the things she coveted most: intellectual life, stimulating society, wealth, and freedom.

These two made a powerful couple. Elisabetta Caminer Turra wrote a poem honoring them in 1773, Andrea for his "civic honors" and "multitude of virtues" and Caterina as a "clear / Example of how much noble intelligence / And knowledge nature has bestowed upon our sex" (Caminer Turra 183). Caterina would do her part as Andrea's companion and wife to aid him with his reforms. Andrea pushed for ecclesiastical changes, including the suppression of some of Venice's monasteries, which he felt had become too powerful and corrupt. When she learned that a number had been closed, Caterina wrote to her husband, "Twenty-six monasteries suppressed? What a comfort!" (qtd. in P. Di Stefano, author's translation). Moreover, she felt that her help to Andrea was particularly useful to her homeland. Caterina's letters show that she stayed abreast of political and religious happenings as well. She wrote, "In this year, 1784, the armies of his Imperial Majesty are more powerful than indulgences," (qtd. in Molmenti, Part III, Vol. 2, 131) showing that she knew not only where the soldiers were moving but also that she could attack these moves with a witty remark about the Catholic Church. "I laugh at the difficulties about the Pope," she had written the year before; "We are not in the ages when popes ruled the emperors" (131). Molmenti characterized Caterina as writing "vigorous and manly phrases" for these pronouncements, (131) showing that women were still not expected to know about nor partake in political life.

However, Caterina apparently had some facility for such involvement. A few months after their marriage, Andrea Tron rose to the rank of Procurator of San Marco. He was second in rank and power only to the doge and in charge of the administration of the Basilica di San Marco, in addition to overseeing programs to protect orphans and the mentally unsound. As Andrea's wife, Caterina acted as "*procuratessa*," keeping her own office in the Procuratie Vecchie, the long row of buildings flanking the Piazza San Marco. In a high ceilinged room with smooth terrazzo floors, Caterina heard petitions and accepted requests from Venetian citizens. She occasionally mediated some of the business that Andrea relegated to her care (P. Di Stefano). Women were not allowed any sanctioned roles within Venetian politics or government, so her work within the *procuratie* was an anomaly. Caterina and Andrea wielded quite a lot of authority, enough that many paid them court in hopes of assistance. Molmenti declared, "For many years she ruled Venetian society by her beauty and her wit, surrounded by flatterers and calumniators" (Part III, Vol. 2, 125). Some may have initially attended Caterina's salon in order to gain favor with her and her husband, though her charm, kindness, and insight enticed them to stay (Gambier).

Caterina's celebrity could be ruinous as well. Andrea Tron aspired to be doge when that post became available in 1779 with the death of Alvise Mocenigo. Andrea and his rival Paolo Renier spent great sums of money and marketed their influence far and wide, but many contend that Caterina's sometimes scandalous behavior marred his chances. There had been that little indiscretion when the Inquisition inspected Caterina's library and called upon her to defend herself—an indiscretion probably muted by Andrea's influence and wealth. The later closure of her salon full of "radical ideas" didn't help either. But the greatest scandal was yet to break.

Caterina's friend Carlo Gozzi recounted in his *Memorie Inutili* (*Useless Memoirs*) an incident involving nobleman Antonio Gratarol that also marred Caterina's career. She was using her influence to support a friend who was running for office. Wanting such patronage for himself, Antonio Gratarol had sidled up to Caterina and her husband, and when favors didn't blossom, he became libelous, saying that Caterina "threatens, persecutes, protects, and dispenses favours by virtue of the decrees of the Senate" (qtd. in Molmenti, Part III, Vol. 2, 126). In other words, she played favorites with her powerful husband's influence. Around this time in 1775, Antonio also had an affair with the actress Teodora Ricci, who enjoyed Carlo Gozzi's friendship and protection. According to Carlo, a series of meddlings, machinations, and misunderstandings led to his play *Love Potions* being seen as a satire that blasted Antonio. After losing the rights to his own play, Carlo turned to Caterina to help suppress it, entreating, "I know that you can settle matters if you like" (Gozzi 266). But Caterina replied, "The kindness of your heart is worthy of all honour . . . but if you knew the whole facts, you would not take compassion on that man" (265). Caterina did not disclose what heinous act Antonio had committed, but it was enough to turn her against him and refuse to help Gozzi. Antonio Gratarol then retaliated with a play maligning Caterina. All of this played out quite publicly in the theaters and salons of the city; Venice is small and gossip is rapid. Caterina was too powerful to be ruined, but such scandal harmed Andrea Tron's chance at becoming doge. Caterina was clearly a force to be reckoned with, someone who took no guff and was able to dish the same.

Despite such an ignominious event, Caterina was known as a kind, amiable, and generous person. Pompeo Molmenti stated that "to all alike she showed herself superior to meanness, but never arrogant" (Part III, Vol. 2, 145). She was a devoted friend to the brothers Gozzi. Carlo wrote about a time when Gasparo was so delirious with fever that he threw himself from a window. Caterina, who was staying nearby, rushed to his side and sent immediately for Carlo, while she fetched doctors. "Save my father!" she cried to Carlo referring to Gasparo as one she looked up to greatly (Gozzi 308). While Gasparo convalesced, Caterina offered to employ her influence to procure a lucrative position for Carlo, taking over Gasparo's job and supporting the family (though Carlo eventually declined). Another close friend, the playwright Carlo Goldoni, so admired Caterina that he dedicated his play *La Bella Selvaggia* (*The Beautiful Savage*) to her beauty and her mind (P. Di Stefano). Demure, passive, and retiring were not adjectives used for Caterina, a woman on the cusp of change in early modern Venice.

When Caterina was young, she made her voice known through her sonnets, but in later years letters she left behind provide samples of her voice. A few hundred letters survive, primarily inscribed to Andrea Tron, but also to Duke Gian Galeazzo Serbelloni. Caterina developed a close friendship with him, who was ten years her junior, and it apparently developed into something more than friendship. In a letter from August 2, 1783, Caterina declared to him, "You are the man my youthful fancy conjured up to make him arbiter of all my emotions and to adore with all my soul" (qtd. in Molmenti, Part III, Vol. 2, 132). She felt that her "heart of forty-six years is but a sorry gift" but hoped that Gian Serbelloni would accept it. But as Gian took longer and longer to respond to her missives, Caterina went from feelings of self-pity to anger, claiming in 1784 that she planned to "declare war" on him (132). By 1786 anything hot between them seemed to have cooled, and Caterina wrote, "All I ask is that an honest man should treat me like an honest man" (133). Caterina characterized herself as having more "masculine" traits when it came to friendship, and she asked for reciprocal and just treatment. Caterina showed that within the social bounds of Venice and her gender, she often wrote her own self-definition. "I am a woman," she later told Gian Serbelloni, "but brought up with all a gentleman's sense of honour" (133). If women were considered to be flighty, insincere, unreliable, then she would not be aligned with those terms. "I am not like the majority of women," she declared (133). She also grew tired of Gian's disregard and finally ended the friendship, stating, "I cannot submit to neglect; my birth, my nature, and my spirit forbid it" (133). After some years of following Gian Serbelloni's lead, Caterina wrote her own rules of engagement.

All of this, of course, occurred while Caterina was married to Andrea Tron and wielded great weight through his office and her own salon, while it was open. She didn't allow society to dictate her behavior. In fact, one telling anecdote reveals how Caterina would not be swayed by public opinion. The Princess Gonzaga flounced into Venice, but because of her dubious reputation, she was not invited into the city's noble houses. Caterina stepped forward to introduce the Princess into noble society, stating frankly, "This is the Princess Gonzaga. She belongs to a noble family, for this I answer; as for the rest, I answer neither for her nor for you nor for myself" (qtd. in Molmenti, Part III, Vol. 2, 145). While Caterina cared for social rank, she wouldn't let this same society condemn a person to ostracism. One might even say that Caterina expected to live her life by the same rules applied to men of her times—in her love affairs, her friendships, her social engagements, and her business dealings.

After Andrea Tron died in 1785, leaving Caterina a wealthy widow, she decided to scale back her social life. Her in-laws contested aspects of Andrea's will, and though he had requested that his "beloved wife" be allowed to continue living in the Procuratie, because she "deserve[s] every respect" (Gambier), Caterina spent more and more time at her property in Padua. She simultaneously rented a *casino* in the Frezzeria and restored her San Marcuola home. Caterina began devising reforms to provide women's education, but sadly none of these documents have survived (Gambier). The country air initially seemed to benefit her health; she had been afflicted by fevers and a nervous temperament all her life. But gradually her sick days grew more numerous. On November 14, 1793, Caterina suffered an aneurism and died in Venice. She was buried in the Church of San Marcuola next to her mother.

Since she had born no children, Caterina distributed her possessions and money to friends and relatives. Her infamous library, which had caused scandal and suspicion, she willed to her nephew Alvise Barbarigo, son of her sister Luisa Tron. Caterina Dolfin Tron's books symbolized her learning, her voice, and her rebelliousness. She would not be foiled or fenced in. Caterina's independence, her ambition, and her social currency elevated her to her full power, a force to be reckoned with.

# Giustiniana Wynne

## A Boundary-Breaking Writer

$I$t took until her middle years, but Giustiniana proved herself right. "Giustiniana was made to do something," wrote Giustiniana Wynne about herself. "Do not laugh, and be patient" (qtd. in Isenberg, "Without Swapping" 162). Giustiniana published her novel *Les Morlaques* in 1788. Professor Irene Zanini-Cordi contends that Giustiniana's book was "what could arguably be considered the first modern novel penned by an Italian woman writer" (womenwriters.nl). Scholars generally agree that the first Italian novel was *I Promessi Sposi*, written by Alessandro Manzoni and first published in 1827. It explores the love relationship between Renzo and Lucia, bracketed by the authority of a hypocritical priest named Don Abbondio and heroic Padre Cristoforo. The novel has been made into an opera, numerous films, and countless editions and translations, read by every Italian high school student for decades.

But what if *I Promessi Sposi* weren't actually the first Italian novel, and what if that distinction actually belonged to a woman? Giustiniana's *Les Morlaques* was published almost four decades before Manzoni's book. Though she was Venetian, she chose to write in French in order to reach a larger international audience, so in that respect hers is not the first novel in Italian. *Les Morlaques* was mostly forgotten, overlooked, and even maligned until recently. Here was an innovative and original author, having to wait most of her life until she even had the opportunity to commence a writing career, then composing something unprecedented, and still not being recognized for her efforts. Giustiniana must have felt frustrated.

Giustiniana Francesca Antonia Wynne was born in Venice on January 21, 1737, and baptized five days later at the Church of San Marcuola, a rather blocky church that never had a finished facade. Her Venetian mother Anna Gazini and British father Sir Richard Wynne had six children (not all of whom survived childhood). The couple did not marry right away and legitimized their offspring several years after Giustiniana's birth. This scandal cast a pall over the Wynne's social life and Anna's and Giustiniana's hopes for a splendid marriage. The family moved in the best circles, both Venetian and foreign, often to be seen at the soirees at British Consul Joseph Smith's Palazzo Balbi on the Grand Canal. Giustiniana later wrote, "Mister Smith shared with me his love for paintings, his antiquities, his library in order to enrich my passion for learning" (qtd. in di Robilant, *Venetian Affair* 24). Early on she loved books and wanted to expand her knowledge, so visiting Consul Smith's palace gave her the opportunity to immerse herself in a literary milieu.

Giustiniana apparently turned the heads of a number of influential and wealthy men besides Smith, who courted her at one point, as did Prince Dimitri Galitzine, Prussian foreign minister Dodo Knyphausen, and the richest man in Paris, Alexander la Riche de la Poupliniere (Isenberg, "Without Swapping" 169 n1). Giustiniana grew into a vivacious beauty. One miniature portrait entitled *Justine Wynne, Countess of Rosenberg-Orsini* shows her with upswept hair studded with pearls. She glows in a pink dress with a white slip and cuffs highlighting the edges, a fur-lined blue cloak, and a jewel-encrusted armband. Giustiniana sits at a table with her book *Les Morlaques* in her left hand and a quill in her right, emphasizing her role as an author. Her eyes radiate warmth.

Filled with Venetian paintings and peopled by Venetian literati and musicians, Consul Smith's *palazzo* was a social hub in the eighteenth century. That's where the fateful meeting took place between Giustiniana, age sixteen, and Andrea Memmo, twenty-four. The Memmo clan came from the oldest original Venetian families, with Andrea considered the pick of his generation. (In fact, he later rose beyond senator, ambassador, and governor of Padua to become the Procurator of San Marco, the most powerful political position next to the doge.) Even though Giustiniana's father hailed from British nobility, her lineage and the scandal surrounding her parents' marriage excluded her from ever having a chance to marry this man she quickly fell in love with. "My passion for him swallowed everything else in my life," she wrote (qtd. in di Robilant, *Venetian Affair* 10). In a letter to Andrea she claimed, "Do you know I have this constant urge to do well, to look beautiful, to cultivate the greatest possible number of qualities for the mere sake of pleasing you, of earning your respect, of holding on to my Memmo?" (34). Giustiniana was still a teenager, thrust early into this heady world, and her passion for life spilled into her passion for Andrea Memmo. But from the beginning, everyone from her mother to her social circle made it clear that her desires would not be fulfilled.

Though she was still quite young and inexperienced, Giustiniana's love for her Memmo coincided with her ambitions to improve herself and have a literary life. Giustiniana and Andrea kept their love secret but managed to dispatch hundreds of love letters—both touching and sizzling—to each other. Though Anna watched over the pair like a Mother Superior and forbade them from seeing each other, the couple still managed to steal away hours and even an occasional night together. Andrea would visit his friends at Ca' Tiepolo (now called the Palazzo Papadopoli) on the Grand Canal so he could gaze across the Rio Meloni into Giustiniana's window at the Palazzo Businello-Giustiani where she lived. Giustiniana once wrote to Andrea, "Come by the canal as my mother doesn't want me to go out, and make an appearance at Ca' Tiepolo as well, if you can" (28). Their relationship is warmly chronicled by Andrea di Robilant in *A Venetian Affair* after he discovered Andrea Memmo's letters among his family's belongings at the Palazzo Mocenigo and pieced together their story by pairing Andrea's letters alongside Giustiniana's. However, the affair was doomed due to the couple's differing social status, and this led to family routs for both the Wynnes and the Memmos, plus barely suppressed public scandal. Anna Gazini Wynne often became apoplectic with outrage, while Giustiniana suffered from headaches and nausea.

Later, in 1758, after countries and years had separated the lovers, and after politics and lineage compelled Memmo to marry, Giustiniana reflected on her first (and probably greatest) love. Writing to him but using the third person, she mused, "Yes, for me Memmo was something too grand." Acknowledging the almost destructive power their love affair had on her life, she continued, "You, my guide in everything. You revealed to me in time the Great Mysteries. You gave thunder to my spirit; you made me sensitive, and either you inspired in me a great soul or you made mine sensitive and noble" (qtd. in Isenberg, "Without Swapping" 167). Popular culture lauded the sensitive soul who suffered; Giustiniana was a woman of her times with acute sensibilities. When she left Venice for London and Paris with her mother and siblings, she found life tasteless and dull; even surrounded by society and entertainments in these grand cities, she remarked, "I am like the queen, and yet I am bored to death" (162). Professor Nancy Isenberg contends that Giustiniana's boredom and attendant illnesses during this period reflect her thwarted ambitions (162). Letter writing gave Giustiniana a healthy outlet, but this was only temporary relief until she could find a place in life where she could exert more control over her circumstances.

Because of her letters, Giustiniana is now immortalized by di Robilant's work. She also shows up in the memoirs of Giacomo Casanova, the famed Venetian most often defined as a great lover but also one of the most important chroniclers of the eighteenth century. Like Andrea Memmo, Casanova met Giustiniana when she was fifteen, though he encountered her in Paris as her mother was bringing the family from London after Sir Richard's death. This vivacious, witty young woman immediately captivated Casanova. He wrote that she "was a beauty, and to the charms of her figure she added those of a cultivated mind, the spell of which is often more powerful" (Casanova 172). On the other hand, Casanova also counted Andrea Memmo as a friend and knew that Andrea "seemed to have the preference" in Giustiniana's heart (172). In 1759, when Anna took Giustiniana off to Paris again—partly to get her away from Andrea and partly to procure her a good marriage match away from narrow Venice—they ran into Casanova. Giustiniana, whom Casanova referred to as "Mademoiselle XCV" in his memoirs in order to protect her reputation, said upon seeing him again, "I have always hoped to see you; and your prodigious escape [from prison] gave us the greatest pleasure, for we were always fond of you" (qtd. in Casanova 172-3). Casanova's avid seduction probably felt exhilarating and straightforward after the complications and intensity of her affair with Andrea.

But one night Giustiniana sent Casanova a letter, confiding in him. She wrote of "a sad burden which weighs on my soul; it is a secret of which I shall feel that I am relieved when it is no longer a secret to you, my only friend at this moment" (186). Though originally Casanova's memoirs were the only source for this story, Giustiniana's letter to Casanova surfaced at an auction in 1999, though some scholars question its authenticity (Isenberg, email). She wrote, "I beg you to assist an unhappy soul who will have no other recourse but to seek her own death if she cannot remedy her situation. There it is, dear Casanova: I am pregnant and I shall kill myself if I am found out" (qtd. in Isenberg, "Without Swapping" 160). Giustiniana felt that an abortion was no worse than suicide, which she would resort to rather than be discovered.

At this time, Giustiniana was actually betrothed to an affluent and elderly French tax official named Alexandre la Riche de la Poupliniere, a good match that would gain her respectability and freedom away from her overbearing mother Anna but in which Giustiniana found no joy. As Casanova tried to help Giustiniana find a way out of her predicament, including convincing her to let him personally administer an "*aroph*" that would bring on an abortion, the two friends became lovers and barely managed to keep a bubbling scandal from boiling over. Casanova eventually found a convent for Giustiniana to escape to, where she gave birth to a boy who was left with a family to be raised. Casanova reported that in her letter, "she told [him] of the peace which her soul was enjoying and her extreme gratitude for all that [he] had done for her" (Casanova 218). To give Giustiniana the benefit of the doubt, it must be remembered that these stories are based solely on Casanova's memoires, which have proven to contain some inaccuracies as he composed his engaging narratives. Giustiniana's marriage plans imploded after this episode, and in 1760 she left Paris to spend a year in London before returning to Venice.

It appeared that Giustiniana's prospects were limited by scandal surrounding her parentage and by her conduct in the affair with Andrea Memmo and later in Paris. But Giustiniana was too talented and accomplished to be foiled by these obstacles. She had received a worthy education, spoke multiple languages, and was always praised for her vivacity. As a child, her father had granted Giustiniana free rein in his sizable library, and she had read broadly, from fables to traveler's tales to history books. If her letters to Andrea are any indication, she was intelligent and thoughtful; for example, she realized that all the prohibitions placed upon her by her mother only made this forbidden affair more piquant. "How could they be so stupid," Giustiniana wrote to Andrea, "not to realize what refinement they bring to our pleasure by imposing all these prohibitions?" (qtd. in di Robilant, *Venetian Affair* 37). She understood the stimulating nature of her relationship while she lived it.

Upon her return to Venice, Giustiniana caught the eye of the Austrian Ambassador to Venice, Philip Josef, Count Orsini-Rosenberg. They married in a small secret ceremony and lived at the Palazzo Loredan on the Grand Canal. Based on a letter, it appears that Giustiniana got pregnant but must have miscarried (270). Because Giustiniana was now the wife of a foreign consul, she could no longer fraternize with Venetian politicians, including her old love Andrea Memmo, who was censured for talking with her about a postal system dispute with the Austrian government. The irony of this rebuke could not have been lost on Giustiniana. The Count, who was a vigorous man though in his seventies, retired from his position, and the couple moved to Austria. Again, due to Giustiniana's questionable lineage, the couple faced social obstacles, and Count Orsini-Rosenberg was unable to procure a meeting with the Austrian court in Vienna. After the Count died in 1764, Giustiniana returned to Venice and took a house near the Piazza San Marco, hoping to find a home where she could once again mingle in a stimulating society.

Giustiniana may have sparkled brightly and beautifully as a young woman, but this was the period when she really came into her own power. She opened her house as a small salon but left time for trips to Paris and London. She brought Count Bartolomeo Benincasa into her household, ostensibly as her secretary, yet there may have been more to their relationship. Giustiniana's niece Elizabeth (Betsy) Fremantle Wynne in her diaries refers to Bartolomeo Benincasa as Giustiniana's "cavalier," (Fremantle 6) and relates a number of amusing stories from their visit to England where the Count danced a minuet with Betsy and her sister, (10) accompanied Giustiniana to have her tooth pulled, (9) and even cross-dressed with her for a masquerade ball (2).

And during this time, Giustiniana wrote.

Probably inspired by Adam Smith's *Theory of Moral Sentiments*, Giustiniana compiled her own two-volume *Moral and Sentimental Essays*, published in both English and French simultaneously in 1785. Topics ranged from gambling, to education, to personal reminiscences. One engaging essay delved into the art of smiling. "Laugh heartily, charming and innocent youth!" she wrote. "The age of smiling will soon be upon you. That will be followed in turn by the years of the expertly contrived smile: an air of peace and serenity will often hide the truly agitated state of your soul" (qtd. in di Robilant, *Venetian Affair* 275). In these lines, Giustiniana seemed to be revealing her inner discontent. In another piece she contemplated her youth, writing, "When I was a pretty woman, I at least had enough intelligence to understand that I would have a long life beyond the brilliant life of youth . . . . Books always remain to me" (qtd. in Wolff 197). Giustiniana dissected herself frankly but with an indulgent wink, cognizant yet forgiving of her weaknesses and foibles.

Besides these essays, Giustiniana penned a few poems, a comedic play titled *Le Nouveau Prejuge a la mode* (Dalton, *Engendering* 158 n8), and an account of Grand Duke Paul I's visit to Venice, which included a description of Venetian festivals. In fact, Casanova sent Giustiniana a letter of praise in 1782 where he wrote, "Madame, the beautiful epistle which Your Excellency has printed concerning the sojourn in this city of the Count and Countess of the North, exposes you to the necessity of suffering yourself to be praised as an author by all those who write" (qtd. in Endore 303). Giustiniana responded kindly, saying, "I am most touched by the sign you have given me of your approbation" (303). Giustiniana must have relished this exchange between two writers, so different from the cat and mouse seduction she and Casanova had played so many years before. She was validated in her ambition to cultivate a literary life.

Giustiniana's writings often stretched the bounds of genres. One such piece was *Altichiero*, a sort of "philosophical guide," as Isenberg puts it, to the villa on the River Brenta owned by Giustiniana's friend Senator Angelo Querini ("Without Swapping" 167-168). The two had known each other for decades, and in the 1780s Giustiniana often escaped Venice to the fresher air and lively conversations convened by the intellectuals who gathered at Angelo's home. Di Robilant reports that while Giustiniana stayed at Altichiero, "she was the lady of the house" (*Venetian Affair* 276). Certainly she reveled in the *conversazione* there, wandering amongst the statues of Rousseau and Voltaire in the garden or enjoying a light pinot grigio from the local vineyards. She published *Altichiero* in 1786 as a tribute to Angelo Querini, as a guidebook to the villa, and as a philosophical journey (Isenberg, email). The essays also touch on the subject of women's education and equality, inviting people to end the inequitable division of the sexes. After travelers on the Grand Tour met Giustiniana and read her work, *Altichiero* was favorably reviewed in Europe. The villa itself has not survived, making Giustiniana's descriptions of it more poignant.

But Giustiniana's most important work came in 1788—her novel *Les Morlaques* about the Slavic people who lived in the rural areas of Dalmatia. After meeting Slavs when she had lived in Austria, and after reading *Viaggio in Dalmazia* by Alberto Fortis, she was inspired to frame her own story. *Les Morlaques* follows "the natural course of ordinary events in a Morlacchi family [that] will make us acquainted with the customs and usages of the nation in a manner more sensitive than the cold and methodical relation of the voyager," she explained (qtd. in Wolff 193). In order to paint an idealized portrait, Giustiniana "offers the image of nature in primitive society" (193). Like Jean-Jacques Rousseau, Johann Wolfgang von Goethe, Madame de Stael, and others at this time, Giustiniana glorified the peasant life for its simplicity and earthiness. While readers with more modern lenses now see that perspective as narrow and limiting, for her time Giustiniana was creating a new genre. Professor Larry Wolff calls this book an "anthropological novel" for its look at social mores and comparative lifestyles (193). But Giustiniana went a step further. Scholar Veronique Church-Duplessis points out that as one of few women writing at this time, Giustiniana "therefore exploits the anthropological aspect of the novel to offer an alternative to the status of women in both primitive and civilized societies" (Church-Duplessis). Though she was writing a fictional novel, one that even contains fairytale aspects, Giustiniana still used this story as an opportunity to denounce the barbaric treatment of women, in favor of more equality between the sexes.

Perhaps this viewpoint also relates to Giustiniana's stance towards marriage. Consider this: her parents' marriage was fraught with impropriety that dogged her heels; her first hope of marriage to Andrea Memmo was thwarted on all sides and was mired in disrepute; her plans for "mercenary" marriages of convenience fell through due to intrigues; and even her eventual marriage to the amiable and good-hearted Count Orsini-Rosenberg still got bogged down in defamation that followed her to Austria. Giustiniana wrote in 1760 that she "hate[s] marriage too much to think about it. Imagine, I wouldn't do it with a man of the greatest fortune whom I could seduce so as not to create my own slavery," she said, referring to La Poupliniere, "and I would not do it with a man who was my friend so as not to risk betraying him one day," meaning Andrea Memmo (qtd. in Isenberg, "Without Swapping" 164). Stilted social mores regarding marriage surrounded Giustiniana, and though she could be a passionate lover, most eighteenth century marriages had little to do with love.

Giustiniana was moving towards her eventual freedom, which she found in her widowhood, when she could read and write to her fill, follow her intellectual ambitions, and spend time with male companions such as Bartolomeo Benincasa or Angelo Querini who brought her contentment and who supported her in her endeavors. Alberto Fortis, who inspired Giustiniana with his travelogue of Dalmatia, was later inspired by her writings enough to declare that she was "a lady endowed with superior talents and solid culture, and therefore very far from all that gives rise to the ridicule of women of letters in our times" (qtd. in Wolff 197). Giustiniana garnered lavish praise from many of the best minds of her times, and moves were made to publish her letters after her death. But because she published in multiple languages and under variations to her name (both English and Italian spellings, and sometimes solely her initials), her works were not collected as part of an Italian oeuvre (qtd. in Isenberg, "Without Swapping" 169 n3). Thus, she was forgotten until the more recent interest in Italian women writers.

But Giustiniana was not forgotten as her life neared its end. "The poor Countess is to die," wrote her niece Betsy on June 23, 1791. "There is no remedy for her. Papa says they are all in a very great distress about it" (Fremantle 67). "Papa" was Giustiniana's brother Richard, who was with her on August 22, 1791, when Giustiniana passed away after nine months of suffering from uterine cancer. She had never raised children of her own, but having her nieces in her life, particularly at its end, must have brought her joy and connectedness. Richard memorialized Giustiniana with a plaque in the Church of San Benedetto in Padua, where she was buried. Similarly, Angelo Querini added a marble bust of Giustiniana to his Altichiero gardens. Andrea Memmo himself had visited Giustiniana's sickbed in great distress to see his beloved friend in such agony.

Like so many learned Venetian women, Giustiniana had suffered from illness related to her thwarted ambitions, but at the end of her life, she had enjoyed acceptance for her merits and love for her character. Over two hundred years after her death, Giustiniana is now gaining recognition as a boundary-breaking writer, author of one of the first—if not the first—Italian novels and credited with originating the anthropological novel. Giustiniana traveled much of Europe, from Italy to Great Britain, France, Austria, and always back to Venice. But it was the passage from passionate lover and letter writer to multifaceted novelist that proved to be her richest journey.

# Maria Boscola

## Una Brava

$M$others come in many wrappings: Business suits. Aprons. Jog bras. Jeans. However, in eighteenth century Venice, mothers of the *popolani* or workers' class would have shared some distinct similarities. Elbows deep in pasta flour. Elbows deep in garden arugula. Elbows deep in laundry suds. Mothers swept the front steps or wiped the stray polenta off Marcolino's chin. Mothers tucked a blanket around the bedful of brothers or patted the back of a crying baby. It being the eighteenth century, mothers dutifully went to church and prayed for guidance. And it being Venice, mothers knew how to row a boat. Mothers were role models and disciplinarians and comforters.

Mothers were also champions.

Maria Boscola, a five-time boat-racing champion whose wins spanned forty years, was also a mother. Maria was born on Sottomarina, a section of Chioggia, an island to the south of Venice proper. She grew her own vegetables, enough to sell the surplus at the markets. History has left scant details about her life, though she is listed as a "smallholder," someone who owns or rents land as a small farm (Stanley). Maria apparently had an independent streak, wanting to run her own business and secure a financial future for herself and her family. She married Bepi Scarpa, probably in the Church of Sant'Andrea on the Corso del Popolo, facing Chioggia's main *campo*. They produced a large family of six: Andrea, Elvira, Teresa, Giovanni, Giacomo, and Elena. Maria must have cultivated the soil of this rural island, pulling weeds, clipping off greens to tie into bunches, bundling onions into bouquets, and loading her reed baskets with eggplants, greens, garlic, beans, onions, and tomatoes. Her children undoubtedly toiled alongside her, probably as soon as they could toddle. She was no stranger to working hard.

For her vegetable business, Maria heaped the baskets aboard her boat and faced a twenty-five-kilometer voyage to sell her goods at the Rialto market. She would first pass the long, narrow island of Pellestrina and the four kilometers of the Murazzi, enormous stone walls fourteen meters thick at the base, erected in the eighteenth century to defend the lagoon from the sea. Maria continued rowing past the islands of Alberoni and Malamocco, heading towards San Giorgio and then up the Grand Canal. Passing under the Ponte di Rialto, she soon reached the marketplace just beyond as the black sky faded into pink and then blue.

Like Venetian men and many Venetian women, particularly of the *popolani* class, Maria would have learned to row a boat since the time she could climb aboard one. She would have rowed standing up, in the traditional Venetian style, with two oars that crossed in front of her chest. With each thrust, she would propel her upper body forward, using the strength in her legs to add force and balance in her small boat. For her market trips, Maria probably rowed the *caorlina*, the most typical market boat of this period as it could hold all her goods. It would have taken over an hour to row to market. Most Venetian boats have no keel below the water line, so they can skim over the shallow lagoon. The *caorlina* is about ten meters long, with a fairly flat hull except for the bow and stern that point up at the corners like a grin. In regattas (or boat races), they require six rowers, though going to market, Maria probably rowed alone until her children became big enough to join her. In which direction did her thoughts turn on those long trips across the lagoon? Of her children or husband or garden? Or of cheering crowds and the glories of the race?

On Chioggia lived fishers and farmers and sailors. Historian Giulio Lorenzetti describes the Chioggiotti as "extremely individual types and among the most expert and intrepid sailors of the Adriatic, high-spirited and sturdy" (849). These were people who worked long hours in the sun, who had to make do with what was at hand, very unlike their counterparts in Venice. The women, like the men, worked laborious lives to support their families; most Chioggiotti were of the *popolani* or workers' class, like Maria. Chioggia also produced more merchants than nobles, though a few handfuls of illustrious doctors, cosmographers, writers, navigators, composers—and the painter Rosalba Carriera—were born there too. For centuries, Chioggia had a government independent of Venice, though it came to her aid in the War of Chioggia from 1378 to 1380, which devastated the island and depleted its power. Chioggia today consists mostly of buildings from the nineteenth century except for its older churches.

Women in these island communities rowed boats for transportation and work, so racing was not a stretch. While Maria Boscola is a remarkable woman champion, she would have had the support of her church and community as well (Stanley). She most likely attended the Church of Sant'Andrea on the Corso del Popolo, near her home. When attending church, Maria probably wore a traditional Chioggia *tonda* of white linen to veil her hair, or perhaps the traditional *indiana*, something that looked like a calico skirt worn round the waist but with the backside tossed up to cover her head like a shawl. Regattas, the boating events that included both parades and races, were encouraged by the parish priest, who blessed the boats the night before the race as the people gathered at the Church of the Salute, bobbing in the Grand Canal like bright corks. Priests offered sanctified oil or candles, and some boats even carried a sacred image for good luck. If a parish's rower won, the red and blue winners' flags were displayed at the church altar. Since the regattas were lauded and encouraged by the church, they became a safe place for women to participate in their community. Maria Boscola was a hometown hero.

It is said that the first regatta celebrated the Feast of the Marias in the thirteenth century, commemorating the rescue of twelve young brides who had been kidnapped by pirates; their rescue coincided with the February 2 feast day of the Virgin Mary, hence the name. Venice loves a show, so regattas were also an excuse to show off boats and rowers to both the populace and the many visitors who constantly streamed through Venice. Jacopo de' Barbari's elaborate birdview map of 1500 even features racing boats. Regattas were organized in the fifteenth and sixteenth centuries by the Compagnie de le Calze, private societies that orchestrated the city's entertainments for festivals such as Carnevale or the Sensa. A regatta could be a stately procession down the Grand Canal to deliver a newly-elected doge to the Ducal Palace, or it could be a raucous race down the length of Giudecca to entertain cheering crowds. Regattas were often used as a way to keep rowers' skills sharp for battle. Racing each other built muscle, and competition kept them hungry. Later, regattas were privately funded by wealthy patrons, even after the fall of the Republic, and in 1841 became publicly funded events. The tradition continues today with racers competing during the summer months at Burano, Murano, Sant'Erasmo, Malamocco, Giudecca, and Pellestrina, with the Regata Storica showcasing historical vessels, or the Vogalonga resurrecting the art of traditional Venetian rowing. Maria is part of this proud history and is one of the few women included in the annals.

In Venice in the eighteenth century, there were a lot of things women didn't do, but *popolani* women, well, they rowed. No private gondoliers for the working class. Every *nonna* knew how to get herself around the islands (Stanley). According to historian Umberto Zane, documents from 1493 record that women participated in a regatta to honor the visit by Leonora, the wife of Duke Ercole I of Ferrara. Zane comments that the women's races often garnered larger bets and sometimes more attention than the men's races. In fact, Zane even contends that Venetian women racers like Maria are among the world's first women athletes (Zane). Racing, in Venice, is not just for the men.

Maria Boscola put her strong arms to work at something besides the dough, vegetables, and suds. She entered the regattas. Who knows what first inspired her: A dare? An encouraging husband? Chioggiotti pride? On May 4, 1740, Maria won her first race on the occasion of a visit from Federico Cristiano di Polonia, a prince and Elector of Saxony. On that day, the regatta included five races, four of them by men either in gondolas or *battelli*, a common lagoon boat that comes in some variations. The women's race that day employed the *batela da fossina*, a boat for two rowers. The book *La Regata di Venezia: Composizione Poetica in Dialetto Veneziano* by Cleandro Conte di Prata lists all the competitors that day. Four teams raced in all: Zaneta Pote with Anna Cabria as a team; Laura Gelmete and her companion from Mestre; and Cecilia Boscola, probably related to Maria, and a friend. Maria's friend Emma, who apparently went by the nickname La Garbina, took the bow, with Maria at the stern (54). Wearing white blouses and long white skirts, the women leaned into their oars and pushed the water behind them in perfect synchronicity. After rowing hard against their competitors, they pulled in fastest, earning a red flag for the first place honors.

A remarkable twenty-four years passed until Maria appears in the records again. *La Regata di Venezia* lists no races from 1741 to 1743, and in 1744 only men raced. Were these Maria's childbearing years? The next regatta is listed in 1751, but again with no women's races. Like a true competitor, the desire to win called Maria back to the boats. To honor Edoardo Augusto, Duke of York, Venice held a regatta on June 4, 1764. Gabriel Bella painted *Regata delle Donne in Canal Grande* (1764), where he depicts the women's black boats barreling down the center of the Grand Canal, the team of two appearing tiny as they pull away from the others. The women racers all wear long white skirts and white blouses with blue bands along their edges, their hair tied into ponytails hanging down their backs. Larger boats, mostly full of men, clog the sidelines in front of the palaces on one side and the Customs House and Church of the Salute on the other. Spectators mill along the *fondamenta* in a colorful array of red skirts, brown breeches, white stockings, and blue coats. The azure canal's surface is whipped into choppy peaks, and clouds like commas twirl across the sky.

Maria was a winner in this race. Could she be one of the women painted by Bella's hand? Canaletto, Guardi, and many other painters immortalized various regattas in oil on canvas. Other racing teams included Lucia Stivella and Ufemia Panela, Anzola and Maria Meneguole (though another source lists Tonina Vianela and Maria Vianela), and Madalena Boscola and Checa Boscola, sisters and also from Sottomarina, possibly related to Maria. But the winning team that day was Maria Boscola and Anzola (Angela) Scarpa, nee Tiozza, her sister-in-law (62). Doge Alvise Mocenigo himself handed them their red flag, honoring their victory. How their hearts must have swelled with pride, to win again after so many years. Cleandro Conte di Prata composed a series of poems in Venetian dialect about the regattas. For this June 4 race, he writes about how "the women of this country know how to emulate manly enterprises" (author's translation). Yet for being described as manly in their strength, the racers are also described as "courteous, lovely, personable, and beautiful."

Maria didn't stop there. Three years later, on June 3, 1767, at a festival honoring Carlo Eugenio of Wurttemberg, Maria won the blue flag for second place. Her teammate was Anzola Tiozza again, though her surname Scarpa was not listed on the roster. In fact, Maria herself is listed as Marieta. Her rival, Lucia Stivella, took first with her teammate Maria Balerina. More of the Boscola women raced again: Anzola and Checa, plus Maria Brava Boscola Tonela (64). What was this family of warrior women like? Did they finish their laundry then run to their *battelli* to play? Did they growl at each other across the Sunday dinner table, challenging each other to a quick after-dinner race? At this regatta, the women tore up the canal with a "great clamor and ruckus," according to the Conte di Prata's poem describing the day. "Lucia came in beautifully for first place," he recounts, while "Boscola and Tiozza, women valued for their passionate rowing, hastily followed" (author's translation).

A number of years elapsed until Maria would win again—but then she won big. Apparently no women raced again for seventeen years. The Boscola and Tiozza women must have been chomping at the bit. Then at the regatta on May 8, 1784, to honor Gustav III, the King of Sweden, Maria raced with a new partner, Checa Boscola this time (69). (There's some confusion here: Cleandro Conte Di Prata lists two sets of race results, yet the winner must have been Maria's team, confirmed by the painting of her at the Museo Correr listing her winnings.) Doge Paolo Renier awarded them the red flag this time. "We admire the red flag of Boscola and Tiozza," the Conte di Prato states, referring to Maria as a "*brava*," a word that means not only good but also worthy, valiant, and strong. Later that month on the 25th, Maria and Checa took first once again, with rival Lucia in second and kin Madalena in fourth (71). Sadly, this was the final race of the Venetian Republic in which women were allowed to participate. Two hundred years would pass and Italy would be united as one country before Venice permitted its women to race in the regattas again.

Thankfully, Maria is preserved for history. Her portrait, the *Ritratto di Maria Boscola* painted by an unknown artist in 1784, hangs in Room 47 of the Museo Correr. Maria stands proudly, a straw hat sitting at a rakish angle on her head, as she clutches her red and blue flags to her chest. She is clad in a simple white blouse and red skirt, with a blue bodice laced in front, her broad shoulders showing where her rowing strength emanates. She wears a curved gold earring and has a sprig of greenery tucked behind one ear. The lagoon sits behind her and a scroll beside her, listing her wins for 1740, 1764, 1767, and the two in May 1784. Maria's gaze is strong but not impudent, steadfast, a mother completing the task at hand. "She knows how to play with spirit and heart," states the Conte di Prata in one poem, and in another, he declares, "The brave Boscola / Leaning so much forward / Makes you admire and enjoy / Her strong rowing" (translation by Giovanni Distefano).

Maria doesn't seem like someone who worried about doing what was safe. She pushed herself to be the best, and she pushed past the limits of what others expected women to do. She must have inspired many young women to follow in her wake and strive to top her record. The women's races were prohibited for many years but returned briefly from 1931 to 1934 when they raced from the slaughterhouse in Cannaregio down the Grand Canal to the fish market. In 1953 the women were racing once again, and the winners that year were the cousins Maria and Teresa Boscolo. No, not a time warp, but the emergence of new racers inspired by the old.

But Maria could be proud indeed of the competition she initiated. Her original record of five wins was eventually broken when women's racing was made a continuous sport. Umberto Zane records that the team of Anna Mao and Romina Ardit had a winning streak of eight races from 1997 to 2004, while the record holder for most wins overall is Gloria Rogliani, with eighteen flags. Women are now a standard part of the summer regatta season, with a new cadre of women—still donning skirts, though ones much shorter than Maria's—pushing at their oars and propelling their boats down the canals, claiming winners' pennants just as the men do. As the Conte di Prata wrote, the Venetian women racers' "reputation will be known throughout the world." Ask any racer or gondolier in Venice—they still cheer for Maria Boscola, *una brava.*

# Elisabetta Caminer Turra

## Into the Limelight

$\mathcal{Y}$oung Elisabetta sat by her mother, poking a needle through the dense fabric, securing the cream-colored ribbon to the felt hat. She still had more ribbons to adhere, then the crisp fabric flowers, before her mother would be satisfied that this hat was complete. Elisabetta's eyes continually darted towards the table piled high with papers and journals, where her father sat translating an article from the French original. "Come help me with this piece about women's fashions," he called to his daughter, and Elisabetta was only too happy to drop her sewing on the chair and join her father in his work.

Benefitting from the fresh ideas of the eighteenth century's Age of Enlightenment, Elisabetta was allowed to forage gleefully amongst her father's books and periodicals. Domenico Caminer was a renowned and successful journalist, running a number of widely-distributed periodicals as well as chronicling historical events and dabbling in theatrical productions. Their house must have brimmed with mounds of books to be read and reviewed, stacks of documents to be typeset. Though Elisabetta was originally trained to sew and create hats, she foreswore ribbons and the needle in favor of pen and paper, following her father into a journalism career. Elisabetta, born July 29, 1751, and baptized at the Church of San Benedetto on August 3, was the oldest of five children born to Domenico and his wife Anna Maldini. The next oldest child, Antonio, also followed his father into the writing profession, helping to edit one of his journals, the *Nuovo postiglione*, and carry on its publication after Domenico passed away. But it was Elisabetta who truly made a name for herself and left a vast, lasting body of work that not only contributed to the world of letters but also vocally advocated for women's equality.

From the time she was quite young to the early end of her life at age forty-four, Elisabetta declared her love for learning and dedicated herself to it. She published her first poem at age twelve, in a collection that honored Gian-Francesco Pisani's new position as Procurator of San Marco. Entitled "Poem on Ambition and the Passing of Time," (1763) she lamented that "For me your clock runs too slowly / And my mind is still too immature / To cut a presentable figure / Among the Apollonian company that I love," already hopefully placing herself among the literati (Caminer Turra 97). She read and wrote voluminously, working alongside her father, and began cultivating literary and scholarly connections of her own. By age nineteen, in a letter to the lawyer and intellectual Giuseppe Pelli Bencivenni, Elisabetta confessed, "I am at an age and in a situation that do not allow me to hope for mediocre knowledge, to say nothing of great learning, and yet I am full of desire to cultivate my mind" (107). Being a woman, she wasn't allowed to attend the university, and not being of the noble class, she wasn't given tutors, but that didn't discourage her. Elisabetta continued in her letter that education "is, if not the only, at least the most useful and constant inner disposition to which I have abandoned myself with joy" (107). She was accepted by other scholars and inducted into the Accademia degli Agiati (The Wealthy) in 1778, with the name Critonilla. Reading, writing, "cultivating her mind," were her life's vocation.

In addition to her first poem, Elisabetta's earliest task was as a copyist for her father in his journalism profession. During her teens her father ran the local paper *Diario veneto*, a gazette called *Europa*, and the literary magazine *Nuova gazzetta veneta*. Though her father recognized and supported Elisabetta's talents and literary interests, he also welcomed her help; theirs was not a wealthy family, and her efforts generated income. For instance, to help make ends meet, the Caminer family had rented out a room in their house to a French tutor, and this was probably where Elisabetta learned the language. Through informal conversations in the hallway to more formal lessons with pen and book, Elisabetta became fluent in French, to the point that she could translate masterfully. Her first major contributions to the magazine, then, were translations of *La princesse de Babilonie* and a letter about smallpox, both by Voltaire.

Elisabetta went on to develop a love and great knowledge of French plays in the bourgeois drama genre, which she felt could inspire empathy and virtuous conduct through their emotional content and modeling of positive morals. She faced criticism from journalist Cristoforo Venier and playwright Carlo Gozzi (brother-in-law to Luisa Bergalli Gozzi), who believed that plays were meant for entertainment not education. But Elisabetta countered by saying "that inviting the people to a lugubrious play does not necessarily mean one is chasing them from cheerful ones" (126). Plays should contain a range of emotions, "in order that the hearts of men might learn to soften," she said (126). At this time, Venice hosted eight public theaters, more than much larger cities such as Paris. It was a rich world much frequented by all members of the citizenry. People attended not only to see the show, but also as a social gathering; they chatted with friends, commented loudly on the singer's merits, or conducted amorous intrigues in the darker nooks. Theaters large and small were sumptuously decorated with gilded boxes and balustrades, mirrors and chandeliers holding multitudes of candles. Venice was a theater-lover's town and a land of opportunity for actors, singers, managers, writers, translators, and directors.

Besides translating three volumes of plays, Elisabetta then began working directly in the theater on these translations, overseeing the productions in the Teatro Sant'Angelo between 1769 and 1771. Women rarely did this kind of work, and Elisabetta handled it adroitly, rolling up her sleeves to tramp through the backstage and to direct the actors. She would have chosen which actors in the troupe would play each role, coaching them to stress certain lines or emphasize certain emotions. She would have hired the musicians and coordinated the set designers in a city known for its elaborate stage scenery. And she would have chosen which plays to mount, handled the theater's finances and advertising, demonstrating a huge range of skills besides her translation work. Elisabetta translated *The Deserter* by Louis-Sebastien Mercier, then had it performed in Venice where she recorded that "it was repeated for twenty-three nights in a row, and it enjoyed equal success in almost all of Italy" (129). She also wrote reviews of productions for various journals, giving honest if not audacious appraisals. For example, in a letter to her friend Giuseppe Gennari, she admitted to him that the play *Antiope* "was a barbarous flop" (106). However, she wouldn't write plays, for she said, "I will never have the temerity to have a work of mine performed if I think it bad or mediocre" (128). She was perfectly busy and well-employed translating and compiling others' words.

Elisabetta was a multi-talented woman of letters: a publisher, translator, journalist, poet, correspondent, editor, theatrical manager, and more. After she married Dr. Antonio Turra on June 20, 1772, and moved to Vicenza, they even started their own press, the Stamparia Turra, in 1780. While Elisabetta's husband financed the company, she made the editorial decisions and reviewed works for her journals. Even after marrying, Elisabetta declared in a letter to a friend that "As far as letters are concerned, whether it is for the better or for worse that I occupy myself with them, and despite my small success, I will certainly never abandon them" (138). She believed that marriage should not prevent women from pursuing their work, and unlike most of the learned women who preceded her, Elisabetta was a prolific writer for her entire life, with no slowdown or cessation due to marriage. She and her husband Antonio never had children; though the reason for this is unknown, according to biographer Catherine M. Sama it may have been part of Elisabetta's design to not disrupt her career ("Volume" 27). What she appreciated most in her husband was "his good soul" she said (Caminer Turra 130), and he supported her career financially, materially, and emotionally.

Influenced by ideas from the Enlightenment, Elisabetta believed that women should be productive, not merely ornamental. In fact, in her review of the *Journal of the Ladies and Fashions of France*, Elisabetta claimed that the author "desires to mask what is useful with what is pleasing"; (197) in other words, clothing fashions focused too much on appearances rather than usefulness. Eighteenth century clothing included heavy dresses layered over underskirts, with capes at the back or hoops to hold out the hip fabric. Necklines and cuffs dripped lace, and tightened bodices restricted women's movements. Elaborate coiffures often included flowers, feathers, bonnets, and sometimes extra hairpieces. Elisabetta lambasted such frivolities, stating, "It is pitiful to see how gallant women torture themselves to invent fantastic decorations and to look like frauds or something worse" (208). Clearly, Elisabetta was not buying that old argument that women must be beautiful to be virtuous, and she used her role as editor to advance her views. She often employed a mocking or sarcastic tone, such as stating that one journal provided "Instructions for the fair sex, in which matters of virtue will be linked together with matters of the toilette" (197). Women had more options and had come a long way from being decorative, mannequins for their husband's wealth—or at least Elisabetta believed that this role was no longer acceptable.

The best way for women to be useful, Elisabetta believed, was to begin by being educated. Just as developing countries know today, an educated woman will "bring no small number of advantages to civil society," she contended, (178) such as managing her household and raising healthy children. Besides, once women have some learning, she sarcastically argued, "it would prevent us from having to blush upon hearing the wonderment people express when a woman is a little less uneducated than usual" (178). Women could contribute to society, to conversation, to (gasp!) politics, and to letters rather than always sitting silently or hiding their talents.

Along the same lines, Elisabetta always wanted to improve herself. In a 1770 letter to her friend Giuseppe Bencivenni, she told him that his corrections of her translations were so valuable because "I use these as instruction, since a nearly innate inclination, I would say, drives me to make studying my only occupation" (104). Years later she had not changed; she wrote to poet and critic Aurelio de' Giorgi Bertola, "I hasten to take advantage of your correction, and I could not have a better guide for improving my ideas" (159). Due to the prohibition against gaining a formal education, Elisabetta could not attend the university but instead honed her critical thinking, parried ideas, and improved her writing through her correspondence with learned and enlightened men. Elisabetta thirsted for such opportunities to grow. She wished all women did likewise.

In 1792 Elisabetta announced in her *Nuovo giornale enciclopedico d'Italia* that a remarkable book had been published in London: *A Vindication of the Rights of Woman* by Mary Wollstonecraft. "Her book proves for the millionth time that women might deserve the honor of being considered part of the human race," wrote Elisabetta, bittersweet joy emanating from her words (189). Mary Wollstonecraft believed that women "should base their power on a better education, on the development of their intellectual abilities, on the cultivation of their reason, and on the knowledge of their own purpose and their own duties," wrote Elisabetta in her book review (189). Venetian women still lacked many educational opportunities beyond elementary reading, writing, and basic math skills, the goal being to read religious books and run a household, (King 171) and only a handful of women frequented the literary milieu. In many ways, little had changed since Elisabetta's predecessors had promoted female passivity and obedience, but Mary Wollstonecraft's *Vindication* seemed to be ushering in a sea-change. Both Mary and Elisabetta recognized that previous women's "power depend[ed] upon youth and beauty" (Caminer Turra 188-9). Elisabetta's reviews of important new books and her support of progressive thinkers helped to eradicate the outworn ways of thinking and escort in the new. She must have held Mary's book in her hands, feeling like she had discovered a box that emanated light.

One of Elisabetta's progressive opinions was that women often contributed to their own oppression. In her "Poem Offering Advice to a Bride and Groom upon their Marriage" from 1774, Elisabetta boldly stated, "It is we [women] who make of ourselves a weaker sex," (203) as they subjugate themselves to idle fashions. In this poem, Elisabetta used the occasion of her friends' marriage to publicly put forth her opinions about equality (Sama, "Introduction" 68). The rise at this time of fashion periodicals, while giving women a place of some agency, also linked them to something superficial and rather useless compared to more intellectual pursuits. In a book review, Elisabetta admonished one anonymous female author for withholding her name and thus not acknowledging her accomplishments. Elisabetta wrote, "Might she be of the opinion, humiliating to her sex, that in cultivating her talent she brings dishonor to women?" (Caminer Turra 190). Elisabetta championed learned women and boldly asked them to come out into the limelight—where she herself stood.

Following this theme, Elisabetta spoke more courageously than most women of her era. "Do not be amazed at this frankness of mine," she wrote in a letter to her friend Giuseppe Bencivenni. "I am not ashamed of it at all: and I would be wrong if I were" (104). Women must learn to trust their words, she believed, cultivate their minds, and share their thoughts. They had every right to. Of course, she wrote this fearlessly in her private correspondence rather than in the more public journals, and in those she often resorted to satire and sarcasm to moderate her message.

In reviewing Mary Wollstonecraft's call for equality, Elisabetta also asked the question: "At what price?" (188). As they fought for equal rights, would women have to risk their physical and emotional safety? A 1792 letter to author and friend Lazzaro Spallanzani outlined how suspected spies had come snooping around the publishing house run by Elisabetta and her husband, asking questions about authors and publications. "Even good people have to fear wicked individuals," Elisabetta wrote as she warned her friend (164). Elisabetta also suffered personal censure, particularly from Carlo Gozzi and Cristoforo Venier as mentioned before. Cristoforo Venier, a writer and editor himself, criticized Elisabetta for her lack of formal education and her arrogance at becoming a literary critic. Looped into his arguments was an attack on her gender; he argued, as did many threatened males before him, that if Elisabetta were so intelligent, she must be sexually promiscuous.

Elisabetta's father Domenico rose to his daughter's defense, taking legal action against Cristoforo that in the end barred him from working as an editor. These charges took place early in Elisabetta's career, when she was but nineteen, and may have contributed to her decision to marry, which provided her with a socially secure and protected position. As researcher M. Gabriella Di Giacomo reveals, writings from the period show other attacks on Elisabetta as a woman who "attempted to destroy the gendered social and cultural watershed" (Di Giacomo). During her career, she was unfairly accused of dishonesty, perversion, promiscuity, and atheism.

Perhaps for these reasons, Elisabetta remained concerned regarding her public persona. When she later had her portrait painted, Elisabetta had herself portrayed in a fashionable, feminine Turkish-style ruffled dress, conscious that such concessions were often necessary to allow a woman to hold a place in men's literary society (Sama, "Introduction" 51). In Marco Comirato's etching of the original painting, Elisabetta's very full hair makes her look larger than life. As she gazes off to one side, her look is wistful, soft, yet hard to decipher. A woman must still appear "womanly" and not too far out of her prescribed position if she were to survive and retain a venue for her work. Or, as another of Elisabetta's letters to Giuseppe Bencivenni attests, it was sometimes necessary for a woman to appear "pressured" by a male colleague to share her work. "I would not have considered republishing and expanding my translated comedies were it not for the entreaties of a printer to whom I yielded," (Caminer Turra 141) she wrote in order to not appear too ambitious. Unlike male writers, women of this era had to worry about such issues. It took considerable perseverance to carry on through a lifetime of such ill treatment.

Whenever she found the opportunity, Elisabetta championed other women. She was in a position, through the journals she edited, to review and promote other women's work. Catterina Boschi was one such woman who benefitted from this patronage. Elisabetta published one of her poems and said such a writer proved that women were "no less capable of sound thinking than men" (114 n57). Elisabetta's editorial and translation work gave her the forum to shape public opinion in both broad as well as particular ways. In a review of the French *Dictionnaire historique portative des femmes celebres* (*Portable Historical Dictionary of Celebrated Women*), Elisabetta outlined numerous remarkable women throughout the ages. She justified her praise, writing, "Moved by this blameless affection for her sex, a woman must think to speak up for all the others in the voluminous work" (168). There is no way to quantify the effects such writing had on women, but almost certainly, in small, everyday ways, those who read Elisabetta's journals could have incorporated her ideas into their worldview, incrementally changing society all the while. Hundreds such journals must have sat on women's dressing tables amidst perfumes and powders, or in kitchens amid the clutter, bringing smiles to the Venetian women who read them and thought, "It's about time!"

Elisabetta's impact can be quantified in other ways, however. She contributed substantially to Venice's and Italy's theatrical worlds with her many translations and productions, particularly fostering the French bourgeois drama genre that cultivated morals into plays. She translated into Italian works by Jean Racine, Voltaire, and other French giants, bringing their compositions to Italian audiences, which promoted Enlightenment ideologies. But perhaps most importantly, Elisabetta's writing and editorial work in her father's and her own journals had the greatest lasting change. As Catherine Sama points out, "Journals were the principal means by which most readers obtained access to new ideas" ("Introduction" 63). Such publications were more affordable and obtainable to the average person than books were. Her editorials and her choices of which works to review wielded great power to influence social discourse and opinion. In a sense, Elisabetta's writing was subversive, using the book review genre to introduce and promote new ideas while getting around the censors. She often addressed weighty topics such as capital punishment, corruption, freedom of the press, and forcing women into convents. Venice produced more periodicals than other Italian cities, and when Elisabetta married and moved to Vicenza, she brought the authority and leverage of this legacy with her.

Elisabetta never did return to live in Venice. Some hints in her letters indicate that she had conflicts in her family life, probably with her husband, that prevented her from corresponding or working for a time. Then she fell ill. Some reports say that she received a blow to her chest that produced a tumor. Whatever the cause, Elisabetta developed breast cancer. In a letter from February 21, 1796, she dictated, "For nearly two months now I have been unable to get out of bed" (Caminer Turra 164). Cocooned in sheets and pillows, she suffered through three more months, unable to eat, crushed by cancer's grip. On June 7 that year she passed away, and she was buried in Vicenza's Church of Santo Stefano, where a plaque commemorated her life. Tireless in her drive to encourage women to step into their well-deserved limelight, Elisabetta had written, "There is no reason for us to hide ourselves" (168).

The Church of San Benedetto

# Isabella Teotochi Albrizzi

## Mirror for Singular Souls

$A$ pigmy, a misanthrope, and a seducer: What do they all have in common?

They are all profiles from Isabella Teotochi Albrizzi's *I Ritratti* or *Portraits*, her descriptions of how men should not behave, published in 1807. First, the Pigmy is a small man, a man with little talent, a man without character who never grows into his potential to be good and just and talented. Second, the Misanthrope is a hater, self-centered, mean in spirit and with his wallet, one who lacks empathy in his drive to procure the best for himself. Third, the Seducer is more than just a rage with the ladies; he is like one who wears a mask, false to others as he tries to gain all for himself. Clothed in a riotous red dress with deep décolletage, her brunette curls piled atop her head and a warm smile on her lips, as shown in Elisabeth Vigee's portrait from 1792, Isabella would have captivated her salon guests as she described these three types of sinister men.

Why would Isabella, an educated and enlightened woman who published her writings and who kept a salon for the nineteenth century's glittering literati, deign to write about these antitheses of the model man? Because she had to contend with centuries of what had come before, namely attitudes that stereotyped women as inferior. In 1721 philosopher Antonio Conti had contended that women couldn't rival men in politics, government, the sciences. A decade later Italian Jesuit writer Saverio Bettinelli wrote that the *belles lettres* genre in Italy, which began to give women authors a voice and a place, had led to a "decline in eloquence" in writing, as Professor Susan Dalton records ("Searching" 96). Over a millennium earlier, Aristotle himself had claimed that women were inferior versions of men, and virtually all men of intellect held Aristotle in the highest esteem, even up to Isabella's century. Worried about the fates of other women and perhaps fed up with their second-class treatment, Isabella probably couldn't resist taking up her pen to warn against men with dangerous characteristics, including in her book the descriptions of these three to look out for.

However, the Pigmy, the Misanthrope, and the Seducer were only three of the portraits Isabella included in *I Ritratti*, which grew into four editions that later totaled twenty-four essays. These three anonymous, negative characters are outnumbered by the positive and instructive models Isabella detailed. In order to honor them, she wrote about the luminaries she knew personally, the men who escorted her to museums, advised her on her writing, battled her in literary dialogues, or inspired her with their art. The list included men like sculptor Antonio Canova, writers like Ippolito Pindemonte, poet George Gordon, Lord Byron, painter Dominique Vivant Denon, and Isabella's second husband, the nobleman Giuseppe Albrizzi. She dedicated *I Ritratti* to their son Giuseppino as instructive moral studies for how a man should behave in the world, even using the informal "*tu*" to cordially invite her readers in (Riviello 7). Isabella admitted that her portraits were prone to "diminish shortcomings and exaggerate virtues" in her friends (qtd. in Dalton, "Searching" 99). In her essay on illustrator and artist Giandomenico Bertoli, she asked, "How can a painter ever capture the form of a man who is never still?" (99). Or in her case, how could Isabella's essays aptly and justly describe the many merits of her subjects? Certainly Isabella was not deterred from trying.

Born in Corfu probably on June 16, 1760, to Greek father Antonio Teotochi and Venetian mother Nicoletta Veja, Isabella was first christened Elisabetta. Isabella lived in Corfu until her marriage at age sixteen to Carlo Antonio Marin, a historian and member of the Venetian Quarantia, a group of forty counselors who acted as a supreme court. A year later the couple had a son they named Giambattista, and they relocated to Venice, in 1778. Isabella launched a literary salon in 1782. Right away her name became known because the male members of this salon wrote about her wit, insights, intelligence, beauty, kindness, and verse. Those who praised her included Melchiore Cesarotti, Aurelio De'Giorgi Bertoli, Anton Maria Lamberti—writers, philosophers, travelers, all considered to be those in the know—and the brothers Ippolito and Giovanni Pindemonte, poet and playwright respectively. Ippolito became a lifelong friend, and Isabella later wrote in her description of him that he was a "clear mirror . . . that is quick to take on the happy or sad tint of the few but dear friends of his heart" (qtd. in Dalton, "Searching" 98). Little wonder that Giovanni Pindemonte would want to spend more time with this woman he called "the painter of singular souls" and "the sculptor of moving bodies" (95). Isabella believed that those who created beautiful things—be they paintings, sculptures, books, or music—were reflecting the beauty in their own souls. These cosmopolitan thinkers brought the larger world into Isabella's salon, which she then helped to enlarge, amplify, deepen, and enliven. This aspect of her life must have been deeply satisfying.

Yet all was not beautiful in her own home life. Isabella's early marriage to Carlo Marin failed, and the couple had it annulled in 1795.

Isabella didn't languish without love, though. She had a brief affair with poet Ugo Foscolo, of which he wrote, "Lover for five days, but friend for life" (Vangelista). Isabella countered in her portrait of Ugo, describing him as "sincere like the mirror that does not delude" (qtd. in Dalton 98). She also had met Venetian patrician Count Giuseppe Albrizzi. His family objected to his relationship with Isabella, fearing that they would lose their patrimony if he married her. The Count sent Isabella on a sojourn to Florence and Rome while his family cooled down. She carried letters of introduction to the famous and the learned, and was even escorted through Rome's galleries by Venetian sculptor Antonio Canova.

Nevertheless, when one of Isabella's admirers proposed marriage, she had to admit that she had already secretly wed Giuseppe Albrizzi. Home to Venice she returned, and the married couple retreated to the Villa Albrizzi-Franchetti in Treviso. They amused themselves by setting up a small theater, where Isabella herself trained with Benedetto Chateauneuf and acted in plays by Voltaire and Claude Crebillon (Riviello 7). Spacious rooms were filled with ornate furnishings, and elaborate stucco flowers, fruit, wheat, and fire gracing the walls represented the four seasons, providing resplendent settings for their plays and gatherings. Other allegorical figures or classic columns gave the villa a grand air. Isabella kept a salon here on the mainland, but the couple eventually moved back to Venice; however, there is no documentation to confirm that she lived in the Palazzo Albrizzi near Campo San Polo. This chapter of Isabella's life provided her with a serene and satisfying interlude.

By this time, the Venetian Republic had collapsed. Centuries of slow decline meant that Venice no longer had the navy or army to defend itself against attack. Napoleon, after running roughshod over much of Europe, pressured the Venetian Senate to disband its government and hand over power to him. In May of 1797, rather than enter into war with the French, Venice's government abdicated. It was a difficult time for Isabella to maintain a literary salon. As Susan Dalton points out, many writers and thinkers were more interested in nationhood and politics than arts and letters ("Searching" 85). With the State in disarray, the publishing process was lengthy and often disrupted, and female writers were still often hindered by male editors and publishers.

But like Veronica Franco and Modesta Pozzo before her, Isabella had influential men as patrons, who helped propel her through the publishing process and who attended and supported her lively salon. Add to her list of admirers Johann Wolfgang von Goethe, Sir Walter Scott, and Sir William Hamilton. Madame de Stael, known for her own outstanding salon in Paris, also called upon the Countess Albrizzi. In fact, Byron used de Stael as the model salon hostess when he wrote, "The Contessa Albrizzi . . . is the De Stael of Venice—not young, but a very learned, unaffected, good-natured woman, very polite to strangers, and, I believe, not at all dissolute, as most of the women are" (qtd. in Vangelista). These luminaries and many others gathered at Isabella's snug and sumptuous salon in the Corte Michiel off Calle Cicogna in the San Marco district of Venice, not far from the Teatro San Moise, the nexus of Venetian nightlife. The building's low ceilinged entryway led to an upstairs that featured a lovely balcony, where guests could get a breath of air while gazing at the soft-colored buildings of the courtyard—the pale yellow, or salmon, or apricot. The real action transpired inside.

The literary salons of the eighteenth and nineteenth centuries were different than their sixteenth and seventeenth century predecessors. Instead of the male-dominated and run academies, now the salons were often hosted by women and brought together both sexes for music, discussion, refreshments, and overall cultural cohesion. At a time when salons in Paris and London were known as dens of gossiping society women, Isabella Teotochi Albrizzi's salon held a higher standard. As researcher Ricciarda Ricorda points out, "For Teotochi, too, it is a moment of self-affirmation and proof of her own potential" (112). The salon's *lingua franca*, as the phrase suggests, was French, though of course Italian, along with its dialects, and Greek were often interspersed as well. While the women generally occupied the seats, the men often stood behind the chairs, though they all mingled in the same room, unlike the more British fashion of segregating the sexes. Tables of inlaid wood were arranged beside chairs covered with embroidered cushions. The cool terrazzo floor added browns, beiges, and blacks below, while Murano glass chandeliers, ever more elaborate, provided color and sparkle overhead. Women's dresses opted for a slimmer line and a high waist, with fabrics that flowed more than the heavy damasks of previous centuries. Due to the waning fortunes of the Venetian Republic, the lemonade might be weaker, the biscuits not as fresh, or the wine of lesser quality, but attendees were willing to forgo such treats to be replaced by scintillating conversation. Salons such as Isabella's kept the arts alive at a time when society was crumbling.

Isabella often chose a topic to start a conversation, and those present volleyed ideas like a lively game of badminton. Typical topics might include ideal love, women's education, or Aristotelian conundrums. Besides writers and artists, scientists, ambassadors, politicians and composers might attend. Isabella, or one of her guests, might read her own verses or scenes for entertainment as well as analysis. She also read from her travel journals; Ricorda comments that "The sober elegance of the pages describing her 'tour' suggests they were destined to be read aloud, an appropriate development for this sophisticated salon hostess" (111-12). Isabella's salon presented an opportunity for her to display her varied talents while entertaining guests. She presided with grace and aplomb, like a cooling breeze against a humid evening.

Scholars often credit Isabella Teotochi Albrizzi, and women in general, with the valuable role of sustaining society and improving culture. The presumed female virtues of "refinement, self-control, attentiveness" placed women in the position to inculcate these qualities in others, both male and female (Dalton, "Searching" 86). Though salons could be hosted by men, these more modern salons became a world where women had a voice and power as arbiters of art and thought. Isabella furthered this role for herself with her portraits in *I Ritratti*. In praising others, she created icons for other men to model themselves upon. "Titian could not have painted a face as [Denon] painted his soul, as he was able to paint truth," she wrote, complimenting the painter Vivant Denon's character (qtd. in Riviello 9). A profile might also include a man's shortcomings, such as her description of Lauro Querini; though he might seem distracted when one asked him a favor, Isabella counseled that "sometimes these [signs] may divert you from the truth; be careful not to trust them" because he was ultimately a generous man (Dalton, "Searching" 92). Yet these descriptions actually delivered backhanded praise, and, again, provided instructive models.

The *Ritratti* were not Isabella's only writings. Besides these essays, Isabella co-authored a book, published in 1809, with Leopoldo Cicognara and Melchiorre Missirini that ran to four volumes about the works of Antonio Canova, the sculptor and her friend. In *Opere di Scultura e di Plastica di Antonio Canova*, she showed her knowledge of the history and principles of art and her ability to critique it. Writer Tonia Riviello points out that Isabella brought a gendered sensibility to her critique; in analyzing the sculptor's *Venus and Adonis*, for example, Isabella noted that it must have been fashioned by a male because Venus begs Adonis to stay with her, while if a woman had made it, Adonis would beg the woman to stay (13-14). Her commentary is cheeky and fresh. After her series of portraits of men, Isabella took on writing accounts of important women. She was commissioned by her editor to write about Vittoria Colonna, one of Italy's best known and most talented women writers. Isabella's piece would be included in a series about famous women that was published in 1815 entitled *Vite e ritratti di donne illustri*. Niccolo Bettoni had previously published Isabella's *Ritratti* and wanted more of her work. Then after the death of salonniere Giustina Renier Michiel, Isabella wrote a profile of her as well, publishing it in 1833. Over and again, Venetian women writers supported their literary sisters with such works, with Isabella eagerly including herself in this sisterhood.

Isabella's portrayals used three measures of a person's character: first, observe the person's facial expression, for "already you know him," she wrote (Dalton "Searching" 90); second, judge the person's taste, which could be taught and refined but displayed the person's values; and third, observe how the person lives, for experiences and actions give clues about character (90-1). For example, of Ippolito Pindemonte Isabella wrote that "his deep knowledge of the human heart, his sensibility, his candor, the saintly and pure qualities of his heart appear in every line he writes" (93); in other words, his literary output shows others his fine soul. While Isabella was not the only person, male or female, to write such portraits in her era, hers show that she herself possessed the character traits to determine who had taste and good moral behavior; Susan Dalton concludes,

> Consequently, while some eighteenth century thinkers argued that women's difference [from men] defined them out of serious political and intellectual forums, others . . . believed that women could play an important social role because of sexual difference. The place that they occupied is illustrated in their social interactions, and the great interest in Isabella's *Ritratti* is the way that it documents these practices, old and new, gendered and not, in all their complexity. (100)

If women were given a narrow, circumscribed role, or only a drawing room in which to develop their voices, then Isabella Teotochi Albrizzi filled her given space fully with her insights, organization, and instructive lessons. "Taste had to be educated," she contended, "but once it had been, it would not only express itself in civil behavior, but also function as a means of identifying morality in others" (91). Her salons fulfilled a deeper societal function than merely a social gathering place; they built character by developing artistic sensibilities, which strengthened society's moral fiber.

But her influence didn't stop there. Isabella inspired others to be their better selves, in addition to inspiring artists to create. In 1811, pleased with Isabella's portrayal of him, Antonio Canova sculpted *Helen,* the Greeks' choicest beauty, and gave this bust to Isabella. Made of smooth, unblemished marble, white as the moon, her soft gaze and hint of a smile evoke grace, while the curls that frame her face add a gentle elegance. The statue stood in Isabella's salon; most who saw it believed she was the model. Lord Bryon was so taken with Canova's sculpture that he composed a poem in praise of it. (He also rated Isabella as one of the twelve top living Italians, the other eleven being men.) This cool marble contrasts with a warmer Isabella, one who could genially welcome others into her home and enliven their evenings. She would have kissed her guests' cheeks, inquired after their health, ushered them into soft chairs, called for servants to bring refreshments, and prompted them to share their insights. Elisabeth Le Brun wrote about Isabella in her heralded memoir and also painted a portrait that provides a lively likeness. Artist Vivant Denon even commissioned Elisabeth Le Brun to paint Isabella's miniature portrait so he could travel with it. Ugo Foscolo was inspired by Isabella to write *Iacopo Ortis*. Isabella's character and her dynamic salon proved to be the catalyst to inspire others. How gratified she must have felt.

Yet smooth oceans always turn to waves. Count Albrizzi fell ill in 1810 and two years later died, leaving Isabella with financial difficulties. She turned to Tomá Mocenigo Soranzo, a friend and previously perhaps more than a friend to Isabella, who helped her through these difficulties and became "guardian in fact if not in name" to her son Giuseppino (qtd. in Wikipedia, author's translation). Isabella spent much of her time in Padua but also traveled during the subsequent years, including time in Paris where she could sip from the cup of revolutionary writings, not to mention French theater and fashion. "The instant she saw friends was the most delightful of her life," wrote her biographer Antonio Meneghelli (Wikipedia, author's translation). But by the 1830s Isabella's health was failing. In 1835 she wrote to her friend Vincenzo Drago, "Not used to being sick, I became so desperate that I could say I was more vegetating than living" (Wikipedia, translation by Claudia Mandelli). To follow such a vivacious life with one of such lethargy must have greatly pained her. Isabella died the following September 27, 1836, and was laid to rest in Padua's Church of Santa Maria delle Grazie, near the Villa Albrizzi.

Isabella helped Venetians navigate through the changes in society at the close of the eighteenth century. As the nobility squandered its wealth, discontinued its hereditary lines through narrowing marriage practices, and lost power as Napoleon gained it, Venice also saw the rise of the *cittadini* class, merchants who amassed fortunes and gained status within the State. People began to believe that taste, gentility, and nobility of spirit could be taught and cultivated, not only born into, and Isabella Teotochi Albrizzi's *Ritratti* furthered these ideas with a blueprint that anyone could follow (Dalton, "Searching" 89). Women were slowly beginning to have more agency in their lives and in the life of their city, with Isabella being one of these cultural arbiters. She gave her generation models for men to follow and to avoid, so they could now rise above being the pygmy, the misanthrope, or the seducer. Isabella helped to shape the new century.

# Giustina Renier Michiel

## Good Soul and Elevated Genius

*W*hen Giustina looked at her three daughters in their nursery, she wondered about their futures. What would society expect of them? What rules would they be governed by? Would they be honored more for their intelligence or their beauty? Would they feel the freedom to put down their embroidery and pick up a pen? Elena, Chiara, and Cecilia, her blond angels with their rosy cheeks and high foreheads might now be playing with dolls or braiding each other's hair. But Giustina wanted to ensure that her daughters would grow up to read the classics—not only Aristotle and Petrarca, but also the Bard, that Englishman William Shakespeare.

"An almost general custom in Italy is to deny Mothers the most precious gift, which is their Daughters' education, which leaves them nothing but the sweet title of Mother" (qtd. in Calvani 10). Giustina Renier Michiel penned this lament in her introduction to her translation of three Shakespeare plays. As a matter of fact, Giustina was the first person to translate the Bard into Italian, with the goal of providing her daughters with a morally instructive set of examples. Her girls—Elena, Chiara, and Cecilia—could learn from the experiences of strong characters who take their fates into their own hands. Marry for love, not custom, like Desdemona in Shakespeare's *Othello*, or direct a kingdom's destiny, like Lady Macbeth, but learn the disastrous consequences of avarice and superstitious belief. Giustina explained that she translated *Othello*, *Macbeth*, and *Coriolanus* to prepare for her daughters "a reading, which can, whenever possible, give them joy and instruction, contributing to their happiness and moderating their growing passion with examples" (10). Or, as Giustina's biographer Susan Dalton, points out, "she often evokes the ideals of civility: of modesty, sensibility, reason, and self-discipline" (Dalton, *Engendering* 84). Much of Giustina's writing focused on these goals and ideals, fueled by her love for her daughters.

In a 1780 oil painting entitled *The Michiel Family* by Pietro Longhi, Giustina poses with her husband, his mother, and his sister. The women are dressed simply but tastefully, with a veil or flowers in their upswept hair, a lace shawl across their shoulders, or a fan in hand. The adults sit around a wooden table with everyday things upon it—some papers, a silver platter, and a brown case. They gaze upon the three young daughters, two of them barely waist-high and the third a babe in the arms of her nurse. Though it's a simple, homely scene, the Venetian-red wall behind them, the family coat of arms, and the portrait of nobleman Pietro Barbarigo on the wall belie the family's patrician standing. Giustina appears to be a noblewoman fulfilling her wifely and motherly duty.

But Giustina Renier Michiel didn't always do what was expected.

Certainly her life began in the traditional ways. Giustina was born on October 14, 1755, to Cecilia Manin and Andrea Renier. About her father, she wrote that "he cannot have more tenderness for me" (qtd. in Dalton, "Conflicting" 82). Giustina came from the noblest of Venetian family lines; in fact, her paternal grandfather Paolo Renier served as next-to-last doge, and her maternal uncle Ludovico Manin served last. Receiving a basic convent education in Treviso, Giustina studied music and art and learned to speak French and English. Giustina is described by essayist Francis Marion Crawford as "a born bookworm, and even in her school succeeded in reading a vast number of books, and in filling her girlish imagination with a vast store of ideals" (Crawford 255). Back in Venice, Giustina continued studying French with a female tutor, and she became completely fluent in three languages to the point where she later worked as a translator.

As a child, Giustina was modest and humble about her abilities and station. She seemed to care little for her noble status, responding to Moliere's comment that "a Countess is certainly something . . . . [But] he should have written that a Countess is very little, or a Count, either!" (qtd. in Crawford 255). Rather than donning the elaborate taffeta or satin gowns of the patrician class, Giustina stated that such clothing was a type of disguise; she instead wore a plain linen or woolen tunic, long and straight and unadorned, though she fastened a crown of roses in her hair (255). But like any child she could be contrary or say outlandish things. In a rather petulant though innocent statement, young Giustina remarked, "I should like to know how everyone does not try to please me, since it would take so little to succeed!" (255). One anecdote relates how Giustina's dress caught fire, but rather than call for help, she rolled herself on the carpet to quell the flames (255). She hated to cause trouble, preferring to be obliging and obedient. That changed gradually over the years.

At age twenty, Giustina married the man the families had chosen for her: Marc'Antonio Michiel. They had actually been promised to each other earlier, and signs pointed to an affectionate union. For instance, at age sixteen Giustina skipped sleeping one night in order to write to her betrothed, "I do not want to let the opportunity pass without taking advantage of it" (qtd. in Dalton, "Conflicting" 82). The newlyweds spent their first year in Rome, accompanying Giustina's father who was appointed Ambassador to Pope Pius VI. (The Pope even presented Giustina with a twelve-pound sturgeon as a gift upon their meeting.) Giustina earned the nickname of "*Venerina Veneziana*," or the "Little Venetian Venus," a reference comparing her to the beautiful Goddess of Love. Giustina's mother-in-law, Elena Cornaro Michiel, sent fashionable dresses and corresponded often with Giustina, smoothing her presentation into the highest echelons of Roman society. Giustina confided to her early on in her first pregnancy, writing, "I can do no less than share with my dear mother my hope of being pregnant, making this confession to you, it being against my nature to keep secrets from those whom I truly love" (qtd. in Dalton, "Conflicting" 83). This child, named Elena after her grandmother, was affectionately known as "Nene" in the family. Giustina enjoyed the company of children, once remarking, "I have hardly any company but that of children. I think very highly of their patience, since there is between me and them the same distance of age which exists between them and me. I find I have nothing in common with them but the taste for '*anguria*,' [watermelon] and this is a good argument for the truth of what I say" (qtd. in Crawford 264). Though a polished lady of society, Giustina enjoyed simple pleasures and remained warm and playful.

Giustina also alluded in her letters to small but growing dissatisfactions in her marriage. After the young couple had returned from Rome, first to the Veneto mainland and then to Venice, Giustina began showing frustration with some of her husband's habits. When Marc'Antonio, away on business too often, neglected to even say goodbye to his wife, Giustina responded, "After having waited many days without receiving a reply which would have been much appreciated by me, I ask that you finally send me some news" (qtd. in Dalton, "Conflicting" 84). It seemed that nearly all of the parenting responsibilities fell to Giustina, with little help from Marc'Antonio. "Our little ones, all well and beautiful, ask for their father, who has run off," complained Giustina in one letter (85). Giustina wanted her husband by her side, sharing in the family duties.

Back in Venice, Giustina began fashioning a life independent from her husband. She set up a literary salon near her home at the Procuratie Vecchie in the Piazza San Marco. Guests gathered in the nearby Corte Contarina, just off the Frezzeria, though reportedly Giustina often set up tables and chairs in the Sotoportego e Ramo Secondo Corte Contarina to take advantage of a freshening breeze. This narrow courtyard surrounded by three and four story buildings provided a secluded refuge a few steps away from the bustling shopping district. White-coated servants must have carried out trays of sweets to the well-heeled and well-educated visitors who stood with their porcelain teacups or Murano glass goblets. If they needed privacy, they could duck into the covered walkway where the low ceiling and thick walls muffled their voices. Following performances at one of the nearby theaters such as the San Moise or San Benedetto, guests arrived after midnight to analyze the actors, the singing, the costumes, and the others in the audience.

Notables like Ugo Foscolo, Antonio Canova, Ippolito Pindemonte, Marina Querini Benzon, Giustiniana Wynne, Madame de Stael, and Lord Byron gathered for *conversazione* and parlor games, and Isabella Teotochi Albrizzi became one of Giustina's dearest friends. In her *Ritratti*, Isabella wrote of Giustina, "Her eyes sparked with a vivacious and at the same time serene radiance, and her rosy lips were constantly parted in a smile that showed the habitual cheerfulness of her disposition. Her slender body seemed all harmony, tending to lean forward attentively, reflecting the kindness which always came naturally to her" (qtd. in Chemello 143). The modest bookworm was blossoming into a woman of letters.

Giustina often took a box at the theater, applauded at concerts, danced at masked balls, or sipped a beverage at the caffes where the intelligentsia congregated. When attending literary academies, she saw herself "like a citizen of the world," she said (qtd. in Dalton, "Conflicting" 86). Unlike most women of her day, Giustina sometimes tackled political topics; her letters are full of the news of the day, such as the Austrian occupation of Venice; "I still firmly believe in peace," she said of the potential French-Austrian armistice in 1800, even though "we are ignorant of all things here, but I who read the English Gazettes see very well the reasons why a new war is impossible" (qtd. in Dalton, *Engendering* 92). Giustina felt that women had an important role to play in the worlds of letters and politics. In a letter to a male friend, she argued that women are naturally involved in events, or else nature "takes vengeance when men attach no importance to women; we are beings precious to nature itself" (78). Giustina then expanded her studies, learning about astronomy, optics, and chemistry, occasionally prescribing herbal remedies to friends (79). She once even developed musk essence with Professor Marco Carburi; Venice had become a hub of perfume production, and Giustina took an interest in this burgeoning art. As her daughters grew older, Giustina filled her days with intellectual pursuits.

However, some of these interests overlapped with a new duty that Giustina fulfilled, that of dogaressa. No, her husband Marc'Antonio had not been appointed to that exalted position; Giustina's grandfather Paolo Renier had. His wife, Margherita Dalmat who had been a dancer, was not deemed suitable to fill the position of Venice's first lady, so in 1779 Giustina was asked to step in. Alongside Doge Renier, she attended state functions, including events like the launching of a new ship at the Arsenale or accepting visits from foreigners. Giustina acted as the doge's consort, not his wife, becoming the female face of Venice.

At this point, Marc'Antonio Michiel was becoming rankled with his wife's independent and busy life. He went so far as to scoff at women's intellectual abilities, for example disbelieving that Giustiniana Wynne had actually authored an essay Giustina showed him, or scorning Giustina when she gained fluency in Latin (Dalton, "Conflicting" 88). Marc'Antonio began to curtail his wife's activities, even demanding that she cease attending the theater. Though in so many ways Giustina Renier Michiel conformed to the roles of a Venetian noblewoman, she was not being as obedient as her husband Marc'Antonio expected. In a 1781 letter to her husband, she despaired that "I usually do the opposite of what pleases you," though she followed by saying, "but in friendship, let us examine the opposition," hoping to discuss the matter with him (qtd. in Dalton, *Engendering* 80). While Marc'Antonio began forbidding her attendance at social events, Giustina grew more despondent. "My miserable situation has reached a point where it requires much deliberation," she told him as she requested permission to leave Venice altogether rather than stay in the city and not be able to socialize with others (80). She actually requested a separation from Marc'Antonio, and the marriage was officially dissolved on August 4, 1784. (This move was not as unusual as it may seem; twenty-five Venetian marriages ended in separation or annulment that year.) (Dalton, "Conflicting" 91) After initial difficulties, the two apparently learned to be on friendly terms for the rest of their lives.

Besides her marriage, Giustina experienced other things falling apart as well. In 1797, Napoleon's troops marched into Venice; the Senate abdicated, and French rule began. This represented a particular blow to Giustina and her family as they lost their positions of government power. A number of patricians gathered at Giustina's home to commiserate. Later, as Napoleon proceeded through the Piazza San Marco with his triumphal entourage, Giustina's cousin Bernardino Renier pointed her out to the French leader as a notable author. Biographer Francis Marion Crawford recreates this conversation between Napoleon and Giustina:

> 'Come, what have you written?' asked the Emperor impatiently.
> 'A few translations.'
> 'Translations?'
> 'Of tragedies,' answered Giustina.
> 'The tragedies of Racine, I suppose?'
> 'I beg your majesty's pardon, I have translated from the English.'
> The eye-witnesses of this meeting say that when the Emperor received this answer he turned on his heel and left the high-born lady standing there. (258)

Napoleon dismissed Giustina's accomplishments as they did not honor his French culture, though little did he know of her multilingual talents. With Napoleon's takeover and the demise of Venetian culture, Giustina reluctantly closed her salon and embarked on a new course.

Without the dogaressa's duties to fulfill but with the means to live independently, Giustina chose to study botany and began the arduous task of translating Shakespeare into Italian. She consulted the work of previous translators, including those by Brumay or Le Tourneur who had translated Shakespeare into French. But Professor and translator Alessandra Calvani, through her detailed analysis of Giustina's translations, notes, and prefaces, has concluded that Giustina used Shakespeare's original English as her primary source (Calvani 1). Shakespeare's work was virtually unknown in early nineteenth century Italy, and few Italians spoke English.

While some male scholars believed that translation work was not "original" work like writing in other genres, Giustina's notes prove that she had to make countless discerning choices in order to create plays that were true to their author's voice. "Soul and wit are perhaps more essential to the accurate transportation of sentiment and taste from one language to another than the ability to write philosophical works," Giustina wrote. "A sprightly and animated style covers and even embellishes the faults; whereas a languid and cold one makes the grace itself vanish" (qtd. in Calvani 8). Giustina made editorial choices, such as omitting racist lines against Othello (Calvani 13), and she eliminated stage directions since she translated the plays to be read, not performed (14). Wherever she omitted lines or changed them drastically to match Italian idioms, Giustina provided the literal translation in her notes and explained her choices. "Most of all," she believed, "it is necessary to strive to make the Authors speak in the language into which they are translated, as they would speak themselves, if they wanted to communicate their ideas in that language" (qtd. in Calvani 8). Giustina was fluent in English, French, and Italian to the point that she could capture the essence of Shakespeare's dialogue, its "soul and wit."

Giustina knew that, though translation work was generally deemed acceptable for women to undertake, she still would face criticism from male scholars. Her own early biographer, Vittorio Malamani, accused Giustina of not actually doing the work herself but of taking credit for Melchiore Cesarotti's work (Calvani 7). Well aware of the prevailing prejudices against women writers, Giustina accepted the advice of Cesarotti, and she quoted previous translators to lend her work credibility. As noted earlier, Giustina chose to translate *Othello*, *Macbeth*, and *Coriolanus* for their educative qualities, both in morals and in emotional insights, particularly on marriage and parent/child relationships. Emotions, she noted wryly, "may be the only topic a woman can discuss without fear of accusations by men" (qtd. in Calvani 9). Calvani also comments that these plays in this order "[offer] to young women the image of a woman's life, from youth till maturity" (10). No reviews survive to mark how the translations were received when they were published in 1798, but the fact that they were reprinted in 1801 suggests that they enjoyed a decent popularity. As Alessandra Calvani contends, "to translate means to have authority over the original text and over the translation reader at the same time" (2). In this way, Giustina created work of the same value as other scholars, despite what any misogynist detractors might have said.

Although being the first to translate Shakespeare into Italian is a unique achievement and a difficult task, Giustina Renier Michiel is actually better known for her other publication: *Origine delle feste veneziane* (*Origins of Venetian Festivals*). She had been approached by the Director of the Biblioteca Marciana, Jacopo Morelli, as well as Count Jacopo Filiasi to fulfill the new French government's request for statistics on Venetian citizens. Giustina agreed to take on the project, but with a format of her own devising: rather than listing Venetian events historically, she would chronicle the city's customs through the lens of its festivals. In this way she could additionally express her patriotic love for historical Venice, the republic that had so recently fallen to Napoleon (Dalton, *Engendering* 76). "This word Festa," she began in her preface to the first volume, "this word of beauty is not pronounced without a true sense of joy" (Renier Michiel 7, author's translation). In great detail, running to six volumes, Giustina outlined the many Venetian festivals, from the Feast of the Marias to Ascension Day and the Marriage with the Sea—the storied past of her beloved Venice.

Giustina employed the guidance of Saverio Bettinelli, Francesco Negri, and Angelo Dalmistro when compiling this work, and yet she received complete credit for her creation. Giustina's contemporary Francesco Maria Francescinis notes that "she offered, as a splendid gift, the history of their festivals, / woven with patriotic love" (qtd. in Dalton, *Engendering* 77). Giustina's work recorded for posterity the grand Venetian Republic before it could disappear from all memories. Writer Susan Dalton notes that "this work was celebrated by men and women alike and was quickly identified as her most important contribution to Venetian Society" (Dalton, "Conflicting" 99). Giustina is memorialized at the Istituto Veneto di Scienze, Lettere ed Arti's Pantheon at Campo Santo Stefano, where a bust of her sits atop a pedestal with over fifty other sculptures celebrating Venice's illustrious male writers, painters, architects, and thinkers. In this depiction, Giustina wears her hair pulled back into a loose bun, some waves cascading down her back. Folds of fabric engulf her shoulders, though her throat is bare. Her large eyes gaze slightly upwards, and her smooth marble face is not broken by a smile, as here she appears more the scholar.

For someone who created such an important work, Giustina remained a humble person. In a written portrait, her dear friend Isabella Teotochi Albrizzi described Giustina as garbed in a simple linen gown, again bedecked by roses (Dalton, "Conflicting" 100). However, Isabella also noted that "Giustina lived in the past, I in the present" (qtd. in Crawford 264). Giustina represented the Venice that was disappearing but that, thanks to her writing, would never disappear forever. She reopened her salon and continued to welcome visitors to her home as evidenced by this note to the Duke of Gloucester as she requested he would "please to accept in advance the thanks for Giustina Renier Michiel for the honour which he intends to do her this evening" with his visit (263). She recalled with mischief their past acquaintance when "he was a child and she was young and pretty; now he is young and charming and she is a little old woman, and also somewhat deaf" (263). Apparently she carried around an ear trumpet to aid her hearing. An 1823 portrait of her by Marianna Pascoli Angeli shows a more matronly woman, her elbows resting on a table before her, a knitted bonnet on her head. A blue scarf on her shoulders brightens up the portrait, though her unsmiling mouth and rounded cheeks look too dour to be the same woman who quipped with the Duke of Gloucester. Despite her usual amiability and generosity, though, Giustina Renier Michiel saw her role as one of conservation—of her city's historical past, of her class' culture, of community cohesion, and of civil behavior.

Giustina lived on into her seventies before she passed away in 1832, surrounded by two of her daughters, her grandchildren, and friends at her home in the Procuratie Vecchie. Her well-educated daughters must have been proud of their mother. Giustina's funeral was held at the Basilica di San Marco with the pomp and presentation practiced by Venetians of the previous century, with a procession to accompany her coffin into the golden nave of the basilica. She was buried on the cemetery island of San Michele, with an inscription near her gravesite in Section 2 that lauds her "good soul and elevated genius." It pays tribute to her writing about Venetian festivals and concludes that she was "beloved by all" (author's translation). Like the mother Volumnia in Shakespeare's *Coriolanus*, Giustina counseled towards peace and unification. As one eulogy noted, "And her ancient spirit, generous and proud, / Released from earthly joy, / Was welcomed among the shadows of the Venetian Heroes" (qtd. in Dalton, "Conflicting" 100). Giustina Renier Michiel did not only leave translated or written works for Venetian daughters—and sons—to learn from, but also her life served as a model of humility, grace, intelligence, and independence.

# Marina Querini Benzon

## Liberty

$A$ smitten paramour croons about the lovely blond woman dozing beside him in their gondola. "The moon peeped out / from behind the clouds, / the lagoon lay becalmed, / the wind was drowsy" (Lamberti). On a perfect Venetian night, in the waning years of the Venetian Republic at the close of the eighteenth century, these lovers slumber benignly, enjoying the gentle rocking of their black boat, "just the suspicion of a breeze / gently play[ing] with her hair / and lift[ing] the veils / which shrouded her breast." She is "*La Biondina in Gondoleta,*" Marina Querini Benzon, whom the song was written for. He is, perhaps, every man who ever loved an impetuous and warm soul or every person who ever loved Venice on a moonlit night, lazing in a sleek boat while the gondolier dips his oar noiselessly to propel them through the black water.

This *barcarola*, a typical Venetian boat song, embodies eighteenth century Venetian life on the water, so often an extension of life in the palaces, one of indolence, delight, and pleasure. Marina, "her little face so smooth, / that mouth, and that lovely breast," renders for listeners a Venice of passion and love. Her paramour croons a final refrain, singing, "So I acted cheekily, / nor did I have to repent it; / for God what wonderful things / I said, what lovely things I did!" (Lamberti). Listeners are left to their imaginations about how the couple behaved in their gondola under moonlight, probably within the privacy of the *felze* that gave them their own little cabin as a nest. Though there's not a record of what Marina thought about this song in which she is the protagonist, she probably relished it. Her own loves show her zest for life. At this time Venetians chortled this maxim: "*Alla mattina una messeta, al dopodisnar una basseta e alla sera una doneta*" ("In the morning a little mass, in the afternoon a little game, in the evening a little woman") (Origo 94).

Besides this famous song, Marina Querini Benzon is often associated with the literary salon she held at her home, the Palazzo Benzon on the Grand Canal near San Benedetto. Its wide and rather plain façade exudes a simplicity that contrasts with Marina's florid nature. Born July 28, 1757, into the affluent Querini family while they resided in Corfu, Marina came to Venice and married Count Pietro Giovanni Benzon on October 7,

1777, at the Church of San Giorgio Maggiore when she was twenty. Her parents, Pietro Antonio Querini and Matilde Da Ponte, had arranged this promising match to secure family ties and wealth, though it's unclear if love was part of the marriage equation. The Querini clan had produced two doges plus a number of honored members of the military, clergy, and government. Marina and Pietro apparently lived separately from each other for some years before his death. But that doesn't mean that Marina had any shortage of men in her life. "*La Biondina in Gondoleta*" pays homage to the kind of love she inspired, whether it was consummated or just dreamed about.

In a portrait of Marina, Pietro Longhi depicts her as slender and petite, though she was said to be taller than her husband "by a forehead" (Rizzo 20). In her dainty hands she holds a teacup and saucer, and her sloping shoulders and tiny waist are accentuated by her form-fitting dress with lace framing her bosom and the gathered sleeves flowing down from her elbows. Her high forehead, thin nose, and narrow face end in a pointed chin, set off by fair, smooth skin and blond tresses piled atop her head. Her mouth seems too small and eyes too suspicious, somehow, out of sync with the descriptions of her warmth and gregariousness. The original portrait was apparently lost, last seen in 1922 at an exposition in Florence, and only a black and white replica remains (20). A strikingly similar portrait by Pietro Longhi of Matilde da Ponte, Marina's mother, gives a hint of what Marina must have looked like later in life, her cheeks a bit heavier, her lips a bit thinner.

A different sort of portrait of her also exists, although it's not a painting. When the Venetian senate abdicated its power and the Republic fell to Napoleon, Marina celebrated, commemorating the event in a great party on June 4, 1797, in the Piazza San Marco. Garlands and flags festooned every window, and no less than four orchestras permeated the air with marches and melodies. A Tree of Liberty that had been erected in the Piazza to welcome the French troops symbolized the new freedom and equality. Marina wore her hair in long braids and sported a short Athenian toga that shockingly displayed her shapely calves and thighs, all the way to her hips (di Robilant, *Lucia* 117). She cavorted with abandon first with Father Pier Giacomo Nani, a Jacobin monk, until, as biographer Tiziano Rizzo records, they both fell on the ground, legs in the air, skirt and tunic over their heads (137). But that didn't deter Marina. With a hand from some French officers, she rose to dance again, soon falling into the arms of Ugo Foscolo, a dashing young Romantic and revolutionary with curly red locks and a dapper suit, until evening fell and candlelight took over the night. A painting now at the Museo Correr by Giuseppe Borsato titled *Festa del' "L'albero della Libertá" in Piazza San Marco* shows a platform erected in the middle of the Piazza, with statues at its corners and the actual tree at its center. Hundreds of people of every social strata fill the square, skirts twirling or arms outstretched in the dance, with a couple dogs cavorting at their feet. But Marina is not depicted here.

No one has left a "tell-all" diary. But it seems that Marina Querini Benzon's *joie de vivre* liberated her from many of the condemnations that women before her had to endure. Certainly, there must have been gossip and shocked whispers behind people's hands, and spies denounced her as a prostitute (Dowling 64). Moreover, the eighteenth century was more relaxed as Venice slid further into hedonism and collapse. Yet, unlike so many other intelligent and spirited Venetian women before her, Marina was not stereotyped as an unchaste or unprincipled woman. Through the way she conducted her long life, she represents a liberated woman in charge of her own destiny.

Like her contemporaries Isabella Teotochi Albrizzi and Giustina Renier Michiel, Marina opened her home to *conversazione*—discussions, entertainment, and refreshments. In contrast to the other two, Marina's evenings were less formal or literary, featuring the topics of fashion, the theater, and art. While some guests such as her poet son Vittore did recite their works, others often sat to play a tune on the harpsichord, surrounded by walls adorned with frescoes or stucco flowers and vines. Marina's salon was not focused on debating philosophical conundrums or dueling with their own Petrarchan sonnets. Evenings at Marina's *salotto* usually commenced around eleven at night, late enough that the entire affair was conducted by candlelight, with guests departing as dawn began to pink the sky. As Rizzo notes, a "generous profusion of mirrors welcome[d] the women and the escorts and embarrassed the husbands" (19). Card players perched on upholstered sofas for a game of *faraone*, draughts, or chess. They availed themselves of a steaming cup of coffee or chocolate in winter, or even hot rum punch. In the hotter months they enjoyed slices of cucumber or cool ices and lemonade, standing out on the balcony, overlooking the Grand Canal where the air was fresh. Marina provided these treats, but due to the privations of life in a failed republic run by the Austrian government, sometimes fresh fare or the tastiest delights were hard to come by. Based on the popularity of her evenings, Marina's guests were not put off by a stale cookie.

Despite the more casual nature of Marina's evenings, she still attracted numerous literary lights. Italian poets Alessandro Manzoni and Ippolito Pindemonte, and sculptor Antonio Canova, who utilized Marina's gracious hands as models, attended (Rizzo 20). Many foreign visitors had heard of Marina as well, and the writers Thomas Moore, Stendhal, and Henry Wadsworth Longfellow all attended the salon. In a letter to his mother, Henry Longfellow wrote, "The Venetian ladies are not handsome, but they have a great deal of vivacity" (qtd. in Littlewood

95). Undoubtedly, Marina would have bristled at this remark. She was about seventy at the time of their meeting and still holding her late night gatherings. In his journal Thomas Moore recorded that his friends said Marina "is one of the last of the Venetian ladies of the old school of nobility—thoroughly profligate, of course, in which she but resembles the new school—her manners pleasant & easy" (qtd. in Norwich 81). There is benevolence rather than censure in this assessment. Visitors admired Marina's openness, were warmed by her generosity, and laughed with her spontaneity, and Rizzo notes that she even had an "intimate" boudoir reserved for private conversations (20). She welcomed Jewish guests as well as Christians, as described in an 1824 letter by Catherine Giovan Broglio Solari (Cameron & Reiman 370). Marina provided a bastion of culture that straddled the turn of the century and change of governments, furnishing a refuge where locals and foreigners could meet and mingle in a cozy atmosphere.

Marina's most important visitor and friend was, of course, poet George Gordon, Lord Byron. As he fled the confines of stuffy England and toured the Continent, he fell in love with Venice and made his home there for a time. Though Marina was about sixty at their first encounter, she still excited Byron's interest, and some contend that they pursued a brief affair (Littlewood 94, Origo 93). Byron had been attending the salon of Isabella Teotochi Albrizzi but found it too sedate and correct. Besides, Byron was peeved that Isabella had written a portrait of him and decided to switch allegiances in April or May of 1818. Some say that Byron was also attracted to Marina because of the gossip that her son Vittore came from an incestuous relationship with her brother; Byron harbored an odd fascination with incestuous relationships (Origo 93). Vittore went on to imitate Byron with his curly locks and Romantic poetry.

Whatever the case, Byron and Marina grew close. In her letters to him, she used the informal and more familiar "*tu*" and often closed with "your Marina" (93). In one letter to Byron she offered her appraisal of him, stating, "In the head, there are some singularities, which are hardly ever lacking in those who possess sublime talents, but that heart of yours is perfect" (qtd. in Origo 99). She included Byron in her smaller family style dinner invitations, more intimate gatherings that she hoped Lord Byron would "be so courteous, as to accept" (97-8). She cherished their relationship, writing to Byron when he traveled to Ravenna, "I have nothing left by me to remind me of you but my constant friendship, which I would never wish to alter" (98-9). Byron loved many women in Venice but chose only a few people with whom to spend time. Marina must have been special indeed to have won his friendship.

For his part, Byron praised her highly, saying to his friend John Hobhouse, that Marina, "without having been one of the chastest—the best of her sex—[was] a Great patroness of mine" (qtd. in Littlewood 65). He didn't criticize her for her lifestyle choices but instead admired her for her singular disposition. Once, however, Byron made the mistake of focusing on her physical attributes. When Marina apparently playfully rebuked Byron for his comments, he wrote to John Hobhouse again, saying that Marina "is <u>right</u>—I ought to have mentioned her <u>humour</u> and <u>amiability</u>, but I thought at her <u>sixty</u>, beauty would be most agreeable or least likely" (qtd. in Cameron & Reiman 369). She was considered a beauty for all her years, but that was not her first concern. Marina once sent these lines to a friend, to be inscribed beneath her portrait: "All my beauty's pride in vain / Time will mow all beauty down / But kind I am, and Time bestows / Upon the kind, the victor's crown" (qtd. in Origo 102).

One of Byron's most famous relationships began with a meeting at Marina's salon. Like a proverbial thunderbolt from across the room, Teresa Guiccioli spotted Byron at Marina's *palazzo* in April 1819, when she entered on the arm of her elderly husband. Byron and Teresa thus began a torrid and lengthy affair. Marina didn't particularly approve of Teresa, who she found coarse after Teresa loudly called across the room, "Mio Byron!" silencing all other conversation. And when Marina and her long-time *cavalier servente* Count Giuseppe Rangone accidentally encountered the couple at an inn while visiting Padua, their relationship cooled. Marina shared her feelings in a letter to Byron, about Teresa "whom I do not approve, you know (for in our parts certain things are not done), but whom I pity and love, on account of the love she bears you" (qtd. in Cameron & Reiman 368). Byron traveled further abroad and wrote less to Marina after this episode. In a letter on heavy paper, sealed with green wax, she admonished him, "And don't you want to know anything more of Venice?" meaning, "Don't you want to know anything more of me?" (369-70). Though she claimed to forgive Byron, the relationship never returned to its earlier warmth.

As the French made off with Venice's treasures, books, and grain stores, and the Austrians crowded into the streets, cafes, and theaters in their smart uniforms, Marina continued to invite guests to visit her salon and to go for glides in her gondola. She became rather plump as she aged, and she earned the gondoliers' epithet, "*Xe qua el fumeto!*" "Here comes the steaming lady!" (qtd. in Origo 102). Wisps of steam emerged from her ample bosom where she had tucked a slice of hot polenta, which she would occasionally pull out and nibble from. Marina was accompanied everywhere by Giuseppe Rangone, affectionately known as her Beppe— her lover, escort, and constant companion. He was "a man of pure gold," she wrote, "the heart of Marina" (103). The adoration was mutual. When once Marina slipped in the Piazza while walking arm in arm with her

Beppe, what was he to do to alleviate her embarrassment? "I?" he replied, "I let myself go with her" (101). On another occasion, when someone asked him how his Signora Benzon fared, he grew dreamy and replied, "Dewy." (102). They had met in 1802, and Beppe relinquished a diplomatic career in order to stay in Venice with Marina. After twenty-four years together, they finally married in 1826, when he was sixty-two and Marina sixty-nine. She penned her happiness to him, saying, "My soul has returned into my body . . . . Blessed above all others the adored and unequalled, sterling golden, healer of all my wounds, Beppe, Beppe" (113). Not every day was as happy as this; many of her letters describe her sadness when Beppe has gone to visit relatives in Padua. In one letter Marina signed off, "Beppe, I am going now, I am going to pray God to help me in everything, in everything—even to keep safe for me your heart, my only treasure. I have so many troubles" (109). Beppe supported Marina through everything, emotionally and financially.

Indeed, a portion of Marina's "many troubles" included her finances. Marina was said to let money slip easily through her fingers (Origo 107). In 1821 a bailiff came to her palace "to value my poor house," she wrote to Beppe, "and then to put it up to auction" (qtd. in Origo 107). This disaster was abated. Marina had even asked Beppe to help her invest what money she had, complaining about her family that "you are all accustomed not to worry about me, and to believe that if I stamp my foot on the ground, money will come out" (107). Also around 1819, Marina worried that the Moro clan her daughter Elena had married into were moving themselves into her *palazzo*. "I knew how to bear great suffering for my children's sake," she wrote, "but . . . I have not, nor ever will have, the strength to sacrifice my freedom for them as well" (106). Her relative solitude could bring her peace, though at other times it weighed upon her. Beppe sometimes left for some days, and Marina might go out in her gondola to call upon her friends around Venice, only to find they were not at home. "I am always alone, creeping miserably round the walls, absorbed in my sad thoughts," (112) she wrote in 1824.

Yet there were many gay times in her life, too. Palazzo Benzon was quite near the Teatro San Benedetto (or Beneto in Venetian), which could hold two thousand spectators for the operas and plays performed there. When Marina's brother Alvise Querini wrote a play that ran there, Marina described it to Beppe as "an uproarious success!" (105). "The theater full as an egg. All my friends. Great, great applause," she explained. "Our box was crowded, and at the end everyone came to congratulate me—even the poor Albrizzi," finished Marina, with sympathy for Isabella Albrizzi, her sometime rival. Good *conversazione*, sparkling guests, both foreign and local, cozy dinners, music, games, and her Beppe—no wonder Marina was best known for her "humour and amiability." "The mansion of this celebrated lady, though she is now in very slender circumstances, continues to be visited by the natives as well as by the foreigners of the first distinction," wrote Catherine Solari regarding Marina's later years. "Her name stands high on the annals of gallantry, both for her extraordinary condescension, and for her easy and indiscriminate compliance, from the prince down to the *bacajuolo* [sic] [boatman]" (qtd. in Cameron & Reiman 370). Marina had a way of welcoming all while maintaining propriety.

Immortalized as "*La Biondina in Gondoleta*," Marina provided an unforgettable portrait of the romantic's quintessential Venice. "If I have not kept my lost beauty," Marina wrote of herself, "my good heart has remained untouched" (qtd. in Origo 108). She passed away on March 1, 1839, a distinct flavor of Venice dying with her. Marina Querini Benzon represented the ancient graces along with the modern liberties, and in her long life of eighty-one years she brought stability to a tumultuous Venetian era while also indulging in some liberties: enjoying love, dancing, gondola rides, and hot polenta.

*Corso delle Cortigiane in Rio della Sensa* by Gabriel Bella

# Andriana Marcello, Maria Chigi-Giovanelli, Anna d'Este, and Cencia Scarpariola

## A Countess, a Princess, a School Mistress, and a Septuagenarian

*A* young sailor, returning to his home island of Burano, brought with him a hank of *halimeda opuntia*, a sea plant found in Greek waters. When he presented it to his fiancé, she was delighted with its delicate deep-green edges and raised ruffles, but she soon grew pensive: It would crumble into dust too soon. She wanted to create something similar that would last as long as their love. She plied her needle and thread to replicate its scallops and whorls in white, and after many tries produced the first lace. This seaweed thereafter became known as "mermaid's lace," and Burano became the center of a thriving lace industry (Cornaro 335-336).

But after centuries as a lucrative business and craft for countless Venetian women, that lace manufacturing would nearly be lost in the nineteenth century, were it not for the combined efforts of four Venetian women: a countess, a princess, a school mistress, and an illiterate septuagenarian.

Despite the charming tale of a sailor's gift, it's unclear when and where lace was first created. Many cities claim this distinction. Historian Doretta Davanzo Poli states that "the origins of needlepoint lace, developed from a type of drawn-thread work, are unanimously attributed to Venice, second half of the fifteenth century" (280). It's well established that Burano, an island about six miles north of Venice, was an important epicenter. Burano is a fishing village, with houses of every shade of blue, purple, yellow, green, and red that give the impression the rainbow ends there. Boats as colorful as the houses line every canal and dock along the island's edges, with nets hung on posts or laid out on the cobbles. Fishermen can still be seen sitting in chairs, mending the nets across their laps. After her 1882 visit to the island, writer Catharine Cornaro wrote, "Lace is a net-work on a finer scale and we can easily conceive how the knitting of nets, first made strong, to assist in getting food, should teach them aptitude for intricate weaving, which in turn should lead the workers into a more decorative class of productions" (335). Cornaro visited Burano's newly reopened lace school and interviewed the countess, recording the story of how lace was saved from oblivion. Davanzo Poli, the acknowledged expert on lace and other textile crafts, points out that only filet lace holds similarities to net making; needle and bobbin lace follow completely different and quite complex techniques (Davanzo Poli, *Lace* 35).

Lace production thrived in Venice and Burano from the early fifteenth century. Because lace was such a luxurious item that it was decimating people's savings as they tried to compete with others for the finest outfits, Sumptuary Laws specifically mention limits for how much lace could be worn by Venetian citizens. Made into cuffs, collars, small shawls, and other adornments, it graced the shoulders and bosoms of women from the upper class, while priests and their altars were draped in lacey vestments. In 1483, Venetian lace was sent to England for the coronation of King Richard III, and throughout the sixteenth century, Venetian booksellers published books of lace patterns and designs. Lace had become the special purview of more than one dogaressa; Dogaressa Giovanna Dandola Malipiero is said to have founded the first such lacemaking school in the mid-1400s (Davanzo Poli, *Lace* 14). Under Caterina Gardin's direction, the school employed 130 women and thus provided a way for many women of the *popolani* class to earn a wage and contribute to household expenses. It's no surprise that a countess and a princess would interest themselves in this industry, since it had been the purview of women of their class for centuries.

Venetian laces were in high demand throughout Europe, particularly the style called "*punto in aria*" or "Venetian point" lace. Burano developed its own particular version of an almost three-dimensional lace with raised rounds of flourishes; women there, like our septuagenarian, learned the technique from their mothers and grandmothers, sometimes with one family specializing in a particular stitch. "*Punto in aria*," translated as "stitch in the air," is constructed entirely stitch by stitch and built up in layers. Davanzo Poli describes the two techniques: "The previously chaotic ground for the *punto Venezia* is now a honeycomb of small bars either bare or with picots [loops], made with buttonhole stitches, while the *punto Burano* is made of a net with a tiny rectangular mesh, rather like vertical sequences of ladders; the net may be *macia*, i.e. 'stained' by tiny geometric elements" (*Lace* 45). It takes a keen eye to see these fine distinctions.

Venetians made other styles and stitches as well, with the island of Pellestrina especially known for its bobbin lace, and Chioggia for filet lace. France, especially, bought it by yards and bolts; it became the highest of fashions. Dignitaries and nobles coveted it, including King Louis XIV who wore at his coronation a Venetian lace collar that had taken two years to stitch and cost 250 gold pieces, making superstars of its creators, Lucretia and Vittoria Torre at the Zitelle hospice (Davanzo Poli, *Lace* 24). The French ambassador reported that France imported 400,000 crowns' worth of Venetian lace (Cornaro 336). Something had to be done before the French completely emptied their purses. So France then imported Venice's women to make the lace for them—and to learn their methods. The industry spread across Europe and competition flourished, with Venetian lace makers next specializing in miniaturization.

A couple of centuries passed thus, with the women of Burano—for lacemaking was exclusively women's work—stitching their way into economic stability. Pattern making, however, involved training in design and was usually the purview of men, with the exception of a pattern book by Isabella Catanea Parasole (Davanzo Poli, *Lace* 16). Within Venice itself, lacemaking became a pastime and trade for nuns in the many convents, and they sold their pieces to earn a few *soldi* for their necessities and niceties. The lace industry also flourished in the *ospedale*, institutions developed in Venice for vulnerable women, whether they be orphans, widows, abandoned wives, women converted to Christianity, the elderly, or redeemed prostitutes. The Casa delle Zitelle on Giudecca island, a home for unmarried women, and the Ospedale dei Derelitti for abandoned women, in particular, employed dozens of women as lace makers so they could earn their keep and hopefully earn a dowry.

On Burano in 1766, the first year a separate census was taken, probably thirty to forty percent of the island's 2,900 women made lace, according to researcher Satya Datta (195, n6). These women did piece work in their homes, for the most part, and were denied the protection of a guild or confraternity like other crafts people. Though lace makers could be at the mercy of greedy merchants who applied severe working conditions, this skill often paid well and allowed countless women to survive (Davanzo Poli, *Lace* 19). That's why, while a countess and a princess were needed to organize and fund the lace industry, it was a school mistress and a lace maker who were indispensible to its survival.

Unfortunately, the lacemaking industry was about to disappear. In an anonymous article titled "Venetian Lace-Makers" from the 1897 publication *The Church Standard*, the author states, "For a variety of reasons, the art gradually declined until in the early part of this century, it was well-nigh lost" (107). After a steady financial and political decline for a couple centuries, the Venetian Republic had fallen in 1797, and the French and then Austrians took over governance. Once-wealthy families could no longer sustain their luxurious lifestyles. Monarchies disappeared, fashions changed, and Europe no longer clamored for Venetian lace; as demand dropped, so did production. *The Church Standard* points out the sad fact that "For centuries there had been families possessed of a skill and dexterity in lace-making, which could only come through generations of practice: families that had a monopoly of certain patterns, which had been designed or first used by their ancestors, and which, by an unwritten law, had become exclusive property" (107). Sadly, as their skills were needed less and less, these talented people were aging and then dying out, and their talents were in danger of disappearing altogether. Only the elderly remembered this art form. On Burano, civic-minded entrepreneurs attempted to found a lace making school in 1757 to give poor children a trade to support themselves, though the effort failed (Davanzo Poli, *Lace* 20).

Then came the winter of 1871 to 1872. The cold was so severe that parts of the lagoon froze over; an anonymous painting titled *Frozen Lagoon at Fondamenta Nuove in 1708* shows citizens in bulky coats and scarves slipping on the ice, pulling sliding friends across the lagoon surface, or hanging out windows along the Fondamente Nuove to watch the spectacle. Fishermen, of course, could not fish, and the people of Burano began to starve. Circumstances were so dire that the Pope and the King of Italy collaborated for the first time, hoping to remedy this disaster. They called upon the people of Italy to organize benefit concerts and performances to raise money for the Buranese. Money flowed in, enough to meet the island's immediate needs, plus a surplus for a long-range plan. A member of Parliament, Paolo Fambri, suggested reviving the lace industry so the people of Burano would have another means of support besides fishing. But did the world still want Burano lace?

Countess Andriana (or Adriana) Zon Marcello and Princess Maria Chigi-Giovanelli stepped forward to establish a new lacemaking school. With civic-minded beneficence, they took up this task in order to help this community in need. Because of their status in the upper stratum of society, these women could influence fashion and urge other women to desire these beautiful laces once again, first among their wealthy friends, and then among the general public. The Scuola Merletti di Burano— the Burano Lace School—officially opened on March 24, 1872, and the Countess and the Princess enticed Italy's Queen Margherita to be president of their new committee. The Queen's name appears on many early labels and advertisements for the school. Traveler Elise Ricci, who interviewed Countess Andriana, describes her as "possessed of singular virtue and qualities—energy, order, culture, spirit, amiability and graciousness" (198). She would need these qualities because the lace industry "was a very dead Lazarus they sought to resurrect" (198). Andriana and Maria now had a plan for a school, but they needed a teacher, someone who still remembered the complicated and decorative stitches that made Burano lace a unique art.

Luckily, Burano is a small island. It wasn't long before these noblewomen found Francesca Memo (nicknamed Cencia Scarpariola and whose name appears with different spellings and variations, including Vincenza). Cencia was elderly and illiterate, but, Andriana reported, "In spite of her seventy years, [she] was able to work the celebrated Burano point-lace stitch" (qtd. in Cornaro 340). A 1905 postcard depicts Cencia seated, with a lace-making pillow on her lap, pausing in her work. Her white hair is parted in the middle and pulled back to the nape of her neck, while her black eyes look off to the distance. A white apron dotted with small flowers covers her dress, protecting the lace she works on. A receipt from June 14, 1875, shows a brown-inked cross in place of Cencia's signature— hands so adept at stitching had no facility with writing (Davanzo Poli, *Lace* 39). Burano has named a short street Via Cencia Scarpariola, where the vivid ochre and mustard yellow walls brighten this woman's name and memory. She must have felt such pride and a sense of usefulness to be sought out for her valuable skills, validated after years of disregard.

In 1882 Catharine Cornaro corresponded with the Countess, who shared these recollections about Cencia and another heroine of the lace industry—Anna d'Este. "As Cencia did not understand the routine of teaching," continued Andriana, "Madame Anna Bellorio d'Este, an energetic and intelligent woman, mistress of the girls' school of Burano, was joined with her and was taught by Cencia in the intervals of lesson hours" (qtd. in Cornaro 340). In many versions of the story, Anna watched Cencia until she had learned to copy the stitches herself. She was focused and intent and sharp, and she must have felt some sense of urgency in her task. Anna then chose eight young women to become her pupils in this "resurrected Lazarus." They were paid by the day until they learned enough skills to create finished pieces. Davanzo Poli writes that the school opened with six students, a director, designer, and master lace maker (Davanzo Poli, *Lace* 40). The industry breathed anew. Cencia and Anna enjoyed a new sense of purpose.

Lacemaking involves several steps, each performed by different specialists, here taken from the article "Venetian Lace Makers" from 1897. First, the design is drawn on parchment placed on layered newspaper over a coarse linen. The design is stitched through all these layers, and this is fastened to a pillow called a *cussinello* over a rounded piece of wood. The woman can work about three inches of lace at a time before repositioning the fabric. The first threads are laid across the lines to cover the pattern; some of these are bound together by loops of thread as the design takes shape. Once the hours and hours of stitching are completed, the lace is cut from its paper pattern with a knife. The loose threads along the back side are plucked out with tweezers or cut until the piece is clean and smooth. The process has changed minimally since then, perhaps employing a razor blade or scissors instead of a knife, or doing away with the layers of newspaper. Modern lace makers of Burano would certainly recognize the work of their venerable sisters. Cencia's hands probably had developed enough muscle memory to complete these steps with little thought needed.

Soon, the eight students that Anna d'Este had trained grew into a much larger lace school, the Scuola Merletti di Burano, housed in the former Palazzo del Podestá. Anna found a replacement at the local girls' school so she could devote herself full-time to the new lacemaking endeavor. After a decade, Catharine Cornaro reported that the school now had 320 workers, paid according to the quantity of lace they produced. The school was divided into seven sections, each focused on one aspect of lace creation, from pattern tracing, to setting the foundation, to creating the various stitches, and finally doing the clipping and mending. Burano visitor Alan Cole explained that in 1881 workers were paid not by the day from then on, "but according to the work each performs. In this way they are equitably dealt with, their gains depending on their individual skills and industry" (804). Countess Andriana added, "in order to assist our scholars to understand thoroughly the different patterns of lace, I arranged that once a week a drawing-master should give them lessons in design" (qtd. in Cornaro 341). Often, it was the married women, who could not work as many hours as their single coworkers, who learned design elements. Andriana also brought in her family's trove of antique laces so that the designs might be copied and studied. The women must have crowded round as Andriana pulled out collars, shawls, ribbons and cuffs, tablecloths, gloves, and tiny baptismal gowns worn by her relatives. These treasures inspired the new corps of lace makers.

The Scuola Merletti continued to grow. In 1897 the school was described as a well-ventilated building with plenty of natural light, divided into large rooms that could hold twenty to thirty workers, though many women actually worked from home. Women sat in rows of wooden seats with a raised footrest and small desk on which to rest their work pillow. The 350 female employees worked six hours a day (seven in summer, taking advantage of the light), wearing white aprons and "oversleeves" up to their elbows to keep their work clean. "The girls are as bright and well-looking a lot of workers as I have ever seen," reported a New York lace merchant who visited the school ("Venetian Lace-Makers" 107). Anna still presided over the school at this time; though Cencia had passed on, her portrait, labeled "Mother of the School," hung on the wall. A marble bust honored Countess Andriana, as can be seen in an old advertisement from the early twentieth century (now on display at the lace museum on Burano).

At the end of the nineteenth century, housing in Burano was inexpensive but still out of reach for many poor fishermen. The revived lace industry empowered young women to improve not only their own lot but also that of the island's men. Cornaro recorded that a small apartment, suitable for a family, cost roughly $120-200 then. A lace maker could save up for such a place and bring it as a dowry to her marriage. "Almost all the young men of Burano seek our work-women as wives," (qtd. in Cornaro 341) wrote Andriana in her letter to Cornaro. Many others reported that this had a positive ripple effect on the island's morality. The parish priest began performing more marriages, double the previous decades and "instead of the twenty-five illegitimate children that, much to his regret, he had to register nearly every year," continued Andriana proudly, "last year but two children were born out of wedlock" (341). In 1874 entrepreneur Michelangelo Jesurum started a lace manufacturing company on Pellestrina that employed scores of women and won awards for its designs (Davanzo Poli, *Lace* 36). A second school was opened in Chioggia in 1904; statistics for 1877 record that over 1,500 women worked in the lace industry (36). Sadly, due to cheaper imported laces that swamped the markets, the Burano school closed in the late 1960s, but the nearly lost art was revived once again by a consortium of artists, scholars, historians, and city officials. In 1981 the Museo del Merletto opened in the historic school's building. When the museum was renovated and reopened in 2011, the portraits of Cencia and Andriana were removed and replaced by a modern sculpture of a traditional lace maker and oil portraits featuring people donning their Venetian lace accouterments.

So often throughout Venice's history, the social classes had few dealings except as masters and servants. In numerous past situations, noblewomen might serve as benefactors for poor and vulnerable women, such as in their administration of the charitable institutions. But in those cases, interactions always flowed from the wealthy to the poor. In this instance, however, the *nobili, cittadini,* and *popolani's* talents were all necessary for this enterprise to succeed. Andriana Marcello and Maria Chigi-Giovanelli brought their affluence, influence, and expertise at leading organizations; Anna d'Este was both the pupil and the teacher, the link between the ends, while without Cencia Scarpariola's precious memories of the original Burano stitches, the whole lace-making history might have been lost forever. The beautiful hand-made gossamer webs that once graced the shoulders of kings and queens, that were coveted across

Europe and denoted one's wealth and prestige, continue to be made today. Countless women bolster their families' income with their handiwork. Venice's priceless heritage was saved.

Satya Datta states, "The voice of my subjects [the lace makers] cannot be heard, but they are not speechless; their voiceless speech and mute language are codified by some pattern" (186). Lace makers didn't write books or preserve their letters, yet their presence lives on in the flowers and flourishes, the infinity of stitches ticked out with their needles. A visit to the lace shops and Museo del Merletto on Burano will illuminate their legacy. Sliding glass-topped boxes contain centuries of handmade lace—cuffs, collars, gloves, shawls, ruffs, borders, table runners, and tablecloths. A baby's christening gown and a bride's lengthy veil display the artistry attained by the Buranese women. Samples of partially-completed lace, with the underlying pattern still intact, demonstrate the countless layers a woman had to stitch to create a finished piece.

The island of Burano has honored these women was well; when visitors disembark from the ferry boats, they generally head straight up Via Adriana Marcello, and the first left leads onto Via Cencia Scarpariola. (The second street on the left honors Paolo Fambri for suggesting revising the lace industry.) Without the collaboration of Cencia, Anna, Andriana, and Maria, these beautiful works of wearable art may have remained something people would only marvel at in a museum, instead of being able to bring home a piece for themselves.

# Acknowledgements

*F*irst and foremost, I must thank Vonda Wells, who generated the idea for *A Beautiful Woman in Venice*. The universe seemed to draw us towards each other, and the result was her sharing this idea with me, which became this book and her tour company and many fun hours of collaboration.

Thank you to the many scholars who helped me in my research on Venetian women and their world. The University of Chicago Press has set a goal to translate and publish the writings of Italian women writers from centuries past, and I relied heavily on their work. A number of researchers responded to my emails and questions, so a special thank you goes to Ranko Bon, Marco Toso Borella, Daniel Bornstein, Andrea di Robilant, Umberto Fortis, Don Harrán, Ian Moulton, Diana Robin, and Guido Ruggiero. The following experts not only answered my questions, but also they read drafts and provided helpful feedback: Patricia Fortini Brown, Gregory Dowling, Claire Fontijn, Nancy Isenberg, Candace Magner, Courtney Quaintance, Anne Jacobson Schutte, and Mickey White. They helped me create a more precise text; any remaining errors are my responsibility. Other friends and researchers helped with details about Venice, so I send a *grazie* to Piero Bellini, Stefano Camilla, Michela Perrotta, Stefano Salvadori, and Elizabeth Salthouse. Thank you also for early and continued encouragement from Adriano Contini, Marco Leeflang, and Judith Summers.

Though I speak some Italian, I often relied on friends to check my work, help me with difficult passages, or translate poems or essays that required more finesse than my language skills could handle. Thank you to Claudia Mandelli and Gregory Dowling for this help. When I needed French articles translated, I have Ruth Benz to thank, while Adriano Contini pitched in with help on Latin, Italian, and Venetian.

My local libraries, the Martin Luther King branch and the Rose Garden branch of the San Jose Public Library, provided much assistance. When those stacks didn't contain what I needed, I reached out to friends for help. Thank you to Tomomi Harkey-Glover, Nick Wilson, and Kate Mast, plus librarian Peter Reinhardt for working some librarian magic. In Venice, I also benefitted from guidance by Laura Zecchin at the Museo del Vetro on Murano and Daniela Brunetti at the Museo Ebraico. Thank you to Susan Chore and Shannon Yule at the Frick Archives in New York for their help accessing the letters of Rosalba Carriera.

These separate categories are not enough to cover the breadth of help I received from my publisher in Italy, Giovanni Distefano. Besides agreeing early to publish this book (which so often gave me the strength to persevere when I was frustrated), he provided so much more. He gave me mountains of books, translated pages of Italian, answered countless emails, read drafts, and provided the biggest welcoming smiles every time I came by his shop. Giovanni called or emailed friends to find the answers to my questions and directed me about who I should include in the book. It's been a wonderful and richly satisfying collaboration, and I thank him for making my dream come true to publish and sell my books in Italy.

I am a writer who cannot work in a vacuum. I rely on people for feedback, and my friends have generously offered responses, advice, and careful readings. Thank you to Usha Alexander for being the first to read the complete manuscript and help me push though many difficult parts. Thanks also to people who read one or more chapters and provided insights: Dayna Barnes, Martha Benco, Kindra Briggs, Justine Carson, Rita Gonzalez, Shawn Matson, Karen Morvay Koppett, Peter Reynolds, Laura Rice, Anna Thomas, Mandy Toomey, and Vonda Wells. My editor Kate Torkaman provided much needed encouragement as I neared the finish line, while she also checked my punctuation and language. I am blessed to have so many who listened and offered so much.

This book, as well as my others, would literally not exist were it not for the superstar talents of my partner, RJ Wofford II. He lets me read to him aloud, and he offers guidance and an island of patient calm. He created cover art, formatted text, and prepared the ebook edition. He lets me run off to Venice when I can't stand to be away, and then he goes there with me for the fun of Carnevale as well as the excitement of promoting my books. RJ's support gives me the confidence to pursue my writing life.

# Bibliography

Adelman, Howard Tzvi. "Sarra Copia Sullam." *Jewish Women: A Comprehensive Historical Encyclopedia.* Jewish Women's Archive. 1 March 2009. Web. 3 April 2014. <http://jwa.org/encyclopedia/article/sullam-sara-coppia>.

Adelman, Howard E. & Benjamin C. I. Ravid. "Leon Modena: The Autobiography and the Man." *The Autobiography of a Seventeenth-century Venetian Rabbi: Leon Modena's Life of Judah.* By Leon Modena. Trans. & ed. Mark R. Cohen. Princeton, NJ: Princeton UP, 1988. 19-49. Print.

Allerston, Patricia. "An Undisciplined Activity? Lace Production in Early Modern Venice." *Shadow Economies and Irregular Work in Urban Europe: 16th to Early 20th Centuries.* Ed. Thomas Buchner & Philip R. Hoffmann-Rehnitz. Wien: Lit Verlag Munster, 2011. 63-71. Google Books. N. d. Web. 15 Sept. 2013.

Aretino, Pietro. *Selected Letters of Aretino.* Trans. unknown, likely Samuel Putnam. New York: Rarity Press, 1931. Print.

Bakic, Jelena. "Ana Maria Marovic, Montenegrin poetess, 1815-1887." *Women Writers.* Oct. 2011. Web. 26 July 2014. <http://www.womenwriters.nl/index.php/Ana_Maria_Marovic>.

Baldauf-Berdes, Jane L. "Anna Maria Della Piéta: The Woman Musician of Venice Personified." *Cecilia Reclaimed: Feminist Perspectives on Gender and Music.* Ed. Susan C. Cook & Judy S. Tsou. Urbana: U of Illinois, 1994. 134-155. Print.

"Barbara Strozzi." *Music Academy Online.* N. d. Web. 19 Jan. 2014. <http://www.musicacademyonline.com/composer/biographies.php?bid=134>.

Barovier Mentasti, Rosa. *Mille anni di arte del vetro a Venezia.* Venezia: Albrizzi, 1982. Print.

"Basilica Del Redentore." *Carnival of Venice.* Omnia Office, 1998-2004. Web. 3 Aug. 2014. <http://www.carnivalofvenice.com/the-city/sestieri/giudecca/basilica-del-redentore?lang=en>.

Bassanese, Fiora A. *Gaspara Stampa.* Boston: Twayne, 1982. Print.

Bella, Gabriel. *Reggatta delle Donne in Canal Grande.* 1764. Oil on canvas. Fondazione Querini Stampalia, Venice.

Bella, Gabriel. *Bajamonte Tiepolo's Conspiracy.* 18th century. Oil on canvas. Fondazione Querini Stampalia, Venice.

Benedetti, Laura. "Introduction." *Exhortations to Women and to Others if They Please.* By Lucrezia Marinella. Ed. & trans. Laura Benedetti. Toronto: Iter, Inc., 2012. 1-38. Print.

Benedetti, Laura. "*Le Essortationi Di Lucrezia Marinella: L'Ultimo Messagio Di Una Misteriosa Veneziana.*" *Italica* 85.4 (2009): n. pag. *Questia.com*. Web. 15 Aug. 2013.

Benson, Pamela Joseph & Victoria Kirkham. *Strong Voices, Weak History: Early Women Writers and Canons in England, France and Italy.* Ann Arbor: U of Michigan Press, 2005. Google Books. N. d. Web. 20 June 14.

Bergalli Gozzi, Luisa. *Componimenti poetici delle piu illustri rimatrici d'ogni secolo: che contiene le rimatrici antiche fino all'anno 1575.* Vol. 1. N. p.: Nabu (reprint), 2002. Google Books. 15 Mar. 2012. Web. 21 June 2014.

Bergalli Gozzi, Luisa. *Componimenti poetici delle piu illustri rimatrici d'ogni secolo: che contiene le rimatrici antiche fino all'anno 1575.* Vol. 2. N. p.: Mora, 1726. Google Books. 29 July 2011. Web. 21 June 2014.

Blashfield, Evangeline Wilbour. *Portraits and Backgrounds.* New York: C. Scribner's Sons, 1917. Print.

Bolognini, Daniele. "*Beata Giuliana Di Collalto Su Santiebeati.*" *Santie, Beati E Testimoni.* N. p., 6 Oct. 2005. Web. 1 Aug. 2014. <http://www.santiebeati. it/dettaglio/92513>.

Bon, Ranko. "Ca' Venier." Web log post. *Residua.* Ranko Bon. 14 Oct. 1996. Web. 16 July 2013. <http://www.residua.org/book-xxi-1996/ca-venier/>.

Borella, Marco Toso. Phone call, Venice, 29 July 2014.

Bornstein, Daniel. "Introduction: A Small World: The Venetian Convent of Corpus Domini." *Life and Death in a Venetian Convent: The Chronicle and Necrology of Corpus Domini, 1395-1436.* By Bartolomea Riccoboni. Ed. & trans. Daniel Bornstein. Chicago: U of Chicago, 2000. 1-24. Print.

Bottecchia, Tiziana. *Views of Venice by Gabriel Bella.* Trans. Sally Bennett. Venice: Fondazione Querini Stampalia, 2003. Print.

Brown, Patricia Fortini. Messages to the author. 2013-2014. Email.

Brown, Patricia Fortini. *Private Lives in Renaissance Venice: Art, Architecture, and the Family.* New Haven: Yale UP, 2004. Print.

Buckley, Jonathan, Rachel Kaberry, & Hilary Robinson. *Venice & the Veneto: The Rough Guide.* London: Rough Guides, 1998. Print.

Calvani, Alessandra. "Translating in a Female Voice: The Case History of Giustina Renier Michiel." *Translation Journal* 15.3 (2011): 1-19. *Shakespeare in Italian.* 20 May 2014. Web. 31 May 2014. <http://translationjournal.net/ journal/57literary.htm>.

Cameron, Kenneth Neill & Donald H. Reiman, eds. *Shelley and His Circle, 1773-1822.* Cambridge, MA: Harvard UP, 1986. Print.

Caminer Turra, Elisabetta. *Selected Writings of an Eighteenth Century Venetian Woman of Letters.* Ed. & trans. Catherine M. Sama. Chicago: U of Chicago, 2003. Print.

Canova, Antonio. *Helen of Troy.* After 1812. Marble bust. Victoria and Albert Museum, London. Web. 3 Mar. 2014.

Carriera, Rosalba. *Self-Portrait as Winter.* 1731. Pastel on paper. Gemaldegalerie Alte Meister, Dresden. *Wikimedia Commons.* Web. 3 July 2014.

Carriera, Rosalba. *Self-Portrait Holding a Portrait of her Sister.* 1715. Pastel on paper. Uffizi Gallery, Florence. *Web Gallery of Art.* Web. 3 July 2014.

Carriera, Rosalba. *Self-Portrait.* 1740s. Pastel on paper. Galleria dell'Accademia, Venice. *Mystudios.com.* Web. 3 July 2014.

Carriera, Rosalba. Unpublished letters. Trans. Anna Kleinman. New York: Frick Art Reference Library Archives. Accessed 2013.

*Cassandra Fedele.* Marble bust. Istituto Veneto di Scienze, Lettere ed Arti, Venice.

Casanova, Giacomo. *History of My Life.* Vol. 5. Trans. Willard R. Trask. Baltimore: Johns Hopkins UP, 1966. Print.

"*Casato Renier: La Storia Raccontata Dai Protagonisti.*" Web log post. *Casato Renier.* Tiscali.it. 2010. Web. 23 Apr. 2014. <casatorenier.blog.tiscali.it>.

Chemello, Adriana. "Literary Critics and Scholars, 1700-1850." *A History of Women's Writing in Italy.* Ed. Letizia Panizza & Sharon Wood. Trans. Peter Brand. Cambridge: Cambridge UP, 2000. 135-148. Print.

Chojnacka, Monica. *Working Women of Early Modern Venice.* Baltimore: Johns Hopkins UP, 2001. Print.

Chojnacki, Stanley. *Women and Men in Renaissance Venice.* Baltimore: Johns Hopkins UP, 2000. Print.

Church-Duplessis, Veronique. "*Les Morlaques Ou Le Roman Anthropologique Comme Moyen Pour Proposer Une Alternative à La Condition Féminine.*" Abstract. *Women Writers.* Feb. 2009. Web. 10 May 2014. <http://www.womenwriters.nl/index.php/Véronique_Church-Duplessis>.

Cohen, Mark R. & Theodore K. Rabb. "The Significance of Leon Modena's Autobiography for Early Modern Jewish and General European History." *The Autobiography of a Seventeenth-century Venetian Rabbi: Leon Modena's Life of Judah.* By Leon Modena. Trans. & ed. Mark R. Cohen. Princeton, NJ: Princeton UP, 1988. 3-18. Print.

Cole, Alan J., and George Bell. "The Art of Lace Making." Lecture. *Journal of the Society of the Arts* 29 (1881): 799-809. Google Books. Web. 7 Oct. 2013.

Comirato, Marco. *Elisabetta Caminer Turra.* 18th century. Etching. In Elisabetta Caminer Turra, *Selected Letters.* Print.

Conte Di Prata, Cleandro. *La Regata di Venezia: Composizione Poetica in Dialetto Veneziano.* 2nd ed. Venezia: Giambattista Merlo, 1856. Forgotten Books, 2013. Web. 9 June 2014.

Cornaro, Catherine. "The Revival of Burano Lace." *The Century Illustrated Monthly Magazine.* 1 (1882): 333-343. Cs.arizona.edu. 3 Dec. 2003. Web. 15 Sept. 2013. <https://www.cs.arizona.edu/patterns/weaving/articles/cen_lac1.pdf>.

Coryat, Thomas. *Coryat's Crudities.* Vol. 1. Glasgow: James MacLehose & Sons, 1905. *Archive.org.* N. d. Web. 28 July 2014. <http://www.archive.org/

stream/coryatscrudities01coryuoft/coryatscrudities01coryuoft_djvu.txt>.

Cotton, Jeff. *The Churches of Venice*. Jeff Cotton. 2013. Web. 2 Aug. 2014. <http://www.churchesofvenice.co.uk>.

Cox, Virginia. "Fiction, 1560-1650." *A History of Women's Writing in Italy*. Ed. Letizia Panizza & Sharon Wood. Cambridge: Cambridge UP, 2000. 52-64. Print.

Cox, Virginia. "Introduction." *The Worth of Women: Wherein Is Clearly Revealed Their Nobility and Their Superiority to Men*. By Moderata Fonte. Ed. & trans. Virginia Cox. Chicago: U of Chicago, 1997. 1-23. Print.

Cox, Virginia. *The Prodigious Muse: Women's Writing in Counter-reformation Italy*. Baltimore: Johns Hopkins UP, 2011. Print.

Crawford, Francis Marion. *Venice, the Place and the People*. New York: Macmillan,1909. Hathi Trust Digital Library. N. d. Web. 31 May 2014. <http://catalog.hathitrust.org/Record/007706166>.

Curran, Stuart. "Recollecting the Renaissance: Luisa Bergalli's *Componimenti Poetici*." *Strong Voices, Weak History: Early Women Writers and Canons in England, France and Italy*. Ed. Pamela Joseph Benson & Victoria Kirkham. 263-286. Ann Arbor: U of Michigan, 2005. Google Books. N. d. Web. 20 June 2014.

Dalton, Susan. "Conflicting." *Italy's Eighteenth Century: Gender and Culture in the Age of the Grand Tour*. Ed. Paula Findlen, Wendy Wassyng Roworth, & Catherine M. Sama. Stanford, CA: Stanford UP, 2009. 79-100. Print.

Dalton, Susan. *Engendering the Republic of Letters: Reconnecting Public and Private Spheres in Eighteenth-century Europe*. Montreal: McGill-Queen's UP, 2003. Print.

Dalton, Susan. "Searching for Virtue: Physiognomy, Sociability and Taste in the Italian *Ritratti*." *Eighteenth-Century Studies*. 40.1 (Fall 2006): 85-108. JSTOR. Web. 5 July 2013. <http://www.jstor.org/discover/10.2307/300534 93?uid=3739560&uid=2129&uid=2134&uid=2&uid=70&uid=4&uid=37 39256&sid=21104783803881>.

Da Mosto, Francesco. *Francesco's Venice: The Dramatic History of the World's Most Beautiful City*. London: BBC, 2007. Print.

Datta, Satya. *Women and Men in Early Modern Venice: Reassessing History*. Aldershot, Hampshire, England: Ashgate, 2003. Print.

Davanzo Poli, Doretta, & Mark Smith. *Arts & Crafts in Venice*. Cologne: Könemann, 1999. Print.

Davanzo Poli, Doretta. *The Lace Museum*. Trans. David Kerr. Venezia: Fondazione dei Musei Civici di Venezia, 2011. Print.

Davis, Natalie Zemon. "Fame and Secrecy: Leon Modena's *Life* as an Early Modern Autobiography." *The Autobiography of a Seventeenth-century Venetian Rabbi: Leon Modena's Life of Judah*. By Leon Modena. Trans. & ed. Mark R. Cohen. Princeton, NJ: Princeton UP, 1988. 50-70. Print.

Deslauriers, Marguerite. "Lucrezia Marinella." Ed. Edward N. Zalta. *The Stanford*

*Encyclopedia of Philosophy* Winter (2012): n. pag. 2 Nov. 2012. Web. 15 Aug. 2013. <http://plato.stanford.edu/entries/lucrezia-marinella/>.

DiGiacomo, M. Gabriella. "Elisabetta Caminer Turra and the "*Giornale Enciclopedico*" in Venice: Gender Consciuosness (conciousness) and Enlightenment between Periodical Literature and Letters." *www.women.it*. N. p., N. d. Web. 25 Nov. 2013. <http://www.women.it/quarta/workshops/writing1/digiacomo.htm>.

Dilnot, Rosie, Mickey White, & Margaret Jackson-Roberts. *Vivaldi's Women*. Schola Piétatis Antonio Vivaldi, N. d. Web. 22 Nov. 2014. <http://www.spav.co.uk/>.

Di Robilant, Andrea. *Lucia: A Venetian Life in the Age of Napoleon*. New York: Alfred A. Knopf, 2008. Print.

Di Robilant, Andrea. *A Venetian Affair*. New York: Knopf, 2003. Print.

Distefano, Giovanni. *Enciclopedia Storica Di Venezia*. Venice: Supernova Edizione, 2011. Print.

Distefano, Giovanni. Messages to the author. 2013-2015. Email.

Di Stefano, Paola. "Caterina Dolfin." *Enciclopedia Delle Donne*. La Societa per L'Enciclopedia Delle Donne, N. d. Web. 29 Sept. 2014.

Doglioni, Giovanni Niccolo. "Life of Moderata Fonte." *The Worth of Women: Wherein Is Clearly Revealed Their Nobility and Their Superiority to Men*. By Moderata Fonte. Ed. & trans. Virginia Cox. Chicago: U of Chicago, 1997. Print.

Dolfino Tiepolo, Caterina. *Sonetti Di Caterina Dolfino Tiepolo in Morte Di Gio. Antonio Dolfino. Internet Archive*. U of Illinois. 21 July 2012. Web. 11 Nov. 2014. <https://archive.org/stream/sonettidicaterin00tron#page/n3/mode/2up>.

Douglas, Hugh A. *Venice on Foot, with the Itinerary of the Grand Canal and Several Direct Routes to Useful Places*. New York: C. Scribner's Sons, 1907. Google Books. 23 Apr. 2008. Web. 15 Apr. 2014.

Dowling, Gregory. Messages to the author. 2013-2014. Email.

Dowling, Gregory. *In Venice and in the Veneto with Lord Byron*. Venezia: Supernova Edizione, 2008. Print.

Ell, Stephen R. "Three Days in October of 1630: Detailed Examination of Mortality during an Early Modern Plague Epidemic in Venice." Diss. U of Chicago Hospitals, 1987. Abstract. *Oxford Journals* 11.1 (1988): n. pag. *Oxford Journals*. Web. 15 Nov. 2013. <http://cid.oxfordjournals.org/content/11/1/128.abstract>.

Endore, S. Guy. *Casanova: His Known and Unknown Life*. New York: Blue Ribbon Books, 1929. Print.

Fedele, Cassandra. *Letters and Orations*. Ed. & trans. Diana Robin. Chicago: U of Chicago, 2000. Print.

Fei, Alberto Toso. *The Secrets of the Grand Canal*. Venice: Studio LT2, 2010. Print.

Ferraro, Joanne Marie. *Venice: History of the Floating City*. New York: Cambridge

UP, 2012. Print.

Ferrazzi, Cecilia. *Autobiography of an Aspiring Saint*. Ed. & trans. Anne Jacobson Schutte. Chicago: U of Chicago, 1996. Print.

Finucci, Valeria. "Moderata Fonte and the Genre of Women's Chivalric Romances." *Floridoro: A Chivalric Romance*. By Moderata Fonte. Ed. Valeria Finucci. Trans. Julia Kisacky. Chicago: U of Chicago, 2006. 1-33. Print.

Fonte, Moderata (Modesta Pozzo). *Floridoro: A Chivalric Romance*. Ed. Valeria Finucci. Trans. Julia Kisacky. Chicago: U of Chicago, 2006. Print.

Fonte, Moderata (Modesta Pozzo). *The Worth of Women: Wherein Is Clearly Revealed Their Nobility and Their Superiority to Men*. Ed. & trans. Virginia Cox. Chicago: U of Chicago, 1997. Print.

Fontijn, Claire Anne. *Desperate Measures: The Life and Music of Antonia Padoani Bembo*. Oxford: Oxford UP, 2006. Print.

Fontijn, Claire Anne. Messages to the author. 2014-2015. Email.

Fontijn, Claire Anne. Personal interview. 28 Nov. 2014.

Franco, Veronica. *Poems and Selected Letters*. Ed. & trans. Ann Rosalind Jones & Margaret F. Rosenthal. Chicago: U of Chicago, 1998. Print.

Freely, John. *Strolling through Venice*. London: Penguin, 1994. Print.

Fremantle, Elizabeth Wynne & Eugenia Wynne Campbell. *The Wynne Diaries*. Ed. Anne Fremantle. Vol. 1: 1789-1794. London: Oxford UP, H. Milford, 1935. Print.

*Frozen Lagoon at Fondamenta Nuove in 1708*. 1709(?). Oil on canvas. Fondazione Querini Stampalia, Venice.

Gambier, Madile. "Dolfin, Caterina." *Dizionario Biografico Degli Italiani*. Treccani, L'Enciclopedia Italiana, 1995. Web. 29 Sept. 2014. http://www.treccani.it/enciclopedia/caterina-dolfin_(Dizionario-Biografico)/>.

Giordani, Paolo. *Venice: Thirty Walks to Explore the City*. Venice: Cicero, 2002. Print.

*Giustina Renier Michiel*. Marble bust. Istituto Veneto di Scienze, Lettere ed Arti, Venice.

Glixon, Beth L. "More on the Life and Death of Barbara Strozzi." *The Musical Quarterly* 83.1 (1999): 135-141. Web. 19 Jan. 2014.

Glixon, Beth L. "New Light on the Life and Career of Barbara Strozzi." *The Musical Quarterly* 81.2 (1997): 311-335. Web. 19 Jan. 2014.

Govi, F. "*La Prima Orazione Accademica Pronunciata Da Una Donna - 1488 - I Libri Che Hanno Fatto Gli Italiani - ALAI*." *A.L.A.I.* Associazione Librai Antiquari D'Italia. 9 Dec. 2013. Web. 1 Aug. 2014. <http://www.alai.it/ita/big_classic/31-la_prima_orazione_accademica_pronunciata_da_una_donna_-_1488.html>.

Gozzi, Carlo. *Useless Memoirs of Carlo Gozzi* (abridged). Trans. John Addington Symonds. Ed. Philip Horne. London: Oxford UP, 1962. Print.

Griffin, Susan. *The Book of the Courtesans: A Catalogue of Their Virtues*. London: Pan, 2003. Print.

Guernsey, Jane Howard. *The Lady Cornaro: Pride and Prodigy of Venice.* Clinton Corners, NY: College Avenue, 1999. Print.

Hale, Sheila. *Titian: His Life.* New York: HarperCollins, 2012. Print.

Harrán, Don. "Introduction." *Jewish Poet and Intellectual in Seventeenth-century Venice: The Works of Sarra Copia Sulam in Verse and Prose, along with Writings of Her Contemporaries in Her Praise, Condemnation, or Defense.* By Sarra Copia Sulam. Ed. & trans. Don Harrán. Chicago: U of Chicago, 2009. Print.

Henry, Chriscinda. "'Whorish civility' and other tricks of seduction in Venetian courtesan representation." *Sex Acts in Early Modern Italy: Practice, Performance, Perversion, Punishment.* Ed. Allison Levy. Surrey, England: Ashgate Publishing, 2010. Print.

"History of Venetian Glass Beads." *The Glass of Venice.* 2015. Web. 3 Jan. 2015. <http://www.glassofvenice.com/venetian_beads_history.php>.

Horodowich, Elizabeth. *A Brief History of Venice: A New History of the City and Its People.* Philadelphia, PA: Running, 2009. Print.

"Isabella Teotochi Albrizzi." *Wikipedia.* Wikimedia Foundation, Inc., 14 Aug. 2014. Web. 4 Sept. 2014.

Isenberg, Nancy. Messages to the author. 2013-2015. Email.

Isenberg, Nancy. "Giustiniana Wynne and the Invention of Eastern Europe." Abstract. *Women Writers.* Sept. 2012. Web. 10 May 2014. <http://www.womenwriters.nl/index.php/Giustiniana_Wynne>.

Isenberg, Nancy. "Without Swapping her Skirt for Breeches: The Hypochondria of Giustiniana Wynne, Anglo-Venetian Woman of Letters." *The English Malady: Enabling and Disabling Fictions.* Ed. Glen Colburn. Cambridge: Cambridge Scholars Press, 2008. 154-176. Print.

Jackson, Barbara Garvey. "Musical Women of the Seventeenth and Eighteenth Centuries." *Women & Music: A History.* Ed. Karin Pendle. 2nd ed. Bloomington: Indiana UP, 2006. 97-144. Print.

Jaffe, Irma B. & Gernando Colombardo. *Shining Eyes, Cruel Fortune: The Lives and Loves of Italian Renaissance Women Poets.* New York: Fordham UP, 2002. Print.

Jeffares, Neil. "Carriera, Rosalba." (2013): 1-5. *Pastellists.com.* 29 Nov. 2013. Web. 3 July 2013.

Jones, Ann Rosalind. "Prostitution in Cinquecento Venice: prevention and protest." *Sex Acts in Early Modern Italy: Practice, Performance, Perversion, Punishment.* Ed. Allison Levy. Surrey, England: Ashgate Publishing, 2010. Print.

Jones, Ann Rosalind & Margaret F. Rosenthal. "Introduction: The Honored Courtesan." *Poems and Selected Letters.* By Veronica Franco. Ed. & trans. Ann Rosalind Jones & Margaret F. Rosenthal. Chicago: U of Chicago, 1998. 1-22. Print.

Jonglez, Thomas & Paola Zoffoli. *Secret Venice.* Versailles: Jonglez, 2010. Print.

*Justine Wynne, Countess of Rosenberg-Orsini.* N. d. Bonhams, London. *Bonhams.*

Web. 10 May 2014.

King, Margaret. "Book-Lined Cells: Women and Humanism in the Early Italian Renaissance." *Beyond Their Sex: Learned Women of the European Past.* Ed. Patricia H. Labalme. New York: New York UP, 1984. N. pag. Print.

King, Margaret L. *Women of the Renaissance.* Chicago: U of Chicago, 1991. Print.

King, Margaret L. & Albert Rabil, Jr., eds. & trans. *Her Immaculate Hand: Selected Works by and about the Women Humanists of Quattrocento Italy.* Binghamton, NY: Center for Medieval & Early Renaissance Studies, 1983. Print.

Kolsky, Stephen. "Moderata Fonte's *Tredici Canti del Floridoro*: Women in a Man's Genre." *Rivista di Studi Italiani.* 165-184. N. d. Web. 12 Aug. 2013. <www. rivistadistudiitaliani.it/filecounter2.php?id=633>.

Konstantinidou, Katerina, Elpis Mantadakis, Matthew E. Falagas, Thalia Sardi & George Samonis. "Venetian Rule and Control of Plague Epidemics on the Ionian Islands during 17th and 18th Centuries." *Emerging Infectious Diseases* 15.1 (2009): N. p. *Centers for Disease Control and Prevention.* Web. 15 Nov. 2013. <http://wwwnc.cdc.gov/eid/article/15/1/07-1545_article>.

Labalme, Patricia H. "Women's Roles in Early Modern Venice: An Exceptional Case." *Beyond Their Sex: Learned Women of the European Past.* Ed. Patricia H. Labalme. New York: New York UP, 1984. N. p. Print.

Lamberti, Antonio. *"La Biondina in Gondoleta." Liedernet.* Trans. Laura Sarti. Ed. Emily Ezust. Emily Ezust. 1995-2003. Web. 23 Apr. 2014. <http//www. recmusic.org/lieder/get_text.html?TextId=9808>.

Landon, H.C. Robbins & John Julius Norwich. *Five Centuries of Music in Venice.* N. p. Minneapolis: Schirmer Books, 1991. Print.

Lane, Frederic Chapin. *Venice, a Maritime Republic.* Baltimore: Johns Hopkins UP, 1973. Print.

Laven, Mary. *Virgins of Venice: Enclosed Lives and Broken Vows in the Renaissance Convent.* London: Penguin/Viking, 2002. Print.

Lawner, Lynne. *Lives of the Courtesans: Portraits of the Renaissance.* New York: Rizzoli, 1987. Print.

Littlewood, Ian. *A Literary Companion to Venice.* New York: St. Martin's, 1995. Print.

Long, Pamela O. *Openness, Secrecy, Authorship: Technical Arts and the Culture of Knowledge from Antiquity to the Renaissance.* New York: JHU, 2003. N. p. Google Books. 2012. Web. 2 Jan. 2015.

Longhi, Pietro. *Matilde Querini.* 1772. Oil on canvas. Louvre, Paris. Web. 23 Aug. 2014.

Longhi, Pietro. *The Michiel Family.* 1780. Oil on canvas. Fondazione Querini Stampalia, Venice.

Lorenzetti, Giulio. *Venice and Its Lagoon: Historical-artistic Guide.* Trans. John Guthrie. Trieste: Edizioni Lint, 1975. Print.

Magner, Candace A. *Barbara Strozzi, La Virtuosissima Cantatrice.* Blogspot. N. d. Web. 19 Jan. 2014. <http://barbarastrozzi.blogspot.com>.

Magner, Candace A. Messages to the author. 2013-2015. Email.

Manetti, Annarosa. *Antonia Bembo: Una Musicita Veneziana Alla Corte Del Re Sole*. Venice: Supernova Edizione, 2008. Print.

*Maria Boscola*. 1784. Oil on Canvas. Museo Correr, Venice.

Mariacher, Giovanni. "Barovier." *Dizionario Biografico Degli Italiani*. Treccani, L'Enciclopedia Italiana, 1995. Web. 3 Jan. 2015. <http://www.treccani.it/enciclopedia/barovier_(Enciclopedia_Italiana)/>.

Marinella, Lucrezia. *Enrico, or, Byzantium Conquered: A Heroic Poem*. Ed. & trans. Maria Galli Stampino. Chicago: U of Chicago, 2009. Print.

Marinella, Lucrezia. *Exhortations to Women and to Others if They Please*. Ed. & trans. Laura Benedetti. Toronto: Iter, Inc., 2012. Print.

Marinella, Lucrezia. *The Nobility and Excellence of Women, and the Defects and Vices of Men*. Ed. & trans. Anne Dunhill. Chicago: U of Chicago, 1999. Print.

Masson, Georgina. *Courtesans of the Italian Renaissance*. New York: St. Martin's, 1976. Print.

Mentasti, Rosa Barovier. *Mille anni di arte del vetro a Venezia*. Venice: Albrizzi, 1982. Print.

Modena, Leon. *The Autobiography of a Seventeenth-century Venetian Rabbi: Leon Modena's Life of Judah*. Trans. & ed. Mark R. Cohen. Princeton, NJ: Princeton UP, 1988. Print.

Molmenti, Pompeo. *Venice: Its Individual Growth from the Earliest Beginnings to the Fall of the Republic*. Part I. Vol. 1. Trans. Horatio F. Brown. Chicago: A.C. McClurg & Co., 1908. Print.

Molmenti, Pompeo. *Venice: Its Individual Growth from the Earliest Beginnings to the Fall of the Republic*. Part I. Vol. 2. Trans. Horatio F. Brown. Chicago: A.C. McClurg & Co., 1908. Print.

Molmenti, Pompeo. *Venice: Its Individual Growth from the Earliest Beginnings to the Fall of the Republic*. Part III. Vol. 2. Trans. Horatio F. Brown. Chicago: A.C. McClurg & Co., 1908. Print.

Moretti, Renata. "*Marietta Borovier: Prima Imprenditrice del Vetro nella Murano di fine '400*." *Professioni al Femminile*. N. d. Web. 3 Jan. 2015. <http://www.donnediorsola.altervista.org/pubblicazioni/Professioni%20al%20femminile.pdf>.

Moulton, Ian. Messages to the author. 2013-2014. Email.

Museo del Vetro. Exhibit texts. Venice: Museo del Vetro, July 2014.

Museo Ebraico. Exhibit texts. Venice: Museo Ebraico, July 2014.

Nadali, G. Paolo & Renzo Vianello. *Calli, Campielli e Canale*. 5th ed. Spinea, Italy: Helvetia Editrice, 2007. Print.

Norwich, John Julius. *The Paradise of Cities: Venice in the 19th Century*. New York: Doubleday, 2003. Print.

Oliphant, Margaret. *Makers of Venice*. New York: Thomas Crowell, N. d. Print.

Origo, Iris. "The Lady in the Gondola." *A Measure of Love*. New York: Pantheon,

1958. 91-114. Print.

"Ospissio Foscolo." *VeneziaMuseo*. N. d. Web. 15 July 2014. <http://www.veneziamuseo.it/TERRA/Castello/Piero/piero_ospz_foscolo.htm>.

Otero, Ellen B. "The Fiction of the *'Rime'*: Gaspara Stampa's 'Poetic Misprision' of Gioanni Boccaccio's 'The Elegy of Lady Fiammetta.'" Diss. U of South Florida, 2010. Ann Arbor: ProQuest. 2010. Web. 22 Sept. 2013.

*Pallade Veneta*. Anonymous poem about Anna Maria dal Violin. Manuscript provided to the author by Mickey White, July 16, 2014. Print.

Panizza, Letizia. "Introduction." *Paternal Tyranny*. By Arcangela Tarabotti. Ed. & trans. Letizia Panizza. Chicago: U of Chicago, 2004. 1-31. Print.

Panizza, Letizia. "Introduction to the Translation." *The Nobility and Excellence of Women, and the Defects and Vices of Men*. By Lucrezia Marinella. Ed. & trans. Anne Dunhill. Chicago: U of Chicago, 1999. 1-34. Print.

Panizza, Letizia & Sharon Wood, eds. *A History of Women's Writing in Italy*. Cambridge: Cambridge UP, 2000. Print.

Paoletti, Pietro. *Raccolta di documenti inediti per servire alla storia della pittura veneziana nei secoli XV e XVI ...: I Bellini, Parts 1-2*. Venice: R. Stabilimento P. Prosperini, 1894. N. p. Google Books. 2011. Web. 30 Oct. 2014.

Pirola, Caterina Piotti. *Portrait of Giustina Renier Michiel*. 1835. Oil on canvas. Museo Centrale del Risorgimento, Rome, Italy. Wikipedia. N. d. Web. 9 Sept. 2014.

Pignatti, Franco. "Fedele, Cassandra." *Dizionario Biografico Degli Italiani*. Treccani, L'Enciclopedia Italiana, 1995. Web. 1 Aug. 2014. <http://www.treccani.it/enciclopedia/cassandra-fedele_(Dizionario-Biografico)/>.

Plant, Margaret. *Venice: Fragile City 1797-1997*. New Haven: Yale UP, 2002. Print.

Pokorski, Robin. "'In Praise of Letters': Cassandra Fedele." *The Newberry*. 14 Aug. 2012. Web. 1 Aug. 2014. <http://www.newberry.org/praise-letters-cassandra-fedele>.

Poli, Doretta Davanzo. *Arts & Crafts in Venice*. Trans. Janet Angelini, Peter Barton, Paola Bartolotti, Jane Carroll, Liz Clegg, Sharon Herson, Caroline Higgitt & Elizabeth Howard. Cologne: Könemann, 1999. Print.

*Portrait of Giovanni Paolo Vidman*. N. d. Oil on canvas. Villa Widmann-Foscari, Malcontenta. *Barbara Strozzi, La Virtuosissima Cantatrice*. Web. 19 Jan. 2014.

Price, Paola Malpezzi. *Moderata Fonte: Women and Life in Sixteenth-Century Venice*. Madison: Rosemont Publishing & Printing Corp., 2003. Print.

Quaintance, Courtney. Messages to the author. 2013-2015. Email.

Quaintance, Courtney. "Defaming the Courtesan: Satire and Invective in Sixteenth Century Italy." *The Courtesan's Arts: Cross-cultural Perspectives*. Ed. by Martha Feldman & Bonnie Gordon. New York: Oxford UP, 2006. 199-208. Print.

Quaintance, Courtney. "Gang Rape and Literary Fame." *The Poetics of Patrician*

*Masculinity.* Typescript of forthcoming book from University of Toronto Press, provided by the author, 30 Dec. 2013. Print.

Quennell, Peter. *Byron in Italy.* London: Collins, 1941. Print.

Rabitti, Giovanna. "Lyric Poetry, 1500-1650." Trans. Abigail Brundin. *A History of Women's Writing in Italy.* Ed. Letizia Panizza & Sharon Wood. Cambridge: Cambridge UP, 2000. 37-51. Print.

Ray, Meredith K. *Writing Gender in Women's Letter Collections of the Italian Renaissance.* Toronto: U of Toronto, 2009. Print.

Remy, Nahida. "Sarah Copia Sullam." *Nahida Remy's The Jewish Woman.* By Nahida Ruth Lazarus. 3rd ed. Ithaca, NY: Press of C.J. Krehbiel, 1895. 141-51. Google Books. 9 July 2013. Web. 3 Apr. 2014.

Renier Michiel, Giustina. *Origine delle feste veneziane.* Vol. 1. Venezia: Tipografia di Alvisopoli, 1816. *Archive.org.* Web. 5 May 2013. <https://archive.org/details/originedellefest05reni>.

Ricci, Elisa. "The Revival of Needlework in Italy." Trans. C. Macfarlane. *The International Studio* 52. March-June (1914): 197-206. *Cs.arizona.edu.* 21 Oct. 2003. Web. 15 Sept. 2013. <http://www.cs.arizona.edu/patterns/weaving/articles/std_ric.pdf>.

Riccoboni, Bartolomea. *Life and Death in a Venetian Convent: The Chronicle and Necrology of Corpus Domini, 1395-1436.* Ed. & trans. Daniel Bornstein. Chicago: U of Chicago, 2000. Print.

Ricorda, Ricciarda. "Travel Writing, 1750-1860." Trans. Sharon Wood. *A History of Women's Writing in Italy.* Eds. Letizia Panizza & Sharon Wood. Cambridge: Cambridge UP, 2000. 107-119. Print.

Riviello, Tonia Caterina. "Isabella Teotochi Albrizzi's Role in Nineteenth-Century Italian Literary Circles." *Revista Di Studi Italiani* (n. d.): 5-18. Web. 15 July 2013.

Rizzo, Tiziano. *La Biondina in Gondoleta: Marina Querini Benzon una nobildonna a Venezia tra '700 e '800.* Vicenza: Neri Pozza Editore, 1994. Print.

Robin, Diana. "Editor's Introduction." *Letters and Orations.* By Cassandra Fedele. Ed. & trans. Diana Robin. Chicago: U of Chicago, 2000. 3-15. Print.

"Rosalba Carriera." *Encyclopedia Britannica.* Encyclopedia Britannica, Inc., 2014. Web. 3 July 2013. <http://www.britannica.com/EBchecked/topic/97038/Rosalba-Carriera>.

"Rosalba Carriera." *National Museum of Women in the Arts.* 2012. Web. 3 July 2013.

"Rosalba Carriera." *Virtual Uffizi Gallery.* 2012. Web. 3 July 2013.

"Rosalba Carriera." *Wikipedia.* Wikimedia Foundation, Inc. 7 Nov. 2014. Web. 3 July 2013.

Rosand, David. *Myths of Venice: The Figuration of a State.* Chapel Hill: U of North Carolina Press, 2001. Print.

Rosand, Ellen. "The Voice of Barbara Strozzi." *Women Making Music: The Western Art Tradition, 1150-1950.* Ed. Jane M. Bowers & Judith Tick. Urbana: U of

Illinois, 1986. 168-90. Print.

Rosenthal, Margaret F., et al. *The Honest Courtesan: Veronica Franco, Citizen and Writer in Sixteenth Century Venice*. Chicago: U of Chicago Press, 1992. Print.

Rosenthal, Margaret F., et al. "Veronica Franco." *USC Dornsife College News RSS*. USC Dornsife College of Letters, Arts and Sciences. 2013. Web. 13 Nov. 2013. <http://dornsife.usc.edu/veronica-franco>.

Ross, Sarah Gwyneth. *The Birth of Feminism: Woman as Intellect in Renaissance Italy and England*. Cambridge, MA: Harvard UP, 2010. Print.

Rossi, Daniella. "Controlling courtesans: Lorenzo Venier's *Trentuno della Zaffetta* and Venetian sexual politics." *Sex Acts in Early Modern Italy: Practice, Performance, Perversion, Punishment*. Ed. Allison Levy. Surrey, England: Ashgate Publishing, 2010. Print.

Ruggiero, Guido. *The Boundaries of Eros: Sex Crime and Sexuality in Renaissance Venice*. Oxford: Oxford UP, 1985. Print.

Ruggiero, Guido. Messages to the author. 2013-2014. Email.

"The Sacred on the Streets: The Venetian *Capitelli*." Web log post. *Daneinvenice*. Blogspot.com. 12 Nov. 2009. Web. 15 Nov. 2013. <http://daneinvenice. blogspot.com/2009/11/sacred-on-streets-venetian-capitelli.html>.

Sama, Catherine. "Volume Editor's Introduction." *Selected Writings of an Eighteenth-century Venetian Woman of Letters*. By Elisabetta Caminer Turra. Ed. & trans. Catherine M. Sama. Chicago: U of Chicago, 2003. 1-74. Print.

Sama, Catherine M. "*Luisa Bergalli E Le Sorelle Carriera: Un Rapporto D'amicizia E Di Collaborazione Artistica.*" *Luisa Bergalli: Poetessa Drammaturga Traduttrice Critica Letteraria*. Ed. Adriana Chemello. Mirano: Associazione Culturale Eidos, 2007. 59-84. *Academia.edu*. Web. 9 June 2014.

Schill, Ben. "Cecilia Ferrazzi." *Women in European History*. 7 June 2009. Web. 14 March 2014. <http://womenineuropeanhistory.org/index.php?title=Cecilia_ Ferrazzi>.

Schmoger, Marcus. "Venice - Historical Flags (Italy)." *Venice - Historical Flags (Italy)*. Flags of the World. 10 June 2011. Web. 18 June 2014. <http://www. crwflags.com/fotw/flags/it-ven-h.html#hist>.

Schutte, Anne. *Aspiring Saints: Pretense of Holiness, Inquisition, and Gender in the Republic of Venice, 1618-1750*. Baltimore: Johns Hopkins UP, 2001. Google Books. Web. 13 March 2014.

Schutte, Anne Jacobson. "Introduction." *Autobiography of an Aspiring Saint*. By Cecilia Ferrazzi. Ed. & trans. Anne Jacobson Schutte. Chicago: U of Chicago, 1996. 3-18. Print.

"*Sotoportego Di Corte Nova Shrine*." *Churches of Venice*. Slow Travel. 11 Jan. 2008. Web. 15 Nov. 2013. <http://www.slowtrav.com/blog/annienc/2008/01/ sotoportego_di_corte_nova_shri.html>.

"*SS. Cosma E Damiano Della Giudecca.*" *Archivio Di Stato Di Venezia*. Ed. Anna Bortolozzi. Archivio Di Stato Di Venezia, 2006. Web. 2 Aug. 2014.<http://www.archiviodistatovenezia.it/siasve/cgi-bin/pagina.

pl?Chiave=5628&Tipo=fondo>.

Staley, John Edgcumbe. *The Dogaressas of Venice*. London: T. Werner Laurie, 1910. *openlibrary.org*. Web. 1 July 2013. <archive.org/stream/dogaressasofveni00stal#pages>.

Stampa, Gaspara. *The Complete Poems: The 1554 Edition of the "Rime," a Bilingual Edition*. Ed. Troy Tower & Jane Tylus. Trans. Jane Tylus. Chicago: U of Chicago, 2010. Print.

Stampino, Maria Galli. "A Singular Venetian Epic Poem." *Enrico, or, Byzantium Conquered: A Heroic Poem*. By Lucrezia Marinella. Ed. & trans. Maria Galli Stampino. Chicago: U of Chicago, 2009. Print.

Stanley, Jo. "Woman Rowing Champ, Venice, 1700s." Web log post. *Gender, Sex, Race, Class—and the Sea*. Blogspot.com. 30 May 2010. Web. 1 July 2013. <http://genderedseas.blogspot.com/2010_05_01_archive.html>.

Steer, John. *A Concise History of Venetian Painting*. New York: Praeger, 1970. Print.

Stevens, Denis. "Orphans and Musicians in Venice." *Cantata Editions*. Baroquecantata.com. N. d. Web. 10 July 2013. <http://www.baroquecantata.com/shared/article.php?article_ID=6&ref=newcantatas>.

Stewart, Pamela D. "Luisa Bergalli." *Italian Women Writers: A Biobibliographical Sourcebook*. Ed. Rinaldina Russell. Westport, CT: Greenwood Publishing Group, 1994. 50-57. Google Books. N. d. Web. 6 June 2014.

Strozzi, Bernardo. *Female Musician with Viola da Gamba*. 1639. Oil on canvas. Gemäldegalerie, Dresden. *Barbara Strozzi, La Virtuosissima Cantatrice*. Web. 19 Jan. 2014.

Sulam, Sarra Copia. *Jewish Poet and Intellectual in Seventeenth-century Venice: The Works of Sarra Copia Sulam in Verse and Prose, along with Writings of Her Contemporaries in Her Praise, Condemnation, or Defense*. Ed. & trans. Don Harrán. Chicago: U of Chicago, 2009. Print.

Syson, Luke & Dora Thornton. *Objects of Virtue: Art in Renaissance Italy*. New York: Getty Publications, 2001. Google Books. 2012. Web. 11 Dec. 2014.

Talbot, Michael. *The Vivaldi Compendium*. Woodbridge, England: Boydell Press, 2011. N. d. Web. 25 Mar. 2015. Google Books.

Tarabotti, Arcangela. "Appendix One:" excerpt from *Paradiso Monacale*, in *Paternal Tyranny*. Ed. & trans. Letizia Panizza. Chicago: U of Chicago, 2004. 155-157. Print.

Tarabotti, Arcangela. *Paternal Tyranny*. Ed. & trans. Letizia Panizza. Chicago: U of Chicago, 2004. Print.

Tassini, Giuseppe. *Curiosità Veneziane: Ovvero Origini Delle Denominazioni Stradali*. Venezia: Filippi Editori, 2008. Print.

Tinelli, Tiberio. *Portrait of Giulio Strozzi*. N. d. Oil on canvas. Uffizi Gallery, Florence. *Barbara Strozzi, La Virtuosissima Cantatrice*. Web. 19 Jan. 2014.

Tintoretto, Jacopo (?). *A Portrait of Veronica Franco*. 1575 (?). Oil on canvas. Worcester Art Museum, Worcester, Massachusetts. *Wikipedia.org*. Web. 31 July 2013.

Titian. *La Bella*. 1536. Oil on canvas. Pitti Palace, Florence. *Kimball Art Museum*. Web. 29 Dec. 2013.

Titian. *Venus of Urbino*. 1538. Oil on canvas. Uffizi Gallery, Florence. *Uffizi.org*. Web. 29 Dec. 2013.

Turra, Elisabetta Caminer. *Selected Writings of an Eighteenth-century Venetian Woman of Letters*. Ed. & trans. Catherine M. Sama. Chicago: U of Chicago, 2003. Print.

Tylus, Jane. "Introduction." *The Complete Poems: The 1554 Edition of the "Rime," a Bilingual Edition*. By Gaspara Stampa. Ed. Troy Tower & Jane Tylus. Trans. Jane Tylus. Chicago: U of Chicago, 2010. Print.

Vangelista, Massimo. "Countess Albrizzi's Venetian Salon, with Foscolo, Canova, and Byron." Web log post. *Letters from the Exile. Byronico.com*. Wordpress. 21 Feb. 2013. Web. 5 July 2013. <http://byronico.com/2013/02/21/countess-albrizzis-venetian-salon-with-foscolo-canova-and-byron/>.

"Venetian Lace-Makers." *The Church Standard* 74 (1897): 107. Google Books. Web. 7 Oct. 2013.

Veniero, Lorenzo. *La Zaffetta*. Paris: Ch. Jouaust, 1861. Project Gutenberg. 23 Feb. 2006. Web. 26 Dec. 2013. <http://www.gutenberg.org/cache/epub/17834/pg17834.html>.

Vicentino, Andrea. *Dogaressa Morosina Morosini Grimani Disembarking at Saint Marks*. 1597. Oil on canvas. Museo Correr, Venice, Italy.

Vidal, Martina. "The History of Burano Lace." *Martina Vidal Venezia*. N. d. Web. 11 Jan. 2014. <http://www.martinavidal.com/storia.php?slang=en.>.

Vigee, Elisabeth. *Signora Isabella Marini Albrizzi*. 1792. Oil on canvas. Location unknown. *Wikipedia*. Web. 28 Sept. 2013.

Vitiello, Justin. "Gaspara Stampa: The Ambiguities of Martyrdom." *MLN*. The Italian Issue 90.1 (1975): 58-71. *JSTOR*. Web. 22 Sept. 2013. <http://www.jstor.org/discover/10.2307/2907201?uid=3739560&uid=2134&uid=2&uid=70&uid=4&uid=3739256&sid=21105417274063>.

*Vivaldi's Women*. Written & directed Rupert Edwards. YouTube. 2006. Web. 10 July 2013. <http://www.youtube.com/watch?v=153WVp8QJQ0>.

Ward, Adrienne. "The Price of Sonnets and Bonnets: How Gender Works in Luisa Bergalli's *Le Avventure Del Poeta*." *Italica* 79.2 (2002): 168-88. *JSTOR*. Web. 4 June 2014. <http://www.jstor.org/discover/10.2307/3655993?uid=3739560&uid=2134&uid=2&uid=70&uid=4&uid=3739256&sid=21105417274063>.

Webb, Megan. "The Lived Experience of the Black Death." Diss. The College at Brockport State University of New York, 2012. 1-53. Web. 12 Oct. 2013. <http://digitalcommons.brockport.edu/hst_theses/5/>.

Weiner, Gordon M. "The Demographic Effects of the Venetian Plagues of 1575-77 and 1630-31." *Genus* Vol. 26, No. ½ (1970): 41-57. Universitá degli Studi Roma "La Sapienza." *JSTOR*. Web. 2 Mar. 2015. <http://www.jstor.org/stable/29787908>.

Weisner, Merry E. *Women and Gender in Early Modern Europe.* Cambridge: Cambridge UP, 2000. Print.

White, Michael. "The Vivaldi Hunters." *The New York Times.* N. p., 21 Nov. 2014. Web. 10 July 2013. <http://www.nytimes.com/2004/11/21/arts/music/21whit.html?pagewanted=print&position=&_r=0>.

White, Mickey. Messages to the author. 2013-2014. Email.

White, Mickey. Personal interview. 16 July 2014.

White, Mickey. "Vivaldi and the Piéta - Oxford Girls Choir." N. d. Web. 13 July 2013. <www.oxfordgirlschoir.co.uk/events/Mickey_White_lecture>.

White, Mickey. "Scenes from the Life of Anna Maria 'dal Violin.'" Unpublished typescript, provided by the author, Nov. 15, 2013. 1-17. Print.

Wilson, Bronwen. "*'Il Bel Sesso, E L'austero Senato'*: The Coronation of Dogaressa Morosina Morosini Grimani." *Renaissance Quarterly* 52.1 (1999): 73-139. *JSTOR.* Web. 15 July 2013. <http://www.jstor.org/discover/10.2307/2902 017?sid=21105576146151&uid=4&uid=3739256&uid=70&uid=2&uid= 2134&uid=3739560>.

Wilson, Katharine M. "Isabella Teotochi Albrizzi." *An Encyclopedia of Continental Women Writers: Vol. 1 A-K.* Google Books. 2012. Web. 5 July 2013.

Wolff, Larry. "'The Morlacchi and the Discovery of the Slavs' From National Classification to Sentimental Imagination." *Venice and the Slavs: The Discovery of Dalmatia in the Age of Enlightenment.* Stanford, CA: Stanford UP, 2001. 173-227. Print.

Zane, Umberto. "History and Glory of the Rowing Champions." *City of Venice.* N. d. Web. 7 Dec. 2014. <http://www.comune.venezia.it/flex/cm/es/ServeBLOB.php/L/EN/IDPagina/71055>.

Zanini-Cordi, Irene. "Defying Genres to Find a Voice: Giustiniana Wynne and the Birth of the Italian Novel." Abstract. *Women Writers.* Feb. 2009. Web. 10 May 2014. <http://www.womenwriters.nl/index.php/Zanini-Cordi>.